George F. Warner

The Voyage of Robert Dudley,

afterwards styled Earl of Warwick and Leicester and Duke of Northumberland, to

the West Indies, 1594-1595

George F. Warner

The Voyage of Robert Dudley,
afterwards styled Earl of Warwick and Leicester and Duke of Northumberland, to the West Indies, 1594-1595

ISBN/EAN: 9783337316471

Printed in Europe, USA, Canada, Australia, Japan

Cover: Foto ©Andreas Hilbeck / pixelio.de

More available books at **www.hansebooks.com**

THE VOYAGE

OF

ROBERT DUDLEY,

AFTERWARDS STYLED

EARL OF WARWICK AND LEICESTER AND
DUKE OF NORTHUMBERLAND,

TO

THE WEST INDIES,

1594-1595,

NARRATED BY CAPT. WYATT, BY HIMSELF, AND
BY ABRAM KENDALL, MASTER.

Edited by

GEORGE F. WARNER, M.A., F.S.A.,

ASSISTANT-KEEPER OF MANUSCRIPTS, BRITISH MUSEUM.

LONDON:
PRINTED FOR THE HAKLUYT SOCIETY.

M.DCCCXCIX.

COUNCIL
OF
THE HAKLUYT SOCIETY.

SIR CLEMENTS MARKHAM, K.C.B., F.R.S., *Pres. R.G.S.*, PRESIDENT.
THE RIGHT HON. THE LORD STANLEY OF ALDERLEY, VICE-PRESIDENT.
REAR-ADMIRAL SIR WILLIAM WHARTON, K.C.B., VICE-PRESIDENT.
C. RAYMOND BEAZLEY, M.A.
COLONEL G. EARL CHURCH.
SIR MARTIN CONWAY.
ALBERT GRAY.
F. H. H. GUILLEMARD, M.A., M.D.
EDWARD HEAWOOD, M.A.
DUDLEY F. A. HERVEY, C.M.G.
ADMIRAL SIR ANTHONY H. HOSKINS, G.C.B.
J. SCOTT KELTIE, LL.D.
F. W. LUCAS.
A. P. MAUDSLAY.
MAJOR M. NATHAN, C.M.G., R.E.
E. J. PAYNE, M.A.
E. G. RAVENSTEIN.
HOWARD SAUNDERS.
H. W. TRINDER.
CHARLES WELCH, F.S.A.

WILLIAM FOSTER, B.A., *Honorary Secretary*.

PREFACE.

LTHOUGH its actual results were insignificant, the voyage of Robert Dudley to the West Indies in 1594 is nevertheless an interesting one. It witnessed the earliest recorded English attempt to occupy Trinidad and ascend the Orinoco; it reflected in a marked degree, and especially from the extreme youth of its leader, the adventurous spirit of the time ; and, above all, it was the starting-point in the active career of a remarkable man.

The romantic element which is so strong in Dudley's life began with the circumstances of his birth, and no account of him can wholly ignore the vexed question of his legitimacy. When this voyage, however, was undertaken, the question had never been seriously raised. If it had not been started in the scurrilous pamphlet generally known as *Leicester's Commonwealth*,[1] it would, perhaps, never have been heard of; but, although the charges there made were published as early as 1584, twenty years elapsed before they were taken up, when the whole tenor of Dudley's

---

[1] *The copie of a leter wryten by a Master of Arte of Cambrige to his friend in London . . . about the present state and some proceedinges of the Erle of Leycester and his friendes in England*, etc. [Antwerp?], 1584. It was attributed, but on no good grounds, to Robert Parsons, the Jesuit. The title *Leycester's Commonwealth* was given to it when it was republished at London in 1641.

life was changed by his futile attempt to prove them. Any discussion therefore of the subject may be deferred till later on ; and meanwhile it will be enough to give briefly what is known of him down to the time when he earned an honourable place among the maritime adventurers of the reign of Elizabeth.

Of his parentage there was never any doubt, for he was acknowledged from birth to be the son of Robert Dudley, Earl of Leicester, by Douglas, widow of John Sheffield, second Lord Sheffield. His mother, who married about 1562, at the age of seventeen, was a Howard, daughter of William, first Lord Howard of Effingham, and granddaughter of Thomas, second Duke of Norfolk.[1] Though some years younger, she was thus first cousin once removed to the Queen, whose mother, Anne Boleyn, was a granddaughter of the same Duke through an earlier wife. Lord Sheffield died in December, 1568 ; and, if the pamphlet above named can be trusted, Leicester was suspected of having caused him to be poisoned. Gervase Holles in his account of his own family[2] tells a still darker story, which makes out that Lady Sheffield was a party to the plot for her husband's death. This was written as late as 1658, and is only worth mention because it seems to have come from a sister of Lord Sheffield, who married Denzil Holles, grand-uncle to Gervase, and is said to have herself detected the plot, though too late to save her brother's life, by picking up a letter from Leicester dropped by her sister-in-law. The earliest strictly contemporary record, however, in which the names of Robert Dudley's parents are coupled is a letter from Gilbert Talbot to his father, the Earl of

---

[1] See an account of her in *Miscellanea Genealogica et Heraldica*, New Series, iii, 1880, p. 368.

[2] The original MS. is at Longleat (Portland Papers, vol. xxiv) ; but the story was printed by A. Collins in his *Historical Collections of the Noble Families of Cavendish, Holles, Vere, Harley, and Ogle*, 1752, p. 77.

Shrewsbury, dated May 11th, 1573.[1] After referring to Leicester's favour with the Queen and his efforts to please her, the writer goes on: "There are two sisters now in the Court that are very far in love with him, as they have been long, my Lady Sheffield and Frances Howard. They (of like striving who shall love him better) are at great wars together, and the Queen thinketh not well of them and not the better of him; by this means there are spies over him." It is clear from this that the writer was unaware of any worse scandal five years before; and it might also be argued that, if Lady Sheffield was already Leicester's wife, or even contracted to him, she might have ended her sister's rivalry by a word, without the necessity for provoking Elizabeth's jealousy by a public avowal. The author of Robert Dudley's life in the *Dictionary of National Biography* gives May, 1573 -the very month in which the above letter was written—as the date of his birth. In this he follows another modern biographer[2]; but the statement is erroneous. Dudley's age was entered as fourteen when he matriculated at Oxford on May 7th, 1588,[3] and the exact date of his birth is given in an authoritative document among Lord Bath's MSS. at Longleat.[4] He is there said to have been born at Sheen House, in Surrey, on August

---

[1] Lodge, *Illustrations of British History*, etc., ed. 1838, ii, p. 17. Frances Howard married, before June, 1582, Edward Seymour, Earl of Hertford. She died, aged forty-four, in 1598, and was therefore at this time only nineteen.

[2] G. Adlard, *Amye Robsart and the Earl of Leycester . . . together with memoirs and correspondence of Sir Robert Dudley*, 1870, p. 279. By an obvious misreading of Dugdale's *Warwickshire*, ed. 1730, i, p. 250, the same writer originated another error, that the alleged marriage took place only two days before the child's birth.

[3] Foster, *Alumni Oxonienses*, 1500-1714. In the Register, as the Keeper of the Archives kindly informs me, the day is written in ink, "Maii 7°," with "rectius 17" added in pencil below, the latter no doubt merely referring to new style.

[4] "Tymes of thinges necessary to be observed in this cause," viz. the legitimacy case in 1604, evidently prepared for the use of counsel (Dudley Papers, Box vi).

7th, 1574. When he sailed in command of an expedition to the West Indies in November, 1594, he was thus actually some months under age. The above date also appears in a deposition[1] of William Clewer, or Cluer, one of Lady Sheffield's household, who adds that the child was born "in a chamber there (*i.e.*, at Sheen House), called the Duke's Chamber." Leicester at the time was in attendance upon the Queen in her progress into the West,[2] and Clewer himself carried the news to him at Gloucester, returning in time to act as proxy for Sir Henry Lee at the christening, the other sponsors, Leicester's brother Ambrose, Earl of Warwick, and Lady Dacre being represented by Dr. Julio and Mrs. Erisa.[3]

If born in wedlock, the boy was Leicester's heir; but there is some doubt whether he was his first child by Lady Sheffield. In *Leicester's Commonwealth* she is said to have given birth to a daughter at Dudley Castle[4] in Staffordshire, and evidence of this, though the sex is not stated, was given in the legitimacy suit in 1604,[5] in which it was alleged that the infant died at, or very soon after, birth, while the mother was hurried back to Court to quiet suspicion. This happened, it is said, eighteen months before Robert Dudley's birth; so that, if the story is true,

---

[1] Dudley Papers at Longleat, Box vii.

[2] Nichols, *Progresses of Queen Elizabeth*, i. She was at Bristol August 14th-21st, 1574 (*Ricart's Kalendar*, ed. L. Toulmin Smith, Camden Soc., 1872, p. 58).

[3] Avice, daughter and co-heir of William Milliton, of Pengersey, wife of Richard Erisa, of Erisa (died 1570), and, in 1600, of Sir Nicholas Parker (J. L. Vivian, *Visitation of Cornwall*, 1887, p. 155). In her deposition in 1604, as Lady Parker, she says nothing about the actual sponsors being proxies. Dr. Julio was Giulio Borgherini, Leicester's Italian physician and the supposed agent in his poisonings.

[4] Dudley Castle belonged, not to Leicester, but to Edward Sutton, al. Dudley, Lord Dudley, who married, as his third wife, after September, 1569, Mary Howard, Lady Sheffield's sister.

[5] Deposition of Dorothy Dudley (Dudley Papers at Longleat, Box vii). It was denied by Lady Sheffield (Answers, June 7th, 1604, Dudley Papers at Penshurst).

the intimacy, whether under contract of marriage or not, must have begun at least as early as June, 1572. But constancy was not one of Leicester's few virtues. When his son was little more than an infant, he wearied of Lady Sheffield and transferred his roving affections to Lettice, Lady Essex. Scandal accused him of an intrigue with her while her husband, Walter Devereux, first Earl of Essex, was serving as Earl Marshal in Ireland; and on the latter's death at Dublin, on September 22nd, 1576, strong suspicions of poison were certainly current. Probably they were unfounded [1]; and in any case they did not prevent Leicester from marrying Lady Essex at Wanstead on September 21st, 1578, just two years later. It is doubtful whether he was altogether a free agent; for, although there had been an alleged earlier marriage, the lady's father, Sir Francis Knollys, is said to have insisted on the ceremony being performed before witnesses in his own presence.[2] But even this marriage, though placed beyond doubt, was supposed to be kept secret from fear of the Queen, whose fury, when it was revealed to her some months later by Simier, the Duke of Anjou's agent, passed all bounds. Elizabeth's jealousy no doubt was more formidable than the charge of bigamy, to which, on the assumption that he was already married to Lady Sheffield, Leicester had rendered himself liable. But, although the offence was not yet actually a felony in English law,[3] it is significant that no steps were taken at the time to assert Lady Sheffield's supposed rights. If there had been a

---

[1] W. B. Devereux, *Lives of the Devereux*, 1853, i, p. 146. The result of an enquiry instituted by Sir H. Sidney, Lord Deputy of Ireland, is printed by Collins, *Sidney Papers*, 1746, i, p. 140. As Sidney married Leicester's sister, his impartiality might be thought doubtful.

[2] So Camden, *Annales*, ed. Leyden, 1639, p. 278.

[3] It was made felony without benefit of clergy, 1 Jas. I (1603-4), cap. 11; but before this it was subject to action in the ecclesiastical courts.

good case, she might surely have counted on powerful support, for Charles, Lord Howard of Effingham, her brother, was Lord Chamberlain and in high favour at Court, while Leicester's enemies would have been only too glad of the chance of bringing him to book. Instead of this, to complicate matters still more, she followed his example by marrying Edward Stafford, of Chebsey, who in 1579 was employed in negotiations in France, and was resident ambassador there from October, 1583 (when he was knighted), until the end of 1590.[1] The date of this marriage has hitherto been in doubt, and injustice has been done to her by the assumption that it preceded Leicester's marriage with Lady Essex. This is a mistake, for Lord Bath's MS. proves that it took place on November 29th, 1579, more than a year later. The step was a strange one, and practically gave away both her own good name and her son's birth-right; nor is the excuse which was afterwards made, that she was terrified into it by Leicester's plots against her life, by any means convincing.

When Leicester deserted the mother, he succeeded in getting the child into his own hands, and there is no reason to doubt his fondness for him.[2] "Robin Sheffield," as he was at first called, is spoken of in 1584 as having been "sometime brought up at Newington."[3] Probably

---

[1] His wife accompanied him, and made a distinguished figure in the French Court (*Miscellaneous State Papers*, 1778, i, p. 196). She bore him two children, who probably died young (Dudley Papers at Penshurst). Stafford died February 5th, 1604-5, and Lady Sheffield, who retained her courtesy title, in December, 1608.

[2] According to Ferd. Heyborne, a former servant of Leicester, the Earl "did to this deponent and unto others in this deponent's hearinge verie often tymes discover his love and care he had of the said Sir Rob. Dudley and the desire he had to have him receyve good usage and educacion," and yet he always styled him "his base sonne and the badge of his synne" (Dudley Papers at Longleat, Box vii).

[3] *The copie of a leter*, etc. (see above, p. i), 1584, p. 35. According to Lady Sheffield, he was called Dudley while with her (Answers, June 7th, 1604, at Penshurst).

Stoke Newington is meant, the manor-house of which was occupied by John Dudley, a kinsman of his father.[1] At ten years of age he is said to have been at school, or with a tutor, at Offington, in Sussex. This place is close to Worthing, and it may have been on the open Sussex coast that he first imbibed his passionate love for the sea. It has recently been stated that his master was Owen Robin,[2] and his attainments were so far out of the common that the name would be of some interest, if it were not a mere figment. We only know of the boy's stay at Offington from one Owen Jones, a witness in the legitimacy case. This man, who had been a lackey to Leicester, deposed that, while he was attending there on Robert Dudley, Leicester, coming once to see his son, commended the latter to his care, with the significant words: "*Owen*, thou knowest that *Robyn* my boy is my lawful son; and as I do and have charg'd thee to keep it secret, so I charge thee not to forget it, and therefore see thou be carefull of him."[3] From this speech Owen Robin the schoolmaster has been evolved!

Apart from such dubious avowals, Leicester until his death seems to have treated the boy consistently as a natural son. If he was ever tempted to proclaim him legitimate, it may have been after the death of Robert, Lord Denbigh, his only child by Lettice, Lady Leicester, on July 19th, 1584. By this event he was left without a lawful, or acknowledged, heir; and, as appeared in the

---

[1] Lysons, *Environs of London*, iii, p. 281; Nichols, *Bibl. Topogr. Brit.*, ii, No. 9. He died in December, 1580, but his widow, who in 1582 married Thomas Sutton, founder of the Charterhouse, continued to reside there.

[2] *Dict. Nat. Biog.*, from a misreading of Dugdale, *Warwickshire*, ed. 1730, i, p. 250.

[3] So Dugdale; but Jones in his answers, May 28th, 1604 (Dudley Papers at Penshurst), after "lawful son" goes on: "I charge thee be carefull of him, and forgett yt not. When tyme serves, he shall remember you."

sequel, Robert Dudley's prospects were materially improved
On May $\frac{7}{17}$th, 1588, he matriculated at Christ Church
Oxford, the register describing him briefly as "filius
comitis," an earl's son. All that is recorded of him while
there is that he was placed under the charge of the well-
known Thomas Chaloner,[1] and a tutor better fitted to
develop his peculiar powers could not have been chosen.
Though not yet thirty, Chaloner had travelled much,
especially in Italy. He was devoted to scientific pursuits,
and had a natural talent for invention; and he even seems
to have had some knowledge of shipbuilding, for which his
pupil afterwards became famous. Dudley no doubt owed
him much; and even his choice of a refuge in exile in 1605
was perhaps determined by the same early influence. How
long he remained at Christ Church, or under Chaloner's
care, is not known. The year in which he went to Oxford
was that of the Spanish Armada; and long after, in the
preface to his unpublished *Direttorio Marittimo*, he declared
that he served as a colonel under his father in the army
assembled at Tilbury.[2] Precocious as he was, this is
incredible; but he no doubt learnt at this critical time the
hatred of the Spaniards which finds curious expression in
one of the narratives of his voyage (p. 31). Personally, he
was more affected by the death of his father on September
4th in the same year. Leicester had made his will when at
Middelburg, in the Netherlands, on August 1st, 1587.[3]

---

[1] He was knighted when serving in France in 1591, and on the accession of James I was made governor to Henry, Prince of Wales. Perhaps his best-known title to fame is his discovery of alum on his estate at Guisborough, co. York, where he opened the first alum works in England (*Dict. Nat. Biogr.*). When Phineas Pett, master-ship-wright at Woolwich, was accused of incompetence in 1609, the technical questions in dispute were referred to him and another for decision (Harley MS. 6279, f. 43).

[2] See the passage quoted below, p. xii.

[3] Printed in J. Temple Leader's *Life of Sir R. Dudley*, Florence, 1895, p. 159 (where it is wrongly dated 1578). The will was holograph,

Though he styled Robert Dudley his "base son" throughout, he treated him liberally, bequeathing to him, after the death of the Earl of Warwick, the bulk of his disposable real estate, including the castle and lands of Kenilworth and the lordships of Denbigh and Chirk.[1] As Warwick died on February 20th, 15$\frac{89}{90}$, it was not long before the property devolved upon him, though he had some trouble with Lady Leicester and her third husband, Sir Christopher Blount.[2] Evidence has lately come to light at Florence, which, if genuine, shows that in 1591 he was contracted to Frances Vavasour, a maid of honour to the Queen.[3] It is in the form of letters testimonial,[4] dated November 3rd, 1592, recording the fact on the evidence of Captain Thomas Jobson, of Colchester, and Thomas Combley, whose names are worth noting, as they both sailed with Dudley on his voyage. The object of the record is not apparent; and, as a matter of fact, at the time it purports to have been made

---

and, according to a deposition of Ralph Moore, one of Leicester's household, was in his keeping until the Earl's death, when he handed it over to Lady Leicester (Dudley Papers at Longleat, Box vii). The term "base son" could hardly have been inspired therefore, as has been suggested, by the latter.

[1] If we can believe Charles Paget, Leicester had a design to marry his "bastard" to Arabella Stuart, which was frustrated by his death (*Cal. State Papers, Addenda* 1580-1625, p. 270).

[2] In *Acts of the Privy Council*, xix, 1899, p. 82, there is a strongly-worded letter from the Council, April 26th, 1590, to Sir Fulk Greville and others, to defend his rights at Kenilworth against Blount's forcible entry. Lord Chancellor Hatton and Lord Admiral Howard, Dudley's uncle, are named in it as two of his trustees.

[3] She was daughter of Henry Vavasour, of Copmanthorpe, co. York, and it was she no doubt, and not her sister Anne, of whom it was written in 1590: "Our new maid, Mrs. Vavasour, flourisheth like the lily and the rose" (Lodge, *Illustrations*, 1838, ii, p. 423). Anne had, in fact, joined the Court before 1584 (*Copie of a leter*, etc., p. 38). Thomas Sherley married Frances before September 21st, 1591, for he had for his audacity been fourteen weeks in the Marshalsey on December 28th, when he wrote an appeal to Burghley (*The Sherley Brothers*, 1848, p. 7; E. P. Shirley, *Stemmata Shirleiana*, 1873, p. 266).

[4] Printed in J. T. Leader's *Life of Sir R. Dudley*, p. 166.

Frances Vavasour had been married for more than a year to the eldest of the famous three Sherley brothers, Thomas Sherley, who got into trouble with the Queen in consequence. Altogether the document, which is not an original, is suspicious; and it is perhaps a forgery, concocted by, or for, Dudley in Italy, when he was trying to induce the Pope to annul his marriage with Alice Leigh on the ground of pre-contract. There is less reason to question his marriage with a sister,[1] or perhaps a cousin, of Thomas Cavendish, the circumnavigator, though little definite is known about it. The first hint of it is given in a letter of October 27th, 1591,[2] in which we read: "Mr. Dudley is forbidden the Court for kissing Mrs. Candishe in the presence, being his wife as is said." Neither the lady's Christian name nor the date of the marriage is recorded. If she was sister to Thomas Cavendish, as Dugdale states, she was a daughter of William Cavendish, of Grimston Hall, Trimley St. Martin, Suffolk; and it is clear from the Cavendish pedigree and the extracts from the Trimley parish register in Davy's "Suffolk Collections"[3] that she was either Anne, baptized October 30th, 1562, or Elizabeth, baptized July 28th, 1567, the younger even of whom was seven years older than Dudley. On the other hand, in a deposition made in 1604 one Thomas Denny[4] mentions incidentally that he was Dudley's brother-in-law. According to Davy, this Thomas Denny, who was of Bawdsey or Mendlesham, married Beatrice, daughter of Richard Cavendish the author, of Hornsey, a younger brother of William. Dudley's wife

---

[1] Dugdale, *Baronage*, ii. p. 225. See also a letter of Lotti, the Florentine Agent, in 1607 (Leader, p. 172).

[2] *Calendar of Hatfield MSS.*, pt. iv, 1892, p. 153.

[3] Brit. Mus. Add. MSS. 19,122, f. 350, 19,087, f. 131. Thomas Cavendish, the year of whose birth is left uncertain in the *Dict. Nat. Biogr.*, was baptised at Trimley, September 19th, 1560.

[4] Dudley Papers at Longleat, Box vi. f. 46: "because I married the sister of Sir Rob. Dudley his first wife."

therefore seems to have been, not a sister, but a first cousin of the circumnavigator. In this case, however, she brought him into a closer connection with Richard Hakluyt, whose first wife was Douglas Cavendish, another daughter of Richard.[1] Whoever she really was, and whenever the marriage took place, she could not have long survived, for Dudley, as will be seen, married again in or before 1597. Although Thomas Cavendish's example was no doubt a potent factor in directing his mind to maritime adventure, any personal intercourse came to a speedy end when Cavendish started on his last fatal voyage on August 26th, 1591. He died at sea in May or June, 1592; and some intimate connection between them is evident from the fact that Dudley took out letters of administration for his estate, a Council warrant[2] of March 18th, 1593, directing the delivery to him of the *Leicester* and *Roebuck*, two of the ships which returned from the voyage. The first name, indeed, rather suggests that he had a share in the venture, and it is possible therefore that he was merely acting as a creditor.

Dudley was now approaching manhood. Young, handsome and accomplished, with a romantic history and a good, though no doubt encumbered, estate, he evidently made a brilliant figure in Elizabeth's Court. The miniature portrait of him by Nicholas Hilliard, which is here reproduced as a frontispiece,[3] apparently shows him as he was

---

[1] Though Hakluyt's biographers mention this first wife, none of them states who she was. Her name, "Duglasse," is given in the entry of her burial, August 8th, 1597, in the Register of Wetheringsett, co. Suffolk, of which he was vicar (Add. MS. 19,090, f. 248).

[2] Adlard, *op. cit.*, p. 282, from the Privy Council Register. The fact is also stated by Thomas Warde, one of his counsel on the occasion (Answers, May 3rd, 1604, Dudley Papers at Penshurst).

[3] The original was formerly at Penshurst. A plate from it, engraved by J. Brown from a copy made by the well-known artist G. P. Harding, was published among Harding's *Ancient Historical Pictures*, 1844, etc., and again in T. Moule's *Portraits of Illustrious Persons*,

a few years later. The classical passage descriptive of him is from Sir William Dugdale[1]: "He was a person of stature tall and comely, also strong, valiant, famous at the exercise of tilting, singularly skill'd in all mathematick learning, but chiefly in navigation and architecture, a rare chymist, and of great knowledge of physic." Anthony Wood's account of him, which was partly derived from his son Carlo in 1673, is on similar lines[2]: "This Robert Dudley ... was a compleat gentleman in all suitable employments, an exact seaman, a good navigator, an excellent architect, mathematician, physician, chymist and what not. He was a handsome, personable man, tall of stature, red hair'd, and of admirable comport, and above all noted for riding the great horse, for tilting, and for his being the first of all that taught a dog to sit in order to catch partridges." These accounts of course refer to his maturity, but they show what must have been the promise of his early prime. In his *Direttorio Marittimo* he himself explains how he came to be devoted to naval affairs. "Suffice it to say," he writes, addressing the Grand Duke of Tuscany, "that he is nephew of three Grand Admirals of England,[3] and that he had from his youth a natural sympathy for the sea, and this in spite of his having in 1588 held the very honorable

---

1869. The collotype here is taken from a proof-copy of this plate in the British Museum. There is a strong likeness to the poet Shelley (see *Dict. Nat. Biogr.*), which was first pointed out, I believe, by Dr. R. Garnett.

[1] *Antiquities of Warwickshire* (1656), 2nd ed. 1730, i, p. 252. Dugdale was born in 1605, the year in which Dudley left England, and he could never have seen him personally. Lotti, the Florentine Agent, describes Dudley in 1605 as "di giusta statura et di barba bionda, et molto gentile in apparenza" (Leader, p. 177).

[2] *Athenæ Oxonienses*, ed. Bliss, 1813-1820, iii, col. 260. Dudley's life was not in the first edition (1691-2), but was added in the second (1721).

[3] He means his two grandfathers, John Dudley, Duke of Northumberland, and William Howard, Lord Howard of Effingham, and his uncle, Charles, Lord Howard of Effingham, afterwards Earl of Nottingham. The word translated "nephew" is no doubt the ambiguous "nipote" in the Italian.

post of Colonel in the land forces, which he exercised under the command of his father, the General-in-Chief and Grand Master of England. He determined at any cost to enter the marine army, on which at that time the reputation and greatness of England depended. He had also a great desire to discover new countries. Therefore from the age of seventeen he gave himself to the study of navigation and of marine discipline and war; in fact, he wanted to blend naval command together with military emprise by land, in India and other parts to which navigation should take him. Therefore he built and manned ships of war, in which he sought to place the best pilots that were to be found, and in whose great knowledge and experience he trusted implicitly. One, the famous mariner Abram Kendal,[1] might be called his master; from him he learned enough navigation for an Admiral."[2]

The first project conceived in his restless brain was to emulate Drake and Cavendish by penetrating into the South Seas. For a young man barely twenty years of age, with no experience of the sea, and with the fate of Cavendish's last venture before his eyes, it certainly showed no lack of self-confidence. Unfortunately, however, he reckoned without the Queen. When his preparations were well advanced, she issued her veto, and he was forced to be content with the shorter and less hazardous voyage here narrated, of which he speaks in an amusing tone of depreciation, as too commonplace to be worth recording. Three independent accounts of it have come down to us, all of which are included in this volume. Practically, it has hitherto only been known from his own brief and matter-

---

[1] See below, p. xv.
[2] J. Temple Leader's *Life of Sir R. Dudley*, Florence, 1895, p. 32, where the passage is translated as above. The original MS. of the work in Italian, mostly in Dudley's autograph, is in Mr. Leader's own possession (*ib.*, p. 19).

of-fact narrative, reprinted here from Hakluyt's *Voyages*; and even this seems to have been hardly extracted from him by its editor's importunity. As there is an evident allusion in it (p. 72) to Ralegh's *Discoverie of Guiana*, it must have been written after the publication of that work in the spring of 1596[1]; but there is no other indication to fix its precise date.

Almost every particular in it is confirmed and amplified by the fuller and more graphic narrative which begins the volume, and which is now printed for the first time.[2] This is contained in Sloane MS. 358 in the British Museum, a small quarto of thirty-six paper leaves, written in a contemporary hand, but apparently not autograph. Though seemingly addressed to some person in authority, who is styled "Right Honorable" (p. 54), it is anonymous in form. The writer, however, more than once betrays his identity, and there can be no doubt that he was Captain Wyatt, the "old and discreet souldier," as he styles himself, who commanded Dudley's "main battle of pike." A curious instance of his forgetfulness in abruptly changing from the third to the first person will be found on p. 50, where he tells us how "Wyatt" was ordered to put some Spanish prisoners on shore, and how they complained of his harsh treatment. In his anxiety to clear himself, he then goes on: "and yeat I protest before God I used them in such sorte as, if my fortune weare to be towched with the like miserie or punnishment ... I would wish to be soe delt withall." It is not so easily determined who this Capt. Wyatt was, and unfortunately he does not even mention his Christian name; but he may have been the Capt. Thomas Wyatt who was Commissary of Musters at

---

[1] It was entered at Stationers' Hall, March 15th, 1595[6], by Robert Robinson (Arber, *Transcr. of Stat. Hall Reg.*, iii, p. 9).

[2] A few extracts from it were given in G. L. Craik's *Romance of the Peerage*, 1849, iii, p. 105.

Bergen-op-Zoom in 1589, and again in Kent in 1595, and who was at the head of one hundred men out of Kent in the Cadiz expedition of 1596, in which Dudley also had a command.[1] He was evidently a landsman, and on his first long voyage; and, to judge from his scraps of Latin and references to classical authors, he had some pretensions to scholarship. In general he writes simply and naturally, and most of his narrative is decidedly good reading. Now and then, however, as when he dilates on the terrible storms which the voyagers encountered, there is more striving after effect, with a tendency, it may be thought, to become bombastic. His grammar moreover is, to say the least, peculiar, but for its worst faults the copyist is perhaps responsible. Much of the matter appears to have been written down from day to day, and has the freshness of a journal; and among other strong points are the writer's evident sincerity and his loyalty to his youthful leader, whose impulsive, chivalrous character is brought out much more clearly than in his own sober account of the voyage.

The third and shortest narrative has had a curious history. It is more strictly nautical in character than the other two; but although mainly a Portulano or Ruttier, recording the variations of the course pursued on the voyage, it includes other matter of less technical interest. Its writer was Abraham, or Abram, Kendall, from whom, as we have already seen (p. xiii), Dudley learned the art of navigation, and who now joined him as his chief pilot or master. Wyatt, no less than Dudley, speaks highly of his skill; he describes him moreover as "excellinge all others in his profession as a rare scholler, a most selldome thinge in a maryner." At the same time, Kendall was clearly not

---

[1] Brit. Mus. Lansdowne MS. 62, art. 47; *Calendar of Hatfield MSS.*, pt. v, pp. 240, 525; pt. vi, p. 206.

popular on board: for when Dudley, as he tells us (p. 73), was eager to ascend the Orinoco in person, the men who were to be left behind mutinied against his going, since they "feared the villany of Abraham Kendal, who would by no meanes go." Only three months after their return to England he joined Drake's last expedition, which sailed on Aug. 28th, 1595, and he died on board the *Saker*, off Porto Bello, on the same day as Drake himself, January 28th, 1596 (p. 14, note). His account of Dudley's voyage was found among the papers he had with him when he died. Afterwards, perhaps by will with the rest of his effects, it came into Dudley's own hands, and an Italian version of it was printed by him fifty years later, as the second of the Portulani included in Book II of his famous work *L'Arcano del Mare*, an account of which will be found further on. As no trace of the original can now be found, this Italian version has here been translated back into English; but there is too much reason to believe that in some places, as on p. 87, Dudley garbled his text, so as to magnify in later life the exploits of his youth. In the *Arcano del Mare* he uniformly mentions Kendall in laudatory terms, coupling him with the better-known Capt. John Davis as the two ablest and most learned seamen England had ever produced.[1] He introduces him again in an interesting chapter on diseases at sea and their prevention.[2] He there attributes to his care and observance of sanitary rules the fact that on this voyage only one man was lost by sickness, adding that on another occasion, when in command of the *Merchant Royal* of London, he cured his crew of scurvy in Saldanha Bay in less than a month, and brought them safely home. As we learn elsewhere, this occurred in 1591,

---

[1] "Questo capitano ed Abram Kendal . . . erono i più valenti e dotti marinari che habbia mai haunto la corona d'Inghilterra, ed erono valentissimi matematici e filosofi" (vol. i, lib. ii, p. 51).

[2] *Arc. del Mare*, lib. iii, p. 31. See also Wyatt's remarks, p. 52.

when the *Merchant Royal* was one of the three vessels which sailed on the first English voyage to the East Indies.[1] Only one of them, the *Edward Bonaventure*, of which we shall hear again, reached her destination. Except in the *Arcano del Mare* and in connection with the voyages already mentioned, Kendall's name does not appear to have been preserved; but there is a curious passage in the Preface to Edward Knight's *Certaine Errors in Navigation*, 1599, which almost certainly refers to him, though his name is suppressed. It is worth giving at length, if only as recording his opinion of Drake's knowledge of navigation, and is as follows :—

". . . . . . . It is not vnknowne to some of good place and reckoning that one of the skilfullest nauigators (as he was by many accounted) of our time and nation, who died in Sir Frauncis Drakes last voyage, when he came to that extremitie of sicknesse that he saw there was no other way but one with him, was reported to haue gathered and bound together into a bundell all his nautical notes and obseruations, and to haue cast them into the sea. But soone after, notwithstanding that foresaid report, there came more comfortable newes by a Captaine that was familiarly acquainted and conuersant with him in that voyage and during the whole time of his sicknesse, in whose armes also he died; who mouing some speach vnto him touching something of Sir Frauncis Drakes that might then after his death be looked for to be brought to light, concerning nauigation : ''Tush (saith he), for that matter there is not much to be looked for at his hands, hee had little skill in that art.' 'Why? and will your self then do any thing?' quoth that Captaine. Wherupon this great nauigator drewe forth a booke out of his

---

[1] Barker, in his account of the voyage, writes : " We left behind [in Saldanha Bay] 50 men with the *Roiall Marchant*, whereof there were many pretty well recovered, of which ship was master and governour Abraham Kendal, which for many reasons we thought good to send home" (*Voyages of Sir James Lancaster, Kt.*, ed. C. R. Markham, Hakl. Soc., 1877, p. 4). In May's account (*ib.*, p. 24) Samuel Foxcroft is named as captain; but Kendall had perhaps succeeded him. On his way back, he left a man on St. Helena, who was taken off eighteen months later by the *Edward Bonaventure* (*ib.*, p. 17).

bosome, and deliuered it vnto this Captaine not long before his death. This booke was shewed by the same Captaine to the R. Honourable the L. high Admirall of England in the Cales voyage, as being made by that famous nauigator, which his Lordship also (as it was reported) thought good should be perused and published. These newes moued some expectation of that booke, so as the right Honourable and my very good Lord the Earle of Cumberland hearing of it was desirous also to haue a sight thereof and remembred me vnto that Captaine, as one not insufficient to peruse and correct the same. And hereupon the booke was brought vnto his Lordship at the time and place appointed at Westminster, and was there also deliuered vnto me, to be perused and corrected. Hauing therefor opened it, & beginning a litle to turne ouer the leaues, to take some generall view what matter mought be conteyned therein, I first espied a Diagramme, the like whereof I knewe verie well I had made in a booke of mine. And herewithall I was the more moued to see if there were any more that I could know as well as the former; turning ouer therefor two or three leaues more, I presently espied another Diagramme also, wherewith I was as well acquainted as with the former; for I found not onely the very same Diagramme, but (that which made me the more to maruaile for the present) folowing also in the same order as I well remembred it did in my booke. Being therefor yet more earnestly stirred vp hereat, and wondering what the reason mought be that we should thus agree, I betooke my self to the reading of that booke. And looking first vpon the first leafe thereof, and afterwardes in many other places, I found it euerywhere to agree with mine, and to be a copie of the same booke worde for worde which I made and presented vnto his Lordship almost seuen yeares before, as the next morning it plainly appeared both to his Lordship and to the Captaine himself that brought it, by comparing it in all poynts with the originall exemplar of the same booke, which I then brought vnto his Lordship."

We thus have the story of Dudley's voyage from three points of view, as told by himself, by his chief pilot, and by one of the captains of his fighting force. When it started, the expedition consisted of four vessels, all of which were apparently fitted out at his own expense. The largest, or admiral, commanded by him in person, was the *Bear*, or, as Wyatt for some reason calls her, the *Peregrine*. Her size is given by Dudley as 200 tons, by Wyatt as about 180, and by Kendall as about 300. The last estimate, however, perhaps exaggerates what Kendall himself wrote. It is repeated in another part of the *Arcano del Mare*,[1] where Dudley states that the vessel was a "galeone riformato" of thirty guns, built for him at Southampton, and that she proved to be very fast. The last point is confirmed by Wyatt, who describes her (p. 13) as being "most singuler for her saylinge." The vice-admiral, the *Bear's Whelp*, was commanded by Captain Monck or Munck, who is otherwise unknown.[2] Of the three narratives only Wyatt's gives her size, but the 80 tons which he allows to her are increased to 140 in the *Arcano del Mare*. Two small pinnaces, to serve as tenders, named the *Earwig* and the *Frisking*, made up the complement. Wyatt, indeed, speaks also of a rear-admiral, called the *Mermaid*, of 100 tons, which was left behind at Southampton to follow later, but no further mention is made of her. Besides Kendall, his nautical adviser, Dudley also had with him on the *Bear* Captain Jobson as his "Lieutenant Generall." He was no doubt the Captain Thomas Jobson already named (p. ix), and a son of Sir Francis Jobson, who married a half-sister of Dudley's paternal grandfather, John, Duke of Northumberland (p. 12). He was older than his kinsman and had served under Drake at San Domingo and elsewhere, and from his relationship

---

[1] Lib. iv, pp. 2, 21. Dudley (ch. ii) divides the vessels of war designed by him into seven symmetries (sette simetrie); the *Bear* was of the first, a plan of which is given in his plate 6.

[2] In the *Arcano del Mare*, lib. iv, p. 3, Dudley speaks of him as a relative (parente dell' autore). His vessel was of Dudley's fourth symmetry (see his plate 12, "Fregate di guerra simetria quarta ò pinnase").

and experience he was Dudley's right hand throughout
the voyage. Captain Benjamin Wood was another well-
seasoned member of the company. He had been with
Amadas and Barlow in Virginia as early as 1584, and was
master of the *Wild Man*, commanded by John Chudleigh,
in an unsuccessful attempt to sail round the world in
1589.[1] He was more fortunate on this voyage with Dudley
than he was in 1596, when the latter put him in command
of an expedition to China, the fate of which was never
quite cleared up (p. 8, note 3). A few more names are also
recorded, chiefly by Wyatt, such as Captains Wentworth
and Vincent, Mr. Lister, Mr. Thomas Comley, Mr. Wright,
Mr. Canter, Mr. Phillips, Mr. Crale and Mr. Norris. Most
of these were musketeers; but "Ancient" Barrow and
"our Generalls page Mr. William Bradshew" were in more
personal attendance upon Dudley himself. The full
number of men originally mustered is not given. Incidentally, however, we learn that, including those taken on
board out of her sunk pinnace, the *Bear* carried nearly
140,[2] who were so cramped for room that sickness soon
broke out. These no doubt made up more than half the
number that started, and at any rate no more than these
actually made the voyage.

Apparently Dudley started on his expedition without any
definite aim. Though Kendall is made to say that it was
to explore Guiana "according as he had order to do from
Queen Elizabeth of England *then reigning*" (p. 84), the very
form of these words shows they are interpolated; and no
doubt there is more truth in Dudley's own statement that
it was "rather to see some practise and experience then any
wonders or profite" (p. 68). He seems, in short, to have set

---

[1] See *Voyages of Sir J. Lancaster*, ed. C. R. Markham, Hakl. Soc.,
1877, p. 19, note.

[2] See p. 69. In the *Arcano del Mare*, lib. iii, p. 31, the number is
given as 200 at least.

out in all the ardour of youth to see the world and seek
adventures, though, to judge from his actions, one at least
of his motives was to capture as many Spanish prizes as
possible. There is some uncertainty also as to his precise
relations with Sir Walter Ralegh, who, with the declared
purpose of exploring Guiana, followed in his wake three
months later and reached Trinidad only ten days after he
had left it. Dudley can hardly have had the deliberate
intention to forestall him, although his proceedings were a
little suspicious. He speaks as if he only formed the
design of "discovering the main" when actually at Trinidad,
from what he heard from Capt. George Popham (p. 71);
but, if such was the case, he must have met Popham before
he was joined by him at Trinidad, which was not until after
his boat had started up the Orinoco (p. 75). It has been
assumed, on the contrary, that he was acting in concert
with Ralegh. There is, however, no evidence of this; for,
although he and Popham waited some time for Ralegh at
Trinidad, it was merely because they "surmized" that he
"had some purpose for this discovery" (p. 75). It is significant that in his *Discoverie of Guiana* Ralegh ignores
Dudley's voyage altogether, and he only once casually
mentions him.[1] After they had both returned home he
showed, in fact, as we shall presently see, decided jealousy
of his interest in Guiana, and did his best to stop his
fitting out another expedition to the same quarter.

Dudley's first and, as it proved, only voyage thither
began badly. Setting sail from Southampton on November 6th, 1594, they first made for Plymouth[2]; but, from
want of wind, it was not until November 19th that all four
vessels met in port, and when two days later they sailed
for Spain, they were speedily driven back, the *Bear* and

---

[1] See below, p. 74, note 2.
[2] The unexplained "business" which Dudley says he had there was possibly to see Popham, or to pick up news as to Ralegh's intentions.

her pinnace into Plymouth and the other two into Falmouth. Sending orders to his vice-admiral to join him at the Canaries or Cape Blanco, Dudley made a fresh start on December 1st. This time the wind was strong behind him; but before he reached the Spanish coast his pinnace was swamped, and he was thus left with only the *Bear*. "Notwithstanding all these crosses, all alone," he says, "I went wandering on my voyage." From the first the *Bear* showed her true character as a privateer, chasing every vessel that came in sight as she ran down the coast on her way to the Canaries. From Wyatt's graphic account, she appears to have recked little of size or number; and, if the three supposed "royal Armathases" which she caught up had really proved to be King's ships, Dudley might have had other grounds for disgust than his inability to meet with any but friends. The only Spanish vessel which they did come across hoisted English colours and escaped into shallow water, and then she mocked them, "the which our generall toke mightelie offensive." This episode, with the abortive night-attack which he planned in revenge on a Spanish harbour, and which was probably not justified by his commission, is only reported by Wyatt; and we also owe to him a lively account of the manner in which they spent Christmas Day near Teneriffe, "a verie hott day, and wee withall becalmed." The Weymouth bark which lay close by, and with whose crew they made cheer, was the second casual vessel which Dudley tried to secure as a consort, but in both cases he was baulked by the "monstrous outragiousness" of the weather.

Soon after this, while still at the Canaries, they at length succeeded in taking two carvels, one of which was smartly cut out close in shore by Jobson under a hot fire. Dudley at once manned the prizes with crews out of his own overcrowded ship, under Captains Wood and Wentworth; and he again begins to talk with pride of his "fleete of 3 sailes."

The addition to his strength was the more opportune as he saw no more of his truant vice-admiral. Monck, as he learned later, had, in fact, returned to England with a couple of prizes—"great and rich galleons," Kendall calls them—and left his leader to pursue the voyage without him as best he could. After waiting some time at the Canaries, and weathering a storm, the horrors of which Wyatt depicts as usual with a lurid pen, Dudley went on to look for him at Cape Blanco, on the mainland of Africa. While there, he landed in company with Wyatt and others to see the country, and both speak in much the same terms of its dreary and forbidding aspect. On the other hand, Dudley is discreetly silent about an action fought by his carvels off the cape with four French men-of-war, only one of which was of any size. It seems that they at first took the carvels, naturally enough, for Spanish fishing-boats; but even when the mistake was discovered, both sides were quite ready to fight the matter out, until the *Bear* interposed with her guns and made the Frenchmen sheer off. The story, which Wyatt tells with much spirit, shows how easily conflicts arose in foreign waters between ships of different nations nominally at peace or even in alliance.

From Cape Blanco, where he left letters for Monck "inclosed in a thinge of wood provided of purpose," Dudley bore away directly for Trinidad, setting sail on January 9th, 1595. According to Wyatt, it was given out that they would touch at Sant' Antão, one of the Cape Verde islands. This was perhaps a ruse for the benefit of those who dreaded being too long out of sight of land; and, at any rate, from fear of the unhealthiness of the place, Dudley and Kendall secretly contrived to run past during the night. For once, wind and weather were fair some twenty days together, and Wyatt therefore found time to study the habits of the flying-fish and its foes. Moreover, he had talks on deck with the "General"; and in an interesting passage (p. 20) he makes it clear that Dudley even at this early age was a skilled navigator and by no means wholly dependent upon his master. Wyatt, indeed, saw in him more than this, for he speaks of him as a hero whose actions "hearcafter will prove to be the worlds wonder."

It was on January 31st, 1595, that Dudley first sighted Trinidad, and the chief interest of his voyage begins from this date. Since Columbus discovered the island on July 31st, 1498, and named it after the Holy Trinity, the Spaniards had attempted from time to time to secure a hold upon it, but without success. Latterly Antonio de Berrio y Oruña had been more fortunate. Descending the Meta and Orinoco from New Granada, where he had married the heiress of the famous Captain-General Gonzalo Ximenes de Quesada, he reached Trinidad about 1584. On his arduous journey he had lost most of his force, but with the help of the Governor of Margarita he subdued the natives and set up some kind of government. In 1591 he fixed his capital at San José de Oruña, which he built six miles east of Puerto de los Hispanioles, now Port of Spain, by the side of a small river running into the Caroni some two miles south. Berrio, however, only valued Trinidad as a foothold for more ambitious schemes. He inherited from Quesada the dream of a kingdom in the interior of Guiana richer in gold than even Peru, and his hopes were all centred in the conquest of this shadowy El Dorado. When Dudley arrived, he was still busied in plans which were fated never to be carried out. In a few weeks Dudley sailed away, harmless and unharmed ; but he was almost immediately succeeded by Ralegh, and before the end of March San José was taken and burnt and Berrio was a prisoner.[1] The

---

[1] Borde, *Histoire de l'ile de la Trinidad sous le gouvernement espagnol*, 1876, i. p. 137 : De Verteuil, *Trinidad*, 2nd ed., 1884, p. 426.

history of these events, however, belongs to Ralegh's *Discoverie of Guiana*, and need not be pursued further here.

To Englishmen at this time Trinidad was probably very little known, although English ships no doubt found their way there in the course of trade or otherwise. One casual visit of more than ordinary interest is recorded in Lancaster's first voyage to the East Indies. In June, 1593, the *Edward Bonaventure*, when she was on her way home, after rounding the Cape of Good Hope and touching at St. Helena, proceeded to Trinidad, "hoping there to find refreshing, but we could not get any by reason that the Spaniards had taken it"; whereupon she sailed out of the Gulf of Paria through the Dragon's Mouth for Puerto Rico, only to encounter further troubles.[1] Dudley was also anticipated by Capt. Jacob Whiddon, who had been specially sent to Trinidad by Ralegh to learn all he could about Guiana and El Dorado. How far he succeeded in his immediate object is not known; but he probably did not stay long after the loss of eight of his crew, who were lured on shore and cut off by the Spaniards in an ambush. In March, 1595, he returned with Ralegh himself, when Berrio paid dearly for his treachery. Whiddon's former visit is dated by Ralegh the year before his own[2]; but as he was there on the arrival of the *Edward Bonaventure*, it was more probably in the summer of 1593. This was some eighteen months before Dudley appeared on the scene; but the latter may fairly claim to have been the first Englishman who landed troops and built a fort; who marched in battle array more than half way across the island; and who, as we

---

[1] *Voyages of Sir J. Lancaster*, ed. C. R. Markham, 1877, p. 29; and see also above, p. xvii.

[2] *Discoverie of Guiana*, pp. 6, 10. The *Dict. Nat. Biogr.* leaves Whiddon's fate doubtful, but Ralegh expressly states that he buried him in Trinidad, "after my returne from Guiana, being a man most honest and valiant" (p. 5).

now know for the first time, formally and ceremoniously laid claim to it in his sovereign's name. More than two centuries, however, were yet to elapse before this claim, such as it was, became a reality by the final cession of the island to Great Britain by the Treaty of Amiens in 1802.

Sailing along the south coast, Dudley passed round the south-western extremity, which, like Ralegh, he calls Point Curiapan, and anchored, to use his own words, " in a bay which was very full of pelicans, and I called it Pelicans Bay" (p. 70). The name does not appear in his map,[1] but its position seems to be marked by an anchor, and no doubt he means what is now known as Cedros Bay. Although Wyatt reports that they only just missed a rich booty by the over-eagerness of the two carvels, there were apparently no Spaniards so far south ; and they soon made friends with the Indians, whom Dudley describes as " a fine shaped and a gentle people, al naked and painted red." Both he and Wyatt give lists of words in their language, from which it is evident that they were of the well-known Arawak tribe, the " Arquachi" of the map. Although the number of words included is small, these vocabularies are of special interest, as they appear to be the earliest on record. As soon as a native was found who could speak Spanish, their first enquiry was for a gold-mine. How they were informed of one some eight or nine miles along the coast, and how they marched thither on February 2nd under Capt. Jobson, and again the next day in greater

---

[1] This map, a photo-lithographic reproduction of which accompanies the volume, is taken from the very valuable atlas which forms the sixth and last book of his *Arcano del Mare*. So far as Trinidad and the mouth of the Orinoco are concerned, it embodies his own observations, as well probably as Kendall's, made on the spot ; but it has the additions which might be expected, seeing that it was not published until 1646. There is another map in the British Museum (Add. MS. 17,940 A) with which it may be profitably compared, and which may perhaps be reproduced in the new edition of Ralegh's *Discoverie of Guiana*, now in preparation. The latter map, I am convinced, not only refers to Ralegh's voyage, but is actually in his own hand.

force under Dudley in person, returning on each occasion laden with ore—this is narrated by Wyatt in his happiest vein. The young General, it is satisfactory to learn, displayed no less admirable qualities on land than on sea; for he bore himself so gallantly under trying conditions of heat, toil, and fear of attack, that all his followers were convinced he would prove the "onlie mirrour of Knighthood." In his own concise valuation, Dudley admits that the ore after all was worthless. "All is not gold that glistereth," he remarks; and it proved in fact to be nothing more than marcasite or pyrites. What time elapsed before this unwelcome discovery was made we are not told; but Wyatt when he wrote was apparently still unaware of it. Some weeks later the same mine was pointed out to Ralegh. By his own account he at once detected its real character, and his remarks on those who had been less astute were no doubt aimed at Dudley and his followers.[1]

It was perhaps the elation caused by this delusive prospect of its mineral wealth that suggested to Dudley to appropriate Trinidad to the English Crown. This he did by the simple device of affixing to a tree near the supposed gold-mine a leaden plate bearing the Queen's arms, with an arrogant Latin inscription, of which Wyatt preserves a copy (p. 26). Wyatt himself played the chief part in the ceremony, which, fantastic as it appears in modern eyes, was evidently regarded by the actors as a serious function. Dudley, indeed, was so well satisfied that a fortnight later he caused it to be repeated still more solemnly by Captain Jobson, the wording of the inscription being slightly varied.

---

[1] "While we abode at the iland of Trinedado I was informed by an Indian that not farre from the port where we ancored there were founde certaine minerall stones which they esteemed to be gold, and were thereunto perswaded the rather for that they had seen both English and French men gather and imbarque some quantities thereof" (*Discoverie of Guiana*, p. xi).

This was on February 18th, when they had more reason to boast, having been nearly three weeks in the island unmolested, and doing there, as Wyatt says, "whatsoever it pleased our Generall to commaunde and liked ourselves best." During this time they had not been idle. On February 6th they moved further north to the Bay of Paracoa, where Dudley resolved to grave and trim his vessels, while the men lay ashore, protected by a "sconce." From its situation on his map, the town of Paracoa was either where San Fernando now stands, or not far off. It was held by the Spanish, though probably in small force; and Captain Jobson was on the point of starting to assault it, when they prevented him by sending a flag of truce and making friendly overtures. Whether they were sincere or not, the haughty letter which Dudley wrote to Jobson, and which Wyatt quotes in full, made anything like amicable relations impossible. It seems strange therefore that just at this time he sent away his two carvels "to try their fortune in the Indies," or, in other words, in quest of plunder. After they had gone, he states that he had only 50 men to oppose to the 300 whom Berrio had procured from Margarita (p. 70), and he must therefore have weakened his already small force by more than a half.[1] As it happened, he never came into actual conflict either with the Spaniards or the natives in Trinidad. The reason he gives for not taking the offensive against the former was that they were both "poore and strong"; while Berrio, for his part, did no more than keep a watchful eye on the invader's movements. His strength, indeed, was probably nothing like so great as Dudley supposed, for he was easily vanquished by Ralegh with only 100 men. The truth is

---

[1] Altogether he had 140 men (p. 69), but it is not likely that the carvels carried so many as 90 between them, and the 50 he speaks of may therefore be exclusive of those left on board to look after the ship. See also below, p. xxxii.

that Dudley's division of his forces, as he himself admits, was a compromise. He was anxious to penetrate into Guiana, but he dared not risk too much in the venture, and he parted therefore with his smaller craft so as not to forego the chance of paying his charges by a lucky capture at sea. What success they met, or what became of them, we do not hear; but as Captain Benjamin Wood, who commanded one of them, is heard of again, they probably reached England in safety.

Gold was the attraction in Guiana, as it was in Trinidad. At the same time, as we know now, there was far better chance of finding it. In the island it has yet to be discovered; but its presence on the mainland opposite is a fact beyond dispute, and in the light of the yearly returns it is hard to realise that it was at one time discredited. So far as appears, the mythical El Dorado—"the imperial city of Manoa"—which fascinated Ralegh and Berrio, was not in the thoughts of Dudley and his fellow-adventurers. Wyatt has not a word about it, and his leader speaks as if he only heard of it later. The more prosaic and practical object he had in view was to obtain possession of a mine; and after threats had been added to promises, Balthazar, the Spanish-speaking Indian whom he kept on board, undertook to guide them to one at Orocoa, the richness of which, as Wyatt assures us, was vouched for by at least a hundred other Indians who visited the ship. In Dudley's map Orocoa is located at the head of the delta of the Orinoco. It corresponds therefore with Ralegh's "Arriacoa, where Orenoque deuideth it selfe into three great braunches"[1]; but, if gold was really to be found there, it must have been obtained from alluvial washings alone. It is a pity that neither Dudley nor Wyatt was in the boat which went up the river

---

[1] *Discoverie of Guiana*, p. 100.

in search of this so-called mine, and we have thus no strictly first-hand report of what happened. Dudley's statement of his own eagerness to go is fully confirmed by Wyatt, who explains that, not only Jobson and Kendall, but the whole company protested against "soe worthie and hopefull a gallant" being hazarded in "soe small and simple a vessell" (p. 35). Dudley's version, as already noted (p. xvi), is slightly different, as it attributes their opposition rather to anxiety on their own account, if they were left to Kendall's mercy in his absence. In the narrative that goes under Kendall's own name it is made out that Dudley did go in person, and that he penetrated "with small boats and frigates" 300 miles within Guiana (p. 87); but, whoever is responsible for them, these statements are plainly untrue. The command of the single boat which was sent was given to Jobson, whose crew of twelve picked men ranged from the two master's mates to "two painfull and able Dutchmen."

The journey up the river, or rather the maze of branches which forms its mouth, cannot of course compare in interest with Ralegh's, though it can claim priority by a few weeks, and with so small a number of men it was certainly bolder. The force Ralegh had with him was much more imposing. Instead of one small boat, he commanded a flotilla, conveying upwards of one hundred men with a large amount of stores, and he was thus enabled to ascend the main stream of the Orinoco as high as the junction with the Caroni; added to this, his story has all the advantage of being told by his own eloquent pen. Dudley's narrative, it will be remembered, was written after the *Discoverie of Guiana* appeared, and there are signs in it of a consciousness that he had been outdone, and that the wind, so to speak, had been taken out of his sails. It is perhaps for this reason that he only gives a brief summary of Jobson's report of his fortnight's wandering, fuller details of which we owe to Wyatt's more curious enquiries. So far as its main object was concerned, the expedition was a failure. Jobson never saw the mine, and it is a question if he even reached Orocoa, as it is not quite clear whether his meeting with Armago, its "captain" or chief, took place there or lower down the river. According to Dudley, this Armago not only declared explicitly that he "had a mine of gold and could refine it," but offered to trade, and as an earnest sent him a few golden crescents and two bracelets of silver; moreover, it was from him they heard of El Dorado and the nation whose bodies were dusted with gold. Less well informed, or perhaps more truthful, Wyatt says nothing of this. He dwells instead on the hardships of the return journey, which are in striking contrast with the picture he gives of the tropical beauties of the scene as they rowed up stream. When Balthazar, after bringing them into a narrow and almost impervious channel, slipped away in the night, their sole guide was a frightened Indian who could only direct them by signs; and when he, too, tried to escape, and had been "stricken by a brown bill," it was with the utmost difficulty that they at length regained the ship, after all on board, except Dudley, had given them up for lost. It was no wonder therefore that Dudley could find no one willing to join him in a fresh attempt. "But nowe," he complains, "they were worse then before . . . for my men came home in very pitifull case, half dead for famine."

As no more could be done in this direction, he left Trinidad on March 12th, 1595, "to see further of the Indies." Though his boat must have returned some days earlier, he records nothing in the interval, except that he waited with Popham for Ralegh. Wyatt, however, fills up the gap with a graphic account of their last and longest march on shore. This was the march which in an earlier passage (p. 71) Dudley describes as extending fifty miles, and from one side of the island to the other, and on which, according to Kendall's narrative (p. 87), he took with him three hundred men ! Wyatt's candour makes short work of these pretensions. He states distinctly that the force comprised about sixty of Dudley's men and ten of Popham's, and that they advanced into the interior no more than some twenty miles; considering, indeed, the nature of the country, and the fact that they were only one night away from the ships, the wonder is that they penetrated the "monstrous thicke wood" so far. In the part where they were, Trinidad is about thirty-five miles across; and it is not only clear from Wyatt's account that they did not reach the further side, but in Dudley's own map Carao or, as Wyatt calls it, Carowa, which was the limit of the march, is placed at some distance from the east coast. They were lured thither, as elsewhere, by stories of gold, for Carowa was reported to be the spot where the ore from the Trinidad mine before mentioned was refined. As usual, too, they got little for their pains. Not an Indian remained; and for evidence of the truth of the report they had to be content with a few melting-pots and some dross. The reason Wyatt gives for the flight of the Indians is a singular one. They were terrified, he says, at the noise the English made on the march, which they did on purpose to attract the notice of the Spaniards, advancing with "collers displaide in honour of England and maugre the Spaniards berd." Though it was partly no doubt from policy, it is to Dudley's credit that he treated the Indians well, giving strict orders that their houses and goods should not be disturbed.

As soon as the *Bear* sailed out of the Gulf of Paria northwards on March 12th, his mind was again bent upon capturing prizes; and "it pleased God to bless him soe," that he took one the very next day on the way to Puerto Rico. She was outward bound, and her cargo of wine linen, hats and such-like shows the nature of the goods which Spain exported to her colonies. Wyatt has much to say of their dealings with her and her crew until she was gutted and burnt off Cape Roxo, this being the occasion, already alluded to (p. xiv), when he taught the prisoners, what Dudley's chivalrous kindness had made them forget, that "they weare to suffer with patience the fortune of the warrs" (p. 50). Dudley, however, was flying at higher game. His plan now was to intercept stragglers from the plate-fleet due, as he learned from some of his prisoners, to leave Havana in April; indeed, Kendall's story is that he had been expressly instructed to do this by the Queen. Accordingly, after lying vainly off Cape Roxo in the hope of catching ships from San Domingo, he made the dangerous passage between that island and Puerto Rico on March 25th. For two days he sailed north-north-east towards Bermuda, and then took a more westerly course. Fortune, however, was adverse; and, in his own words, "the fleete I found not, but foule weather enough to scatter many fleetes" (p. 76). The other two narrators tell the same tale, Wyatt quite surpassing himself in his description of their miseries. For a whole month, it seems, they were driven at the mercy of wind and wave, and the *Bear* must have been both stoutly built and ably handled to have survived. According to Wyatt, they ran up the coast of Florida and Virginia, and found themselves at last near Labrador; but the highest latitude marked by Kendall is 40° 10', and from this point they flew before a gale across the Atlantic to the Azores, which they reached in safety on April 28th.

As victuals by this time were running short, Dudley resolved to make at once for England, and on the way, in lat. 45°, on May 6th, he met the crowning adventure of the voyage. In his own brief report of the two-days' fight with a Spanish ship of war he describes her as being of six hundred tons. This is just double Wyatt's estimate; but otherwise they are in close accord, and Wyatt merely fills up the other's outline with picturesque details. On a smaller scale, the fight was a repetition of what happened in the Channel with the Spanish Armada in 1588, the active *Bear* " working warelie to keep the wind" and pouring shot into her heavier antagonist, who " went upright as a church." With a storm-battered vessel, a crew of barely fifty men, only four guns fit for use, and only nine barrels of powder unspoiled by water, it was a daring step to provoke an action; nor did they draw off until their powder was exhausted and boarding was found impossible. Dudley's hope, no doubt, was that the enemy would yield in good time; but, for reasons which Wyatt explains, this was not to be, and the only fruit of victory was the conviction that she must sink before she reached land. Although the *Bear* herself by no means came off unscathed, only one man, strange to say, was wounded by a shot. Dudley does not mention his own very narrow escape; but both Wyatt and Kendall tell how his " leading staff" was knocked to pieces in his hand. From the former we also hear of another curious incident, that in the very thick of the fight Jobson, noting the bravery of Dudley's page, Bradshew, led him up to his master and declaimed some aptly-chosen lines from Kidd's popular *Spanish Tragedie* in his praise. Such a " fine conceipt" was thoroughly in harmony with the taste of the time, and Dudley was just the man to appreciate it.[1] Leaving the Spanish ship to her fate, he now resumed his

---

[1] Something of the same kind occurred during Rodney's famous action with the French fleet off Dominica in 1782. While the fight was raging round the *Glorieux*, Sir Charles Douglas, Rodney's flag-captain, exclaimed: " Behold, Sir George, the Greeks and Trojans contending for the body of Patroclus!" " Damn the Greeks and damn the Trojans! I have other things to think of," was the Admiral's reply. A few minutes later, however, when victory was secure, he added: " Now, my dear friend, I am at the service of your Greeks and Trojans and the whole of Homer's *Iliad*, or as much of it as you please" (*Mundy, Life of Rodney*, 1830, ii, p. 304).

course for England, and, after narrowly escaping the rocks of Scilly in a fog, he landed at St. Ives, in Cornwall, at the end of May, 1595, after a voyage that lasted just six months. During this time he had seen and learned much, and had amply proved his courage and fitness for command; but beyond this he had little to show on his return. At the close of his narrative, the most he claims is that he and his fleet had taken or destroyed nine Spanish ships,[1] and his own feeling in the matter is expressed in his final words, "which was losse to them, though I got nothing."

An interesting letter written by him to Sir Robert Cecil just after his return is preserved at Hatfield. A copy of it here follows, and by the kindness of Lord Salisbury a collotype facsimile is also given. As it was dated from Wilton, Dudley was probably breaking his journey there with Lord Pembroke on his way up from Cornwall to London, and its tone shows his anxiety to secure a powerful patron.

"Most honorable Sir Robert Sileet,[2]

"How much I honour you and how infinitly I thinke my se[l]fe tyed vnto you for your manie honourable fauours, which I vnderstande by my mother, I cannot chouse for them but make my self your voued seruant by luines (?)[3] and allso by the vttermost of my seruice and dewtifull affection striue in some measure to make satisfaction of your honours kindnes. Sir, my true louing and honoring you is all the recompence I am able to make, which though it be not of worth sufficient to counteruayle the least parte of your honours kindnes, yet I humbly beseach you take it, as all he is able to doe that vnfaynedly honoreth you. And that, I assure your honour, you shall allway commaunde more then anie gentillman in Englande. Let me intreate you not to take me as a complimentall courtier, but as a playne dealing saylor,

---

[1] The three unaccounted for (p. 77, note) were possibly taken by the carvels after they parted.
[2] This is a singular corruption for "Cecil," but it is so also in the address on the outside.
[3] I can make nothing else of this word, but it is unintelligible. Possibly it is the name of a messenger.

that hath learned to loue them honestly and vnfaynedly that he is so much bounde to as to your honour. The discourse of those matters I haue seane I leaue till I wayte vpon you, which shalbe when I haue in some reasonable sorte recouered my health, which hath bine not alltogether the best sence I came ; I am stronge inouf, but somthing dulled with the sea fare. The best thinges I knowe I shalbe glade to make knowne vnto your honour. So intreating perdone for my bouldnes, I humbly take my leaue in mannor as best becometh me. From Wilton, this 11th of Junne, 1595.

Your honors poure frende to commaund in
all dewtie and seruice,
Ro: Duddeley.

"I beseach Gode sende your fortunes as greate as I shall allway wish them, which shoulde be as great as your selfe can desier them.

"Lett me intreate your honour to excuse my not writting to my Lord your father, for I am affrayde I shoulde be trowblesome vnto him ; but I humbly pray you to assure him that I am one that honoreth him and his house as much as anie man shall doe."

What effect this letter and the subsequent interview had does not appear ; but it was not long before adverse influences were at work in the same quarter. On November 10th, 1595, Ralegh in his turn wrote to Sir Robert Cecil, and in the course of his letter he remarked :—

"What becomes of Guiana I much desire to hear, whether it pass for a history or a fable. I hear Mr. Dudley and others are sending thither ; if it be so, farewell all good from thence, for, although myself, like a cockscomb, did rather prefer the future in respect of others, and rather sought to win the kings to her Majestys service than to sack them, I know what others will do when those kings shall come simply into their hands. If it may please you to acquaint my Lord Admiral therewith, let it then succeed as it will."[1]

---

[1] *Cal. of Hatfield MSS.*, pt. v, 1894, p. 445. This was before the publication of his *Discoverie*.

These ill-natured reflections apparently had the result intended, for whatever plans Dudley may have formed for another venture to Guiana, they came to nothing, and his vessels, the *Bear*, the *Whelp*, and another, are next heard of on their ill-starred voyage to China under Captain Benjamin Wood,[1] at the beginning of 1597.

Dudley himself served in the expedition against Spain under the Earls of Essex and Nottingham in 1596. He there commanded the *Nonpareil*[2]; but in the contemporary accounts he by no means plays the prominent part which he arrogates to himself in the *Direttorio Marittimo*.[3] On the contrary, in the actual attack upon the fleet in Cadiz harbour on June 21st even the command of the *Nonpareil* appears to have been taken out of his hands, as Lord Thomas Howard, the Vice-admiral, removed into it out of his own *Honor de la Mar*, which drew too much water.[4] After the capture of Cadiz, his services were rewarded by knighthood. This honour, however, was not conferred upon him, as upon so many others, in Spain, but at Plymouth, on Aug. 8th, on their return, "in the open streete when the Lords Generall came from the sermon," the same account[5] which mentions this eulogising him as having "so many good parts of a woorthy gentleman as the like are seldome seene to concurre in any."

---

[1] It was perhaps in connection with this expedition that a warrant was issued on January 22nd, 1596-7, for the Queen's usual reward to Dudley, among others, as owners of a newly-built ship (*Cal. of State Papers*, 1595-97, p. 351).

[2] He was appointed a captain in March (*Cal. of State Papers*, 1595-97, p. 190).

[3] "He took the command of the great English fleet in 1596, in the absence of his uncle, the Earl of Nottingham, High Admiral. The year following (*sic*) he was Admiral of the English vanguard in the battle of Cadiz, in Spain . . . Then he besieged Faro, in Algarna [Algarve], in Portugal, and next took command of the English galleons sent to the rescue when Calais was besieged by his S. H. the Archduke of Mentoza" (Leader, *Life of Sir R. Dudley*, p. 33).

[4] W. B. Devereux, *Lives of the Devereux*, i, p. 361.

[5] Hakluyt, 1598, i, p. 146.

This was Dudley's last active service at sea, and no more perhaps need be said by way of preface to his early voyage. At the same time, it will not be out of place to explain briefly the circumstances under which his talents were lost to his own country, and devoted for the best part of his life to the interests of a foreign state. His hapless attempt to prove his legitimacy, and so establish his right to be Earl of Leicester and Warwick, was begun in 1603, when he was in his thirtieth year. In such a case motives, laudable and otherwise, are not far to seek. With his proud and sensitive nature, he would naturally seize any opportunity of removing the stigma on his birth ; and there is little doubt that he was also spurred on by the ambition of his second wife, Alice Leigh,[1] and her father, Sir Thomas Leigh, of Stoneleigh, co. Warwick. The story, as hitherto known, comes solely from Dugdale, who tells it both in his *Warwickshire* and his *Baronage*, adding in the latter a summary of the adverse judgment delivered in the Star Chamber on May 10th, 1605. Although he says of the alleged marriage, " I shall leave it dubious," he hardly conceals his own belief in it, and modern writers have been still more outspoken. There is a good deal notwithstanding to be said to the contrary. Whether Dugdale had access to all the documents is doubtful ; his account is certainly incomplete, and he practically confines himself to the evidence on one side. To judge the case fairly, careful attention must also be given to the numerous depositions and other papers which have lain unnoticed at Longleat[2]

---

[1] He probably married her after his return from the Cadiz expedition in 1596, his eldest daughter, Alice Douglas Dudley, being baptized at Kenilworth September 25th, 1597 (Vaughan Thomas, *The Italian Biography of Sir R. Dudley*, p. 74).

[2] Dudley Papers, Boxes vi-viii, being three (A, D, H) out of eight books referred to in a synopsis of the case, which is included. An exemplification of the judgment is in Box iv, No. 88. These papers descended to the Marquis of Bath from the sister and heir of Robert Devereux, third and last Earl of Essex. The Dudley Papers at Pens-

and Penshurst, and which at least prove that there were reasonable grounds for doubt.

Seeing that his claim involved two earldoms, besides Warwick Castle and other valuable properties, it appears strange that Dudley did not move in the House of Lords or in one of the superior courts of law; but legal technicalities perhaps stood in the way. Instead of this, he began by procuring on May 20th, 1603, a commission to examine witnesses from the Court of Audience of Canterbury. This was executed quietly at Stoneleigh, under the eye of his father-in-law; and he then followed it up by a more or less collusive action in the Consistory Court of Lichfield on September 27th against one Buswell for calling him "bastard," the object being, as it appeared, to get the marriage formally put on record by means of *ex parte* testimony. News of this, however, leaked out, and on October 10th the Privy Council issued a mandate to quash the proceedings, and to compel Dudley to begin afresh in one of the higher ecclesiastical courts, where all parties interested might be heard. Those who were chiefly affected, morally and materially, were Lettice, Leicester's reputed widow, and Robert, Lord Sidney of Penshurst, whose mother, Mary Dudley, was sister and, in default of lawful issue, co-heir to both Leicester and Warwick.[1] Less open, but perhaps even more dangerous, opposition might also be expected from the Crown, to which some of the lands in dispute had reverted by escheat. It seems that Lady Leicester did not wait for any further proceedings on Dudley's part. Acting presumably within her rights, but with what looks like sharp practice, on February 10th, 160¾, she filed a bill in the Star

---

hurst, comprised in three bound volumes, belong to Lord De Lisle and Dudley as representative of the first Lord Sidney.

[1] Robert Dudley was thus first cousin to Sir Philip Sidney, as well as to Lord Sidney.

Chamber against Dudley, his wife and mother, and his principal witnesses and agents, for conspiracy and defamation. The effect of this was that the issue really tried was not so much the truth of the marriage as the legality of the methods used to get up the case; indeed, according to Rowland White, writing just after the judgment, "the matter of marriage was not handled at all: only the practise was proved in the proceedings."[1] But, although the main question was, perhaps of legal necessity, left to the ecclesiastical courts, and was in fact never judicially determined, the evidence on which Dudley relied was fully set out in the depositions in the Star Chamber, and much of it is still available. To examine it in detail here is of course impossible.[2] Putting aside a mass of hearsay and loose gossip, which was largely the reflection of Leicester's unpopularity and an echo of the malignant attack upon him in 1584, the really material witnesses were Lady Sheffield herself, two of her former household, who declared they were present at the marriage, and Owen Jones. It is noteworthy that, as she admitted, Lady Sheffield was strongly opposed to the question being raised, at least while she was alive. The false position in which she had placed herself by marrying Sir Edward Stafford is enough perhaps to account for this; otherwise it might be suspected that she had good reasons to know the weakness of her son's claim. Be that as it may, on her examination her story was precise and circumstantial enough.[3]

Briefly, it was to the effect that she was contracted to

---

[1] Letter to the Earl of Shrewsbury, May 13th, 1605 (Lodge, *Illustrations*, iii, p. 160).
[2] There were no less than ninety witnesses on Dudley's part and fifty-seven on the Attorney-General's; but the evidence of the majority is only found in a summary form, in papers entitled "A State of the Sute," etc.
[3] It was given in the form of answers to interrogatories at her residence at Sudeley, June 6th and 7th, 1604, copies of which are at Penshurst.

Leicester in 1571 in Canon Row, Westminster, and lawfully married to him in the winter of 1573, at night, in her own chamber at Esher House. Who the "minister" was she could not say, nor could any of the witnesses; but she actually named no less than ten persons who, *besides others*, were present. The most important of them was Sir Edward Horsey, who, as she said, gave her away, and the rest were chiefly her own servants. One of the two alleged eye-witnesses now produced was Henry Frodsham, who had been her gentleman-usher. His evidence has not been preserved, and beyond its general purport we hear little of him, except that he was brought out of Yorkshire in order to give it by his cousin, Magdalen Salisbury. The latter plays a very dubious part in the existing papers. She declared[1] that, as Magdalen Frodsham, she was Lady Sheffield's gentlewoman for five or six years from about 1572, until she married Thomas Salisbury, but she refused to say how or where she had lived since. In 1603 she was in a humble position, if not in penury, lodging, apparently rent-free, in a house which by a curious coincidence belonged to Thomas Ward, who was employed by Dudley as a proctor. In some unexplained way she there became known to Thomas Drury, a man of good family[2] but of notoriously evil character, who in the judgment of the Star Chamber originated the whole conspiracy to establish the marriage. He died of the plague on August 26th, 1603, before the Star Chamber proceedings began; but, unless his widow and other witnesses[3] lied, his dealings with the woman Salisbury, whose statement was taken

---

[1] Answers, May 15th, 1604, at Penshurst.

[2] He was brother of Sir William Drury, of Hawstead, Suffolk, who married a sister of Sir Edward Stafford, Lady Sheffield's husband (Brit. Mus. Add. MS. 19,127, f. 179).

[3] Answers of Elizabeth Drury, Will. Reeve, and Will. Rowse, at Longleat (Box vi). The last deposed that, when he was sent to fetch the woman, she said, "What would they have me to doe? I was very

down in his room and sent by him to Dudley, were open to the gravest suspicions. His object plainly was to extract money, and a letter from him to Dudley on August 8th, saying he had made her "subscribe to the noate," and that "she is verie forward to depose for a further consideracion," is so cynically frank that it is difficult to believe it genuine.[1] Salisbury's account of the marriage agreed with that of her mistress, and, if it was false, they must have been acting in concert. One element of doubt is that she seems to have explained her presence in two different ways. In her answers of May 15th, 1604, she said she was nineteen at the time and was commanded by Lady Sheffield to "attend upon her"; while according to Thomas Ward, a friendly witness, her story to him was that she was of "verie tender yeares" and that "she came into the chamber by chaunce and woulde have gone out, but one Frodsham wished her to staie there as well as others."[2] It was deposed also, though there was equally evidence the other way, that she did not enter Lady Sheffield's service until after Dudley's birth; and in support of this Lady Parker, the intimate friend of Lady Sheffield, who was with the latter for a fortnight at her lying-in and whose evidence is transparently honest, disclaimed any knowledge of her until later.[3]

Although it was Drury's discovery of Magdalen Salisbury that set the case going, Owen Jones, if he spoke truth, had offered his testimony to Dudley about four years

---

young and I cannot remember anything." According to Mrs. Drury, her husband "reminded her [Salisbury] of manie things, which she straight verified and confessed, but did not tell them before." There was no doubt a good deal of false swearing in the case.

[1] It is quoted among "matter to discover the practise" in a paper at Penshurst, and ends, after allusion to his own "travell" in the business, "As I like of your answere and dealing, soe I shall proceede; if not pinchingly [*i.e.*, grudgingly or stingily], I am yours. Mora trahit periculum." The handwriting was proved by T. Denny.

[2] Dudley Papers at Longleat, Box vi, f. 34.

[3] Answers, January 10th, 1604 (*ib.* Box vii, f. 146).

earlier.[1] Since Leicester's death he had lived a roving life in the wars and at sea, and had finally returned to his home in Wales. As to his character witnesses differed; but he was needy, and when he sought out Dudley it was apparently in the hope of relief. The story with which he introduced himself to his favour has already been noticed (p. vii). Apart from the discrepancy in the two versions of Leicester's alleged speech to him, at best it is too glaringly improbable to be taken on trust, for it compels us to believe that the Earl confessed to his footman what he studiously concealed from the rest of the world down to his death. There is one point, however, in Jones's favour. In his evidence he makes no pretence of having witnessed the marriage; and it is the more curious therefore that Lady Sheffield in her answers of June 7th, 1604, includes him among those who were present. But this may have been a mere slip, or even a clerical error, and it need not be unduly pressed.

But the crucial evidence was Lady Sheffield's own; for either it was true, or Dudley must have convinced her, as well as himself, that all means were lawful which would redress the wrong they had both suffered by his father's duplicity. That Leicester promised her marriage, and basely used the Queen's jealousy as an excuse for delay, hardly admits of doubt; but even if the engagement was as formal as she affirmed,[2] the balance of probability is against its ever having been legally carried out. There is no hint of any family pressure, as later in the case of Lady Essex. According to Lady Sheffield, indeed, the "principal

---

[1] Answers, May 28th, 1604, among the papers at Penshurst. He is elsewhere described as "base and pore, a knight of the post ... a comon drunckard," etc.

[2] Her deposition as to the contract is at Longleat (Box vi, f. 48). She says that seven or eight witnesses were present, before whom the Earl said, "I doe vowe to have no other wife but you," and further, "I doe take you to be my wife," and so on.

mover" in the marriage was her kinsman, the Duke of
Norfolk; but he was beheaded on June 2nd, 1572, eighteen
months before its alleged date. Her own account was
that, suspecting herself (some two years after the contract)
to be with child, she desired the Earl "to performe his
promise and to marry her, which hee perfourmed"; at the
same time, as if this was not enough, although he insisted
on absolute secrecy, he had the marriage solemnized
before a dozen or more witnesses, and those not specially
selected for their discretion, but called in almost at
random. Magdalen Salisbury went further, and deposed
that the priest showed a "licence or dispensacion" from
the Archbishop; if so, some official record was presumably
kept, but neither this nor any other documentary evidence
was produced. Granting that Leicester's persistent denial
goes for nothing, one of the strongest arguments against
the marriage is Lady Sheffield's behaviour when he cast
her off and married her rival. If proof was really so
abundant, her neglect to avail herself of it at the time
is more than ever inexplicable. Although she may have
been "the pitifullest abused that ever was poore ladie,"[1]
she was not a simple, country-bred girl, such as Amy
Robsart is depicted in *Kenilworth*, but a woman of the
world, brought up at Court and having powerful connections, and the notion that she was paralysed by fear is not
easily credible. Yet it was actually not until after the Lichfield proceedings of 1603, when without her testimony the
marriage was thought to be established, that, at her son's
suggestion, she wrote to her brother, the Earl of Nottingham,
protesting that she had been Leicester's lawful wife. Her
friend Lady Parker "believed in her conscience" that she
was married, and so understood from her; but, although
she recalled her tears and distress and her bitter complaints

---

[1] *The Copie of a leter*, etc., p. 36.

that Leicester had "falsified his faith to her," she pointedly
abstained from saying that she ever had from her any such
account of the marriage as she gave five-and-twenty years
later, and the whole of her evidence is consistent with the
existence of a promise of marriage only.[1] Whether Lady
Sheffield had real grounds for asserting that the Earl had
tried to poison her, so that she was "moved for saufgard of
her liffe (liffe being sweete) to determyne to marry," is
impossible to say. She was bound to offer some explanation of her becoming the wife of Sir Edward Stafford; but
her true motive may have been the wish to rehabilitate
herself, in which happily she seems to have succeeded.
Stafford died while the case was in progress, but not before
he had made a deposition, which, if true, shows almost
conclusively that there was not even a binding contract.
As it is given in an abstract of evidence at Penshurst, he
declared that, after his marriage, the Queen pressed him to
"importune his wief whether theare were a contracte
betwene her and the Erle of Leicester, which if it were,
then she would make him make vpp her honour with a
marriage or rott in the Tower, and would better the estate
of Stafforde. She aunswered with greate vowes, greif and
passion that she had trusted the said Erle to[o] much to
have any thing to shew to constraine him to marrie her.
The like she did to the Queene, and the like to the Erle of
Sussex; and that she had tould Stafford the trueth before
she married him." Elizabeth's hatred of Lady Essex,

---

[1] On her way to Cornwall, a month after Robert Dudley's birth, she
met his father at Salisbury, where he was attending on the Queen.
He asked her, "How doth my lady and my boy?" which is the nearest
approach to an admission of the marriage reported on trustworthy
authority. But the term "my lady" applied to Lady Sheffield is
ambiguous, and so long as there was no actual marriage, Leicester
was no doubt ready enough to save her reputation. Lady Parker,
moreover, though she read the letter of which so much was made in
evidence, could not say that it was signed "Your loving husband," as
alleged. The Queen and Leicester were at Salisbury on Sept. 5th,
1574 (Lodge. ii, p. 43).

whom she would gladly have humiliated, is quite enough to account for her intervention; while the mention of the Earl of Sussex shows that Leicester's enemies were equally ready to champion his victim's cause, if she could have substantiated her claim to be his wife.

In the judgment given on May 10th, 1605, the Star Chamber found that Dudley had been the dupe of Drury, who, "to work his own private gains," had induced him to believe that his mother's marriage could be proved, having overcome his first doubts by the statement which had been obtained "by large promises" from Magdalen Salisbury. Drury's death had put him beyond reach; but for later developments Sir William Leighton,[1] who appears to have been Dudley's chief agent in the business, was held mainly responsible. He was accordingly fined £300, while Dr. Babington, judge of the Consistory Court at Lichfield, was mulcted in 100 marks, Magdalen Salisbury[2] and Henry Frodsham in £100 each, and Owen Jones in £40, all of them moreover being committed. What was still more serious for Dudley's claim, the last three were "to be ever after held suspected in their testimonies," and all depositions and other documents were impounded. Dudley and his mother were acquitted without even a censure; but there was nothing against them, Lady Sheffield's depositions in particular not having been made until after the Lichfield suit, beyond which the inquiry did not extend.

---

[1] He was author of two poems, *Vertue Triumphant*, 1603, and *The Teares or Lamentations of a Sorrowfull Soule*, 1613, the latter reissued with . . . . *Musicall Ayres and Tunable Accents*, 1614. His fortunes must have been at a low ebb, as he was sued for debts in 1608, and outlawed in 1610, and seems to have passed his later days in prison (*Dict. Nat. Biogr.*).

[2] Lady Sheffield seems to have taken her into her service again, and she left her some of her body-linen in her will (*Misc. Gen. et Her.*, iii, 1880, p. 370). The will, dated Sept. 14th, 1608, includes a bequest of a black velvet bed, etc., to her "honorable and beloved son Sir Robert Dudley," who, it will be noticed, is not designated under his assumed titles.

Whatever was the precise legal effect of this judgment, practically it barred Dudley from all further prosecution of his claim. Although the Court of Arches was still open to him, the stigma put upon his witnesses was evidently regarded as an obstacle, for a motion was made[1] to modify its terms in such a way that, whereas "they were censured as suspected, they should be set down only as 'subject to suspicion.'" The distinction does not seem vital; but, in any case, it was a misfortune that the question of the marriage was not argued out on its merits, if only to remove the impression of a miscarriage of justice. This hope having failed, Dudley gave up the contest, and on June 25th he obtained a license to travel for three years abroad. When he left England shortly after,[2] he made a fresh sensation by carrying away with him a young maid-of-honour and noted beauty, Elizabeth Southwell, disguised as his page[3]; and, to add to the scandal and complete the ruin of his fortunes in his native land, after they had both declared themselves Catholics, he formally married her,[4] although his second wife, Alice Leigh, who had borne him several daughters, was still living. There is no doubt that he was passionately attached to the girl who had thrown in her lot with him, and he continued so until

---

[1] Letter of P. Sandford, June 7th, 1605 (Lodge, iii, p. 163). The Earls of Salisbury and Dorset and the Chief Justice spoke against it, and the Earl of Northumberland in its favour.

[2] He apparently set out July 4th (Leader, p. 177), and certainly before the 6th (Lodge, iii, p. 167). Adlard and *Dict. Nat. Biogr.* say he was still in England, and meditating a renewal of his suit, four months later, but the true date of his letter to Sir A. Atye, on which they rely, is Nov. 2nd, 1603, not 1605, and it refers to his intentions after the Privy Council stopped the case at Lichfield.

[3] She was his own first cousin once removed, being a daughter of Sir Rob. Southwell, of Woodrising, Norfolk, by Elizabeth, daughter of Charles Howard, Earl of Nottingham (Brit. Mus. Add. MS. 19,149, f. 292).

[4] As they were cousins, he procured a Papal dispensation, but in applying for it he appears to have suppressed the fact that he was married already (Leader, p. 50). Later he tried to induce the Pope to annul the earlier marriage, but it is not clear whether he succeeded.

they were parted by death ; but, in his disgust at the issue
of the trial, he may also have felt a malicious satisfaction
in doing what his father, as he contended, had been allowed
to do with impunity. This marriage, undoubtedly bigamous,
although it was acknowledged abroad as valid, is said to
have taken place at Lyons ; but after a short stay there
he made his way to Florence, which became his home until
his death in 1649.

Fascinating and full of romance as the story of his life
in Italy is, it is too large a subject to be fully treated here,
and little more can be done than to direct attention to the
valuable new materials for it which are to be found in
Mr. Temple Leader's recent work. It was not the case, as
might be thought, that on leaving England he shook its
dust off his feet in disgust, with the resolve never to return.
At least down to 1618, the chief cause of his remaining
abroad was the resentment of the King, fostered no doubt
by the malice of his enemies and by his own folly. On
Feb. 2nd, 1607, his license to travel was revoked, with the
plainly-expressed intention of calling him to account for
his doings abroad.[1] His answer, addressed to his kinsman,
Henry Howard, Earl of Northampton, on April 29th,[2] is
so curious and characteristic that, as it has apparently
never been printed, it may find a place here.

" MY LORD,

"The Ambassadour to his Maiestie at Venice[3] sent hether
to mee a Privye Seale, which beinge a writinge of Recorde and the
labell of superscription derogating from my due pretences and
right which I clayme, being lawfull sonne and heire to my father,
I durst not open as consenting to, so to receave the same Privie

---

[1] See the Privy Seal, printed by Adlard, p. 287.
[2] Preserved in a contemporary copy in the Public Record Office
(*Cal. of State Papers*, 1603-1610, p. 347). The copyist, as will be
seen, failed to decipher some of the words.
[3] The well-known Sir Henry Wotton, who was certainly not a
" vain, fantastical man," as Dudley slightingly describes him later on.

Seale, least in so doing it might bee preiudiciall to my right and tytle for the premisses. Therfore [I] doe with all humilitie returne it herein, which I would not, if it had beene a private letter and no Recorde. But with this aunswere I doe returne it, that whatsoever it shall please his Maiestie to command mee I doe most willingly obey, as his faythfull and obedient subiect, and the least note of any of his Maiesties Councell shall bee sufficient to me to obey his Maiesties pleasure and command in all thinges. Furthermore, I am to entreat your Lordship to informe his Maiestie that these commaunded to delyver the Privie Seale, as one Mr. Rooke and one Mr. Winnebancke and Captayne Yorke and Mr. Cockeyne, that came with him, and Mr. Stone, these amongest them spred abroad that I was recalled in it to bee heynouslye punished, and that I was one in such disgrace with his Maiestie and so hatefull to him and so much mistrusted as the Englishe Marchauntes were by them or of them chidden for at all comming to mee and commanded not to come to mee in peyne of loosinge what they hadd. Mr. Mones, an Englishe Marchaunt, came to testifie the same. This is a great disreputacion for mee, to bee published over Italy for a traytor and worse, having deserved no ill of his Maiestie, I protest to God, in the leest thought. Besydes I hold the same course not very honourable for his Maiestie to have bruted in his Maiesties name such scandalls to a subiect before tryall. I knowe not how his Maiestie findeth the service of his Ambassadour, but here the wisest count him a vayne fantasticall man, busye enough, but so full of Cornelius Tacitus in his phrases and affection as I may forbeare to write or meddle with the censures.

But to returne to the matter, what are the treasones manifested against mee by them? 1. That I am a Roman Catholique; so I saye is 20,000 professed in England and good subiectes. 2. That I have made a marriage, they saye, questyonable; so did the Earle of Devonshire,[1] one of his Maiesties most trusted Privie Councellours, and the like questiones (they suggested) are in questione daylie in the Arches without offence to the state. 3. That abroad I take vppon me the tytles of my pretences; to which I aunswere

---

[1] Charles Blount, who in 1605, against the canon law, married Penelope, the divorced wife of Lord Rich. Dudley's case was not analogous, as there had been no divorce.

I maye better doe it abroad, being my vndoubted right, thoughe questioned by his Maiestie, then the Lord of Westmerland, the Lord Beauchampe and the Lord Mounteagle did, before he hadd the graunt from the King, and did it and doe it at home daylie, not only by the examples of this tyme but all other. But I may saye I have more reasone to doe it here in all Catholique partes then they, bycause I have not only made my full proofe thereof in England and past the assaye of the Starchamber and have the same examinacions as evidence to defend my right, as no other nobleman hath more but these to defend them, but also publique storries doe give sufficient testymonie to all the Catholique partes of the world by there lawes to account mee lawfull sonne and heire to my father, and so consequently Earle of Warwicke and Leicester. Yf I hadd no other proofe but that, it were sufficient and no more excepted at here then that my Lord of Arrundells younger sonne is called Count Arrundell over Germanie.

Yf these bee all the allegacions my enymies have made against mee to his Maiestie, as I presume no man can bee so horrible a lyar to speake worse against me, I hope his Maiestie will account my enymies report [*blank space in original*] and not competent witnesse not [*blank space in original*] disgrace me over the world by recalling mee vppon these reportes, whereby the world will censure them true and me so vilde as they reporte. God knowes my hart is faythfull to the Kinge and State and not to bee withdrawne from it. Therefore my knowledg of myself maketh mee presume with confydence this peticion to his Maiestie, that I maye both staye abroad with his leave to repayre my reputacion abroad and at home, that I am his loyall faythfull subiect, and heareafter by that demonstracion given to returne contentedly with hope to deserve his Maiesties gratious favoure and not to live thus a living death withowt it to returne dowbtfully censured in disgrace with his Maiestie and so to bee daily wronged by mine enymies, which I cannot endure, and the least of these would bee to mee the same death. Also I desire most humbly to have leave to give my best assistaunce and service to the great Duke of Florence, his Maiesties faythfull frend, in all his designes against the Turke, or if not leave, that it will not be ill taken. Therebye I shall better manifest to his Maiestie how farre I am able to serve him and my master the Prince. And thus desiring your Lordship to make this relacion for mee in my behalf to his

Maiestie, I humbly take my leave. From Ligornia, the xxixth of Aprill, 1607.
                    Your Lordshipps most faythfull and
                    affectionate kinseman,
                        WARWICK AND L[EYCESTER]."

" I further pray his Maiestie I may not bee so vsed by his Ambassadours and by their spies and ministers."

One of the charges against him being his assumption of the title of an earl, his surrender might have been the means of re-opening the whole question of his birth. His mad passion for Elizabeth Southwell had, however, put a new difficulty in his way. A trial for bigamy now involved a greater risk than he probably cared to face[1]; anyhow, he did not obey the order of recall, and his estates were thereupon sequestrated for contempt. The precise nature of his transactions with Prince Henry,[2] who ultimately bought Kenilworth from him for considerably less than its value,[3] is somewhat obscure; but he seems to have saved something from the wreck of his fortune, and it is satisfactory to learn that some provision was also secured by her friends for his deserted wife[4] and family. All through it is clear that he was anxious to return, if only he could first obtain a plenary pardon; but, in spite of Prince Henry's good offices, this could not be arranged except under conditions. Writing to him on July 30th, 1612, his former tutor Sir Thomas

---

[1] " If he do marry Mrs. Southwell, it is felony by these last statutes" (Letter of Sir F. Leake, July 6th, 1605, Lodge, iii, p. 167). See also above, p. v, note 3.

[2] See an account of them in *Cal. State Papers*, 1623-1626, Appendix, p. 546.

[3] In a letter to Sir J. Cæsar, Oct. 18th, 1612, he writes: "this is my first purchase, and no ill bargain as I conceive" (Birch, *Life*, 1760, p. 319). It is doubtful how much of the purchase-money was actually paid.

[4] She was created Duchess Dudley in 1644, by a singular patent, in which her husband's legitimacy was admitted. The circumstances, however, under which the patent was granted much weaken the force of the admission. The Duchess died January 22nd, 1669, aged 90. Of her seven daughters, five were alive in 1616 (Adlard, p. 286).

Chaloner, now Chamberlain to the Prince, enclosed articles agreed upon by James and his son, by "submitting dutifully" to which, as he says, "you may forthwith receive that gracious pardon which you so much thirst for."[1] The terms thus sent have not been preserved; but, so far as their purport can be gathered from Chaloner's letter, they were not unreasonable, and, if Henry had not died on November 6th following, a reconciliation might perhaps have been effected. Left to himself, James was probably less disposed to be lenient, and he was no more capable of appreciating Dudley's highest qualities than Ralegh's. At the same time, besides other grounds for displeasure, he would have shown less than his usual shrewdness if he had not seen in the violence of his political views the advantage of keeping him at a distance. The notorious "Proposition for bridling the impertinency of Parliament," which was one of Dudley's expedients for gaining favour, seems to have been seriously meant, and it no doubt did far more harm than good to his cause. This unprincipled scheme for a military tyranny in England on the worst mediaeval Italian model was sent to James under cover to Sir David Foulis in 1614, and submitted to him by the Earl of Somerset. In spite of his own tendencies to absolutism, it must fairly have staggered him, and nothing more was heard of it until the outcry raised by the discovery of a copy in Sir Robert Cotton's library in 1629.[2]

It was more to Dudley's honour, as well as more relevant to the subject of the present volume, that in 1612 he sent to the Prince a short paper on the importance to England of naval supremacy, the first part enforcing by examples

---

[1] Adlard, p. 311, where the year is wrongly given as 1621. Chaloner died in 1615, little more than two years after Prince Henry, and Dudley thus lost his two best friends.

[2] S. R. Gardiner, *Hist. of England*, 1603-1642, vii, p. 138.

the dictum that "whosoever is patron [master] of the sea commandeth also on land," and the second dilating on the merits of two new vessels of his own invention.[1] One of these, styled a "gallizabra," was of light draught, carrying fifty guns, and driven either by sails or oars; while of the other class, or "galleys royal," he says that they "row as swift and sail faster than the English galleys, and in draught nearly equal; but for force to fight so far surpassing, as one of these, carrying 60 pieces of good ordnance, is able to beat 20 galleys." Two years later he offered to the king the design for a third new ship of war, termed a "counter-galliass," which was "of so wonderful consequence of force and swiftness as I dare boldly say the like was never known to the world, and wonderfully far beyond those I mentioned in my discourse to the Prince."[2] The fullest account of this vessel is given by him in a letter from Pisa, May 8th, 1614, to Sir David Foulis, where he declares plainly: "One thing I resolve yow, that, if it please his Majesty to harkin to this greatnes to himselfe, I must pretend to desyre to be generall (with that tytle) of such a squadron of these vessels as his Majestye shalbe pleased to have, and to be a command and goverment by itselfe, not to be under the Admirall of England, but as the gallies is in France, a different command at sea, nor hazard the reputation of my owne workes under the discretion or skill of another."[3] In connection with the same subject he condescended to solicit the interest of the Earl of Somerset, the royal favourite, to whom he wrote in these terms:

---

[1] Printed by Adlard, p. 299. It was enclosed in a letter to Sir David Foulis, the Prince's Cofferer, from Florence, November 14th, 1612.

[2] From a letter to a friend in London, perhaps Mr. Yates, in Jan. 161¾ (Adlard, p. 304).

[3] *The Fortescue Papers*, ed. S. R. Gardiner, Camden Soc., 1871, p. 6. He wrote again to Foulis on the subject on July 15th (*ib.* p. 11; and Adlard, p. 307).

"My verie good Lorde,

"I haue herde by manie, but espeacially by one that respecteth you much of the worthie courses your Lordship taketh for his Maiestie his contries honor and good. For the which, as I cane not chouse but honor and loue so much virtue and worth, so doe I desier and am bould (though vnknowne to your Lordship) to incorage your willingnes to walke in such worthie steppes, to your perpetuall fame and the comforte of them that thirst after nothing more then all happines to his gratious Maiestie and his seede for euer, vnto which if my affection or labers can adde anie talent, I shalbe allway readie to lay it downe as a tributorie dewty at his Royall feete, and therefor will begge at your Lordships hands that by your good meanes I may be acceptably made a happie instrument of his Maiesties and contries good. I hope that the care of my own reputation wilbe able to maynteyne the trust that shalbe put in me concerning the performance of what lately I offered his Maiestie for his service, wherein my worthie friende Sir Dauie Foules cane informe you more particularly. And that offer I made first to his Maiestie nearly ought of love and devetie, more then particular eandes (*sc.* ends), for else perchance care this I might haue spede my fortune sufficiently in other partes. My reputation and skill (withought ostentation) I doubte not, with the concurrence of your Lordships fauour, shall inable me sufficiently to performe what I offered, though it might seame strange and difficult by reason of the great consequence and importance of the matter for the state of England and the securitie thereof, towards which I have made longe practise and stvdie, and therefor apply it hereby vnder the protection of your greatnes, that I doe most honor by the fame of your worthienes, and so not to trowble you with more impertinent discourse, I will remayne

Your Lordships faythfull frende to
serue you,
Warwick & Leycester."

To this letter,[1] the expressions of esteem in which were no doubt as thoroughly insincere as they were undeserved,

---

[1] In the Public Record Office, with the paper below (*Cal. State Papers*, 1611-18, p. 233).

Somerset sent a guarded reply on Sept. 12th. Dudley's own letter is undated, but it must have been written about the same time as the following explanatory paper, dated May 11th, which perhaps accompanied it.

"What I promise touching the vessell offered his Maiestie, if he please to accepte it.

"*First.* That the vessell shalbe lesse charge a great dealle then anie of his great shippe[s] of 600 tonne, this vessell not passing that burthen, but rather lesse.

"2. That this vessell for swiftnes shall oughtsayle anie shippe or pinace in Englande, anie way by or large (*sic*), and at the least to spare them a mayne topsayle. This I cane promise, though I expecte much more.

"3. That this vessell shalbe exceadingly stiffe-sided as anie ship whatsoeaver, and sufficiently well conditioned for the English seas, to defende the stat and, if neade be, offende farther of, and shall not passe in draught, being laden, 10 feet or 11 at most, and most harde or impossible to be sunck with the enimies ordinance under water.

"4. That these vessells may be kepte in an arsinall, like Galliazzes, vnder arches, dry, and so kepte with littell charge and induer longe.

"5. That this vessell shall carie 90 or 100 peices of brasse, whereof the least a saker; and [the] lower tyer shall carie 40 or 44 Italian Demicanos of 30 *l.* waght Italian bullet, which is 20 *l.* Inglish, which peace (*sc.* piece) for the sea passeth all other Demicannos, and made after my fassion will not passe 300 *l.* waght Inglish or thereaboutes, and be most secure, by profe she shal carie at least 30 demicolverins, the rest sakers. The lower tyer at the mid-shippe or lowest parte wilbe 3 feet from the water or thereaboutes.

"6. That the vessell shall nauigate on square sayles and is contriued to rowe as well as the ancient Galliazzes; yet you may vse the same vessell withought owers at your pleasure; in fine it hath the benefitte of one and the other.

"7. That these vessell haue much more succor for men then Galliazzes, but lesse then shippes, caring (*sc.* carrying) littell carueld worke, to make them rowe and sayle so fast as promised, which qualitie at sea gayneth the victorie, so as with this ordinance promised and swiftenes she may well fight with anie 2 shippes, I meane not to borde them, but with the advantages of her qualitie and ordinance to sincke them, and therefor are intended for battayles principally to defende the statte or offende an enimie or principall seruises.

"8. These [vessells] nauigated with owers neade 700 men at least, rowers and all, but withought owers 300 men wilbe sufficiente, soe this vessell cane nauigate eather with owers or withought. This vessell nauigating with owers cane not carie aboue 3 or 4 months vittells, as a Galliaze doth, but withought rowers may carie for 9 months vitling with wine and water.

"9. The infinite vse and benefit of these vessells his Maiestic may iudge of, eather to offende or defende, by there fletenes, swiftnes and great force of ordinance, which is all the secret in this manner of garbe and proportion, to make a vessell carie so much ordinance withought hindring her sayling or good qualities.

"10. That this vessell is builded by a new meanes of arte and architecture, which I have proued in other vessells, but far different and [with] more difficultie then that of Inglande or Italy or anie other conterie, but by so sure a rule as served by making one the master carpenter cane not fayle to make the same qualities in as manie as he maketh, which is a matter of wonderfull consequence allso; for the best carpenters of Englande, if they make 20 shippes, they wilbe all different in qualities one from the other, and so in other contries, because these rules are not secured, and the shippes of Englande, being the walles of Chr[istendom], shalbe a securitie of the greatnes thereof. The offer performed, as I am secure to doe what [is] here written (and wilbe a meane to make good), his Maiesties wisdome cane best iudge of the consequence hereof and what the seruice deserueth. Therefor [I] doe subscribe it and write it with my owne hande as an obgligo (*sc.* obligo) by my worde to be able to performe what [is] here written. Dated, the 11 of May, 1614.

"Ro. Dud[ley] & L[eicest]er."

Whether the result would have quite answered Dudley's promises is extremely doubtful. So far as appears, James took no notice of his offers of service, even so far as to lay them before experts; and it is useless to speculate what might have been the effect upon the English Navy if he had been allowed full scope for his inventive genius, but somewhat too vivid imagination, in its dockyards.

From his first going to Italy, probably at the end of 1606, he applied himself to shipbuilding more seriously than there is any reason to believe was the case before he left England. He arrived in fact at Florence at an opportune moment, when the Grand Duke Ferdinand I, assisted by the Knights of St. Stephen, was bent upon ridding the Mediterranean of the Barbary and other corsairs which preyed upon its commerce. The singular appeal which Dudley addressed to him for protection is one of Mr. Leader's most interesting documents,[1] and nothing in it was better calculated to ensure its success than the prominence it gave to his practical knowledge of shipbuilding and naval affairs. Whatever view Ferdinand may have taken of the applicant's grandiose scheme to make him absolute master of the Levant, he was quick to appreciate his talents and personal charm, and the favour he showed to him was fully continued, after his own death in February, 1609, by his son, Cosmo II. As early as March, 1608, Dudley had built the *San Giovanni Battista*,[2] of sixty-four guns, which, as he boasts, became from her speed and powerful armament the terror of the Turks; and there could hardly be a more striking proof of the Grand Duke's high opinion of him than the attempt in 1607 to entice to Italy his old instructor, Matthew Baker, master-shipwright at Deptford.[3] Nor were his services limited to the construction and improvement of the Tuscan

---

[1] Leader, p. 181. It is in French, and bears no date.

[2] Leader, p. 54. She was a "rambargio" of his second symmetry, of which the curious in such matters may see a description and plan in the *Arcano del Mare*, lib. iv, p. 22. He gives an instance of her prowess in lib. iii, p. 13: "For example, the *S. Giovanni Battista* was a "rambargio" of the author's invention; and with one or two companions of small consideration she fought with the armada of the Grand Turk, numbering forty-eight galleys and two *muone*, which are Turkish galliasses, and put them to flight with great loss of Turks, as is very well known."

[3] Letter of Lotti, the Florentine Agent in London, May 23rd, 1607 (Leader, p. 55).

navy.[1] He is said to have at once recognised the advantages of developing Leghorn as a commercial port, so that, in Anthony Wood's words, "Leghorne, which was a small town, grew by his endeavours a great city on a suddain." "And I have heard," the same writer proceeds, "from some living who have frequented those parts that this our author R. Dudley was the chief instrument that caused the said Duke not only to make it firm, but also to make it a *scala franca*, that is a free port, and of settling an English factory there, and of drying the fens between that place and Pisa." In these statements there is probably some exaggeration. The rapid growth of Leghorn was undoubtedly due to the enlightened policy of Ferdinand I,[3] who had the true commercial instincts of the Medici; if he was influenced, however, by Dudley, it could have only been in the last two years of his reign (1587-1609), when the prosperity of the port was already achieved. At the same time, it is undeniable that Leghorn was the scene of some of Dudley's engineering feats. In the *Arcano del Mare*[4] he claims the credit of designing the mole, and he enlarges still more upon the subject in a remarkable account of himself and his family, written in 1628, when he was called upon to prove his son Antonio's nobility. He there boasts that he had completed the work at comparatively small expense and within twelve years, whereas similar works had taken ages and cost millions of *scudi*;

---

[1] Much matter of interest on this subject will be found in Mr. Leader's two chapters, "Dudley as a Shipbuilder," and "Dudley as Master of Marine," with the appendix of documents.

[2] *Athenæ Oxonienses*, iii, col. 259.

[3] Galluzzi dates its rise from the shelter given there by Ferdinand to English privateers during the war with Spain in the reign of Elizabeth (*Istoria del Granducato di Toscana*, 1781, iii, p. 509). See also Gino Capponi, *Storia della Rep. di Firenze*, 1875, ii, p. 495.

[4] Lib. vi, p. 5, and map vi. For a facsimile of the autograph document of 1628, see Leader, p. 134.

and, as the facts at the time must have been well known, he probably spoke no more than the truth.

As his position and emoluments at Florence became more assured, and his family by Elizabeth Southwell increased,[1] he must have chafed less at his exile, and during the last thirty years of his life he was practically an Italian noble bearing an English title. The hopelessness of its ever being recognised in England was strongly impressed upon him in 1618, when his old opponent, Lord Sidney, already Viscount Lisle, was created Earl of Leicester, and on the same day (Aug. 2nd) Robert Rich was created Earl of Warwick. Dudley's retort to this affront was ingenious and characteristic. Through his influence with the Grand Duchess Maria Maddalena, whose Grand Chamberlain he was, he procured from her brother, the Emperor Ferdinand II, on March 9th, 1620, a patent which enabled him, with some show of authority, to assume the still higher title of Duke of Northumberland. The character of this patent, a copy of which was prefixed to the *Arcano del Mare*, has, however, been somewhat misunderstood. In effect, it is not creative, as it is generally described, but merely declaratory, the Emperor recognising Dudley throughout his dominions as Duke of Northumberland[2] on the ground of his being legitimate heir of his grandfather, whose attainder was ignored. At the same time, Dudley's personal merits were fully set forth in the preamble, being made to include not only his " singular integrity of life and morals, prudence, knowledge of affairs, and rare and

---

[1] In all he had by her seven sons and five daughters, the second son, Carlo, succeeding him in 1649 as Duke of Northumberland. The Duchess, his wife, as she was always reputed at Florence, died September 13th, 1631 (Leader, p. 108).

[2] "Tanquam descendentem ab avo suo paterno Joanne, comite a Warwich, libere et *inconfiscabiliter* creato Duce Northumbriæ." The patent, in the wording of which Dudley's hand is plainly visible, is printed also by Leader, p. 197. Leicester's name is not mentioned.

ingenious inventions," but his more questionable sufferings for the Catholic religion. Although by this crowning act of presumption[1] he finally cut himself off from all hope of pardon, he did not cease to press his pecuniary claims upon the English Government through the Florentine Agent, Salvetti. As his efforts were unsuccessful, he had recourse, in 1627, to an extraordinary measure for obtaining redress; for, in order to recover the full value of his estates with interest, he obtained from the Ecclesiastical Court at Florence a sentence for reprisals upon English merchants, not being Catholics, at Leghorn.[2] It is difficult to see what point of religion was involved, which would justify the interference of the Church. Dudley, however, always posed abroad as a Catholic martyr, and the feeling against the concession of trading privileges to heretic strangers was evidently not yet extinct. Nor was the sentence intended to be merely an empty threat. Naturally enough, the then Grand Duke, Ferdinand II, was not disposed to sacrifice the English trade, and perhaps risk a war, for Dudley's private benefit; but, even when he opposed execution, Dudley did not desist. Assured of the support of the clergy, he carried the matter to Rome, where the sentence was confirmed, and it required unwonted firmness on the Grand Duke's part to nullify its effect. Whether in consequence of these proceedings or in spite of them, it appears that, in 1633, Salvetti after all succeeded in obtaining for Dudley some compensation for his losses.

The rest of Dudley's life belongs solely to Italy and may be passed over, but, before concluding, a few words must be given to his magnificent work *L'Arcano del Mare*, which is his most enduring memorial. As Mr. Leader has

---

[1] Salvetti, writing from London, pointed out the folly and impolicy of it, ridiculing Dudley's fondness for empty titles (Leader, p. 93).

[2] Galluzzi, *op. cit.*, iii, p. 502; Leader, p. 94.

pointed out, the germ or basis of it is to be found in three manuscript volumes preserved, with some of his nautical and other scientific instruments, in the Specola, or Museum of Natural History, at Florence. The first two of these volumes are in English, and were written about 1610; the third, in Italian,[1] seems to have been added ten years later, as the author speaks of himself as a Duke and of Cosmo II, who died in 1621, as still living. A prefatory note in it, after referring to the seven "symmetries" in shipbuilding, which it apparently attributes to Abram Kendall, goes on thus:

"As to the art of Architecture, in regard to the above said symmetries, the Duke has written an entire volume with figures of many kinds of vessels, but it is written in the English language. About the fortifications of Ports, and the method of doing so, he has also written in English, for at that time, about 1610, the Duke did not know enough of the Italian tongue to write that volume in the *Volgare* but perhaps he will do so when he has the leisure. He has also written a larger volume than these, on the true and real art of navigation; but this was written in England, with many curious mathematical and astronomical figures, and other things never before seen, such as nautical Instruments for the observation of the variations of longitude and latitude, and others for the horizontal and spiral Navigation, and about the Great Circles. Of these, however, common sailors understand little, as also about the marine management and discipline, and about sea fighting and squadrons, which are amply treated in these volumes."

The mention of a treatise on navigation written before he left England is of special interest, as this is the only knowledge we have of such a work; and it is to be hoped that, attention having now been called to it, the manuscript may yet be recovered. With regard to its matter, this was no doubt embodied later in the *Arcano del Mare*, as was the

---

[1] So Mr. Leader (p. 60); but, although he quotes its title in Italian and translates the prefatory note, he gives the opening passage in English which is evidently the author's own.

case with the contents of the three volumes at Florence. The latter deal with no less than thirty-four "symmetries," or classes of vessels, as well as with the "fortefiing and ordering of ports" and other kindred subjects, the whole corresponding to the third and fourth books of the *Arcano del Mare* as given below. The author's high opinion of his own work was frankly expressed, as was usual with him, and an interesting passage in the introduction to the third volume thus concludes:

"Not to diverte the reader from the matter, I will only secure him that whatsoever is conteyned in this worke is different from the orders of all others in these simetries, as well from those in England as in these other parts, and not taught me by anie, but invented merely (with God's assistance) by the practise, experiens and knowledge it hath pleased his Infinite Goodness to imploy in me and afforde by my practise, contemplations and studies herein, and therefor [I] doe desier the practise and imploymente thereof may be cheafly for God's service to the suppression of all, as I intend, infidelitie."

Another unpublished work from Dudley's pen, the *Direttorio Marittimo*, has already been mentioned (p. xii). It is described by Mr. Leader, the present owner of the original MS., as having been written for the use and instruction of officers of the Tuscan navy, and includes most of the subjects treated in the *Arcano del Mare*, such as navigation generally and great circle sailing, the discipline and management of a fleet, etc. As Mr. Leader quotes from it a reference by name to the larger work, it can hardly, as he supposes, have preceded it, but must be an abridgement.

It was not until 1646, three years before his death, and when he was seventy-two years of age, that Dudley began to publish to the world the result of his fifty years' study and practical experience of all matters connected with the sea. The comprehensive character of his work may be seen from its title-page, as follows:

DELL' ARCANO
DEL MARE,

DI D. RVBERTO DVDLEO DVCA DI NORTVMBRIA,

E CONTE DI VVARWICH,

LIBRI SEI;

Nel primo de' quali si tratta della Longitudine praticabile in diuersi modi, d'inuenzione dell' Autore,

Nel Secondo, delle Carte sue generali, e de' Portolani rettificati in Longitudine, e Latitudine,

Nel Terzo, della Disciplina sua Marittima, e Militare,

Nel Quarto, dell' Architettura sua Nautica di Vascelli da guerra,

Nel Quinto, della nauigazione scientifica, e perfetta, cioè Spirale, ò di gran Circoli,

Nel Sesto, delle Carte sue Geografiche, [Corografiche][1] e Particolari.

AL SERENISSIMO

FERDINANDO SECONDO

GRAN DVCA DI TOSCANA

suo Signore.

(*Here is a plate of an elaborate Mariner's Compass*).

In FIRENZE, Nella Stamperia di Francesco Onofri. 1646.

Con licenza de' SS. Superiori.

---

[1] This word was accidentally omitted and has been supplied from vol. iii, pt. ii.

In English: "Six Books of the *Secret of the Sea*, by Robert Dudley, Duke of Northumberland and Earl of Warwick; in the first of which he treats of longitude to be found in various ways, of the author's invention; in the second, of his general maps and of portolani rectified in longitude and latitude; in the third, of his maritime and military discipline; in the fourth, of his naval architecture of vessels of war; in the fifth, of scientific and perfect navigation, that is spiral or by great circles; in the sixth of his geographical maps, [chorographical] and particular. Dedicated to the Most Serene Ferdinand II, Grand Duke of Tuscany, his lord." Of the three volumes, the first two, containing Books I-IV, are uniform in size (12 ins. by 9 ins.) and were published together in 1646; the third, published in 1647, is in two parts, the first part (18½ ins. by 13 ins.) containing Book V, and the second part (21½ ins. by 15½ ins.) containing Book VI. Unlike the *Direttorio Marittimo*, the work has no autobiographical dedication. Without a word of preface, the author begins with the statement that the secret of navigation is the finding of the longitude, and proceeds to give various rules for it, which he claims to have himself discovered. In the second edition, published after his death in two huge quartos[1] at Florence, 1661, a preface is supplied with the title "Delle Scienze Matematiche che entrano nell' opera dell' *Arcano del Mare* Discorso proemiale del Duca de Nortumbria." In the first edition this discourse is placed at the end of the whole work as an appendix.

Although much of the matter throughout is of too

---

[1] They are of the same dimensions as vol. iii, pt. ii of the first edition, so as to include all the plates without folding. One of the two copies in the British Museum is dedicated, not to the Grand Duke of Tuscany, but to the Republic of Venice, and includes a dedicatory epistle to the Doge by the editor, Antonfrancesco Lucini (*cf.* Leader, p. 121). Lucini, who engraved the plates, states that he had spent twelve years on the work, and used no less than 5,000 pounds of copper.

technical a nature for its originality and scientific value to be determined by any but experts, no one can fail to be struck by the extent and variety of the author's learning, and the pertinence of many of his observations. At the same time, the text is not the most bulky, or even perhaps in some respects the most important, part of the work.[1] Its value is greatly enhanced by the very large number of engraved plates, which include all kinds of nautical, astronomical and mathematical instruments, diagrams for navigating and other purposes, plans of ships, fortifications, etc., and, above all, maps or charts. Some of the last are included with the curious Portolani, or books of sailing directions, which, with chapters on winds, currents and tides, changes of weather, etc., form the contents of Book II; but the majority, numbering 127 in all, make up the separate atlas in Book VI, fifty-four of them being devoted to Europe, seventeen to Africa, twenty-three to Asia, and thirty-three to America, with an explanatory note, frequently of some length, in each case. A fair idea of their character and utility may be obtained from Map xiii of America, which has been reproduced for this volume; and an English version of the accompanying text, from which it appears that the map was first published by Dudley in 1637, is printed as an appendix (p. 93). The text referring to Map xiv, which continues the coast of Guiana and Brazil to the east of the Amazon, will also be found in the same place, its chief value lying in the particulars which it gives of an otherwise unknown voyage of exploration to Guiana by Captain Richard Thornton, who was sent out by the Grand Duke Ferdinand I in September, 1608. Probably owing to Ferdinand's death before his return in June, 1609, nothing came of the expedition, but the fact of its being made so soon after Dudley's arrival at Florence affords

---

[1] Vol. iii, pt. i, for instance, has 117 plates to thirty-four pages only of text, which contain little more than brief explanations of the figures.

curious proof, not only of his continued interest in Guiana after he left England, but of his success in impressing his views upon his Italian patron.

One other feature of the *Arcano del Mare* calls for some notice. The work offered a wide field for the display of the author's excessive vanity, which must be taken into account in all his statements about himself. It was this foible, as much as anything, that brought about his misfortunes, and it seems to have grown upon him as he advanced in years. At the same time, the brilliant talents and other personal advantages which under a happier fate might have raised him to eminence in his own country were marred by more serious faults of character. Any suspicions that attach to him in relation to his attempt to prove his legitimacy may be disregarded as unproven, but nothing can excuse his heartless desertion of his wife and family, and the utter lack of principle shown in the political project which he laid before James I justifies Horace Walpole's reflection,[1] that his exile was perhaps fortunate both for himself and the state.

In conclusion, grateful acknowledgment is due to the Marquis of Bath and to Lord De Lisle and Dudley for the loan of their important papers bearing upon the question of Robert Dudley's birth; and to the Marquis of Salisbury for permission to include in the volume a facsimile of the letter to Sir Robert Cecil, his ancestor, which is printed on p. xxxv. I have also to thank Mr. William Foster, Honorary Secretary to the Hakluyt Society, and my colleagues, Mr. Edward Scott, Mr. A. Hughes-Hughes, and Mr. J. E. Herbert, for friendly assistance in other ways.

G. F. W.

---

[1] *Royal and Noble Authors*, ed. 1806, v, p. 339. Lord Roos, writing from Florence, Nov. 25th, 1612, no doubt expressed the opinion of many of his contemporaries in the words, "I love many good parts that are in Sir Robert Dudley, but dislike many evil ones" (Birch, *Life of Henry, Prince of Wales*, 1760, p. 321).

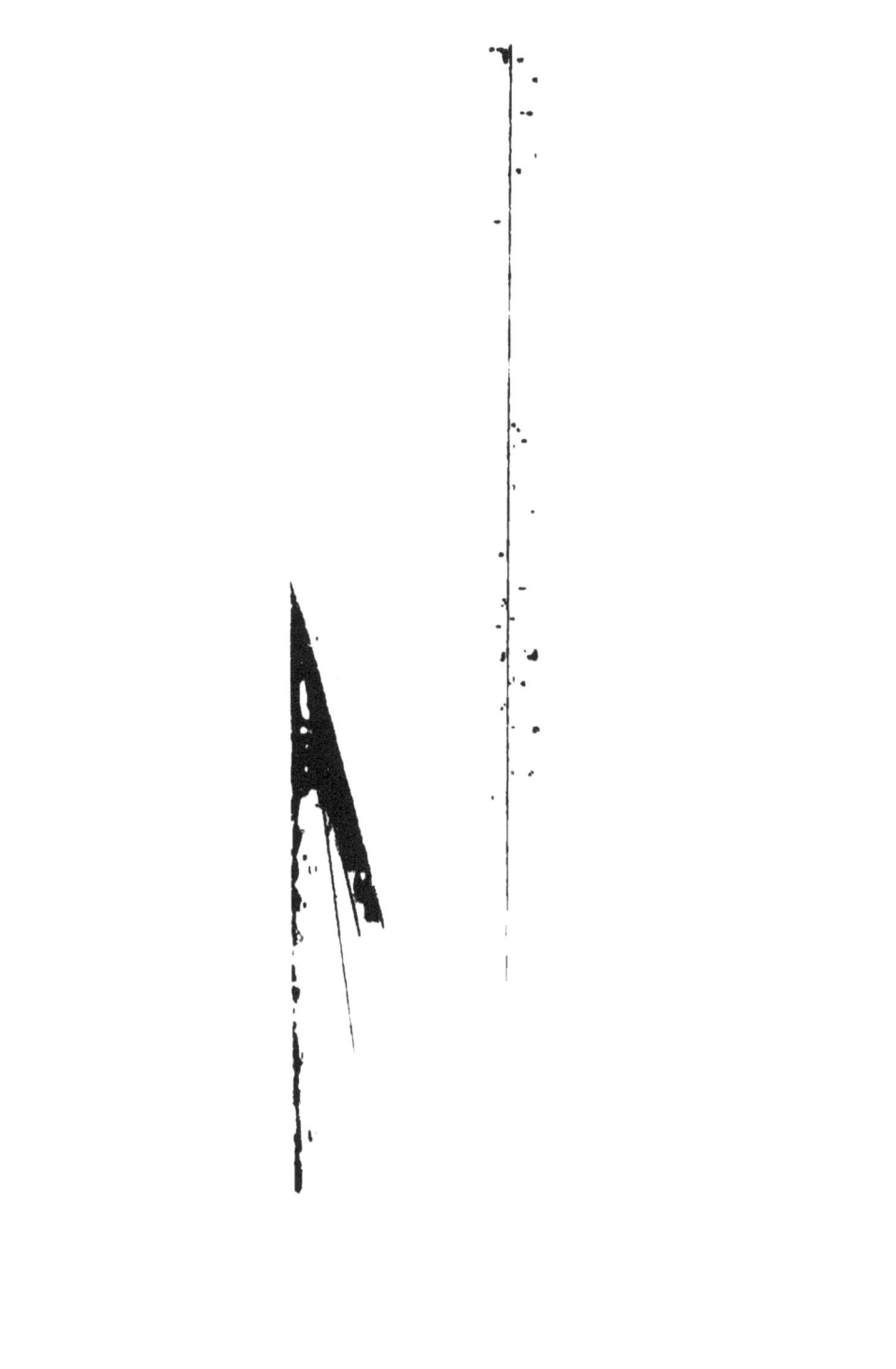

Most honored Sir: Robert Sidney hath much of honour you, and how
infinitely I think my self tyed vnto you, for ma[n]y favorable favours
I vnderstand by my mother. I cannot choose but make my self
yo[u]r avowed S[er]vant by [h]onor: and also by the vttermost of my service
or dutyfull affection. fyine in me weaknes to make satisfaction
of y[ou]r kindenes. So my bare loving, or honoring you is all the recompence
I[']able to make. no thing but to not of worth sufficient, to
counter ways the least part of yo[u]r honours kindnes. yet I humbly
beseech yo[u] to beseech you take it, as all tho[ugh] is able to doe That vnfayne[dly]
honor[e]th you. And that I assure yo[u]r hon: you shall allway
comau[n]d more then anie gentleman in England. Let me
intreat you not to take me as a complementall Courtier, but as a playne
dealing Saylor. that hath learned to sewe them honestly or
confayntely. that he is so much bounde to as to yo[u]r honour, this
discourse of those matters I haue some. I haue still tymays to repose
you: on shall[?] when I haue in some reasonable ord[er] recovered my
health. w[i]th lost time, altogether the best force I came through first
but something disliked w[i]th the for fore. / the best things I know
I shall be glade to make knowne vnto yo[u]r honour, So intreating
pardon for my boldnes I humbly take my leaue in manner
as best becometh me. / this 1[?] June 1595.

I beseach god sende yo[u]r
fortunes in greate yo[u]r yo[u]r honors power, bound to command in
shall euer my wish: then all dewtie or service
of he can defier them[?]

R. Sidney

Let me intreat yo[u]r hon: to gratifye
me in writing a line to yo[u]r father
forth an assurance, it shall be [illegible]
of honor: and that I humbly pray you
to assure him that I am one truly
honor[eth] him as far forth as anie man shall doe /

ROBERT DUDLEY'S
VOYAGE TO THE WEST INDIES,
1594-1595,
NARRATED BY CAPTAIN WYATT.

N the yeare of our Lord God 1594 a voyage was determined by that Honorable gentleman Robert Duddeley, sonn and heire unto the Right Honorable Robert, Earle of Leicester, [Leiftenante of all her Majesties fortes and forces beyonde the seas, Lord High Stewarde of all her Majesties Howscholde, Knight of the most honorable order of the Garter,][1] for the South Sea; but man pourposeth and God disposeth, for so it fell out by the proceedings of this noble gentleman, who, havinge allmost finished shippinge serviceable for that viage, was forste to surcease that and to begin other more convenient for his viage newlie pretended, which was unto the West Indies, beinge by speciall commaunde contradicted of her Majestie from the former, as tenderinge[2] the ripenes of his yeares, and

---

[1] The words within brackets have been scored through with a pen. Leicester died on 4 September, 1588.

[2] In the sense of "prizing" or "valuing highly," as in Shakespeare, e.g., "He shall not die, so much we tender him," *Com. of Errors*, v. 1.

ROBERT DUDLEY'S
VOYAGE TO THE WEST INDIES,
1594-1595,
NARRATED BY CAPTAIN WYATT.

N the yeare of our Lord God 1594 a voyage was determined by that Honorable gentleman Robert Duddeley, sonn and heire unto the Right Honorable Robert, Earle of Leicester, [Leiftenante of all her Majesties fortes and forces beyonde the seas, Lord High Stewarde of all her Majesties Howseholde, Knight of the most honorable order of the Garter,][1] for the South Sea; but man pourposeth and God disposeth, for so it fell out by the proceedings of this noble gentleman, who, havinge allmost finished shippinge serviceable for that viage, was forste to surcease that and to begin other more convenient for his viage newlie pretended, which was unto the West Indies, beinge by speciall commaunde contradicted of her Majestie from the former, as tenderinge[2] the ripenes of his yeares, and

---

[1] The words within brackets have been scored through with a pen. Leicester died on 4 September, 1588.

[2] In the sense of "prizing" or "valuing highly," as in Shakespeare, e.g., "He shall not die, so much we tender him," *Com. of Errors*, v. 1.

yealdinge, allthough hardlie, unto the latter, not doubtinge but that experience might worke a most excellent perfection in him, whome nature had made singuler. Thus licensed of his most gratious soveraigne, he toke his leave from courte, with the consente of a few for his departure, but with the praier of all for his safe returne. Havinge allreadie sent his provision unto Southampton by his servants the which shoulde give attendance on him in this viage, hee sett forwarde himselfe and came unto Hampton, where retayninge a sufficient and able companie, not without his great chardge for the througlie manninge of his shippinge for the viage, [hee] gave a speciall commaundement unto all his companies that they shoulde generallie provide themselves to goe with him the Sonday followinge, beinge the thirde day of November, to the church and theare accompany[1] him for the reverent receavinge of the Holie Communion, and after at his chardge to dine with him all togeather, as members united and knitt togeather in one bodie. The which beinge accomplished, on the Wednesdaie followinge, beinge the sixte of the same moneth in the yeare aforenamed, [hee] caused his shippinge to disanker from the Rode afore Hampton (the which amonge the marriners, beinge the first breakinge of grownde, is adjudged the beginninge of the viage) unto Heeve,[2] a harber more convenient, as well both for the doublinge of the maine continent of Englande over against the Ile of Weight, as allsoe for the receavinge aborde of such victuall the which was to be transported from thence for our viage, lyinge in this harber aborde the

3 Nov.

6 Nov.

Dudley was only twenty-one at the time. In his own account he modestly attributes the Queen's refusal to her fears for those whom he would have taken with him on so hazardous a voyage.

[1] MS. accompaninge. The author, as will be seen, has a special fondness for the present participle, which in order to make sense must be changed into a finite tense.

[2] Hythe, on the western side of Southampton Water.

good shipp called the *Peregrine*,[1] beinge admerall, of the burden of nine score or theare abouts, and his vice-admerall called the *Beares Whelpe*, of the burden of foure score, with two small pinnesses, all of his owne proper chardges, leavinge behinde him in the rode of Hampton the shipp called the *Mermayde*, of the burden of an hundred, to com after him, beinge his reare-admerall.

Havinge laine in this harber of Heeve untill the xvi. of this moneth, the winde cominge abouts, he determined to sett saile, fallinge somthinge nearer unto the pointe untell the next day; the which beinge the xviith day of the same monthe, and for that it was a day of triumph for the Queenes coronacion,[2] it was sollemnised by us with all our great ordenance, the which was re-answeared by the Queenes ordenance out of Callshott Castle, and under which castle wee then did anker, for that the ebb drew on soe fast, and night approchinge our master thought it not good to turne downe the channell, the tide beinge soe far spent, with a shipp of soe great a burden. Wheare-upon our Generall concluded that the vice-admerall with her pinness should sett saile and make for Plimworth before, theare to take aborde such provision of victuall which was theare provided for the throughlie furnishinge of her for her viage. The which commaunde was noe sooner given him in chardge, but with as great speed [it] was accomplished, leavinge us at an anker under Callshott

16 Nov.

17 Nov.

---

[1] This is one of the rare occasions on which Wyatt's narrative of the voyage is at variance with the other two. Dudley calls his ship the *Bear*, of 200 tons; but perhaps this was merely a change of name, suggested by his father's well-known device of the Bear and Ragged Staff. It will be seen below (p. 28) that he gave the name Port Peregrine to a bay in Trinidad. He says nothing of the *Mermaid*, but he adds that the *Bear's Whelp* was commanded by Captain Munck, and he gives the names of the pinnaces as the *Frisking* and the *Earwig*. Kendall speaks of the *Great Bear*, of 300 tons, and the *Little Bear* only.

[2] Her accession is meant; she was not crowned until 15 January, 1559.

Castle, wheare wee lay untell the last of the ebb, and soe, takinge the benifitt of the tyde and winde, wee doubled the pointe and came up as far as Gurned,[1] wheare wee lay that night, hopinge to pass the next day through the Needles with the less daingcr.

18 Nov. And the next morninge, beinge readie to sett saile, wee might discry two great shipps comminge down the Channell, the which shipps when they weare discried by our companie to be noe English shippinge, and withall beinge judged to be men of war and that of noe small burden, our Generall commaunded to wave them, and halinge them with his noyse of trumpetts made them know theire dwtie unto our English collers by vailinge theire topsailes, and withall caused a bote to be manned forth and sent aborde them two of his companie to know what they weare, from whence, and wheather (*sc.* whither) they weare bownde. Who made us this answear, that they weare of Anserdam, and that they came from the service of Brest, and withall delivered the truth of that honorable, allthough blooddy, service theare accomplished by our Englishmen,[2] and how they had left five of the Queenes shippinge in Plimworth Rode, wheare wee fownde them when wee theare aryved. Returninge with thease advertisements unto our Generall, wee plied for Plimworth, and wee had noe soener passed the Needles but wee mett with the Scottish and Burteus[3] fleet bownde for Scotlande

---

[1] Gurnard Bay, in the Isle of Wight, west of Cowes.

[2] In August, 1594, an expedition in support of Henry IV was dispatched under Sir John Norris for the relief of Brest, which was besieged by the Spaniards. Sir John's own Journal of his proceedings from his landing on 1 September to 12 November is in Brit. Mus. Stowe MS. 166, fol. 159. The Spanish fort near Crozon was besieged from 1 October to 7 November, when it was taken by assault with some loss. Sir Martin Frobisher, who commanded at sea, was among the wounded, and died soon after reaching Plymouth. See also the pamphlet *Newes from Brest*, 1594 [5].

[3] No doubt for "Burdeus," *i.e.* Bordeaux. "Burgis" is the district of Bourgès, with capital Bourg, on the Gironde and Dordogne. "Le vin surtout du Bourgez est fort estimé" (Expilly, *Dict. Geogr.*, i, p. 758).

from Burgis, of whom our Generall had a hogsehead of
new Gaskin wine bestowed on him. The which beinge
taken aborde, wee spedilie sailed and safelie arived in the
Sownde of Plimworth on the xixth day, beinge Twseday, 19 Nov.
wheare wee mett with our vice-admerall. Who havinge
receaved commaundement from our Generall to this effect,
that he shoulde give summans to his men to com aborde
for that they shoulde sett saile for the cost of Spaine, the
winde beinge soe fayre, the next Thursedaie, beinge the
21 day, our admerall disankored and hoysed saile, not 21 Nov.
doubtinge but it woulde be a cause to make our vice-
admeralls men the more willinge to hasten forwarde;
whose negligence caused our Generall to turne to wind-
warde and lie at hull betweene the Deadman and the
Ediston all that night with much winde, and withall to
send his pinness to hasten them away. The next day,
beinge Friday, both the *Beares Whelpe* with the two 22 Nov.
pinnesses came and mett our Generall, and all togeather
wee sett forwarde towards the cost of Spaine. But wee
had not run past some fifty leagues into the sea but wee
weare incountred with a most bitter storme, with the winde
soe contrarie unto our courses that wee weare forceablie
driven perforce to make back againe for the cost of
Englande, and, beinge seperated, wee with our pinness
[came] into Plimworth, our consort and her pinness into
Famouth. And while the winde was thus contrarie unto
our courses, our Generall laie in Cattwater, refreshed his
men, and withall renued his store of victuall, lyinge theare
in this harber of Plimworth untell the first of December, 1 Dec.
beinge Sonday. Upon which day, havinge a north-east
winde, wee once againe disankored and sett saile for the
cost of Spaine, havinge two daies before dispatched a post
by land unto the vice-admerall that they shoulde likewise
sett saile, first for the Canaries and then Cape Blanke.

And thus puttinge forth into the sea, the winde in-

creased[1] in soe outragious a manner that night that it bred
some dislike of our men beinge aborde the pinness, which
caused them all to com aborde the admerall, determininge
to towe the pinness; but the billowes of the sea weare
throwne up with such vehemencie of the winde that they
quicklie overwhelmed her, and beinge suncke into the
unsatiable bowells of the merciles sea, wee weare without
hope of ever recoveringe her againe. Thus havinge lost
her, not without the great sorrow of our men, wee passed
on forwarde towards Spaine, givinge chase everic day,
untell wee came unto the cost of Calitie,[2] the which wee
discried on Twseday, beinge the thirde of December. The
next day, beinge Wednesday, runninge to make the lande,
wee founde it to be the Groyne; the next lande was Sysarck,
then the Staggs of Mountjoye, and soe alonge the cost to
Cape Finister. The which Cape wee had noe sooner doubled
but wee had sight of viii. or ix. great saile of shippes, the
which had they not bin discovered to have bin Flemmings
wee had given them chase. Our Generall, unwillinge to
lose anie time, plied up alonge by the high lande of
Camena[3] and soe to the rock, wheare wee had the first
chase that wee might justlie aver the reprisoll of, yett not
failinge anie day before of his chase, if they had bin such
whereof[4] wee might without violatinge the injunctions of
our commission have avowched the takinge. But this
before-mentioned Spaniarde, perceavinge the imminent
dainger ensewinge and seinge noe way to avoyde it but
either by submission expect for mercye at the conquerours
feet or by subverssion of his enimie make himselfe free

3 Dec.

---

[1] MS. increasinge.
[2] Galicia. "Sysarck" below is for the Sisargas Islands, west of Coruña or "the Groyne."
[3] Caminha, to the south of the mouth of the Minho, the "rock" being Cape Roca.
[4] Interlined, the original reading being "as that," with "of them" at the end of the sentence.

from beinge captivated, lefte both thease waies, as not fittinge his proud humor, eschewinge the one as unwillinge to brooke servitude and shunninge the other as not able to withstande our forces, [and] made triall of a thirde, which was to worke theire safetie by desaitefull pollecie, a fitt subject for base abjects to worke strainge stratagems, yett the usuall occupation of Spanish practises. But to my purpose. Beinge in this dilemma, and driven withall to this forced conclusion by necessitie, they bore up with us, puttinge forth an English flagg, keeping his men soe close that they might not soe much as seeme to bee Spaniards. But wee seinge her to be a flibote[1] standinge with us, bearinge in her top the English collers, supposed them at the least to be some Irishmen bounde for Lisborne; neither might anie have perswaded themselves otherwyse of them, soe freindlike did shee presume of our courtesie. But beinge noe sooner past us, and perceavinge that, if wee should cast aboute after them, wee might hazarde the bouldginge[2] of our selves, beinge a shipp of soe great a burden and withall soe neare the Rock, they then begin to disclose themselves, abusinge that most contemptuouslie which before they had most safelie, allthough craftelie, used for theire safegarde, by takinge theire English flagg, by whom they had theire safe pass, from theire top and hanging[3] it at theire sterne most disdainefullie. The which our Generall toke mightelie offensive, yeat at that time coulde not remedie it, but with himselfe concluded a revenge, the which he determined to put in execution within a few daies followinge.

---

[1] A fly-boat, the Dutch *Vlieboot*, the real derivation of which, according to Murray's *New Engl. Dict.*, has no reference to speed, but to the Vlie, or channel out of the Zuyder Zee, where such small vessels were employed.

[2] To bulge = to stave in the bottom of a ship (*New Engl. Dict.*).

[3] MS. hanged.

Thus passinge alonge the cost by Cascales[1] and soe by Cape Pitcher, then by Mounte Checo, [wee] made[2] such expedition that by the xii[th] of this moneth wee weare at Cape St. Vincent, and passinge by Cape Saker wee came unto the bay of Lawgust, which was the place wheare our Generall had determined to crie quittance for that abuse offred unto us by the Spaniarde ; which was after this manner. In the caveninge he sent of (*sc.* off) his bote, committinge the chardge unto Captaine Wood,[3] sendinge with him Mr. Comley, Mr. Phillips, Mr. Crale, Mr. Norris, with divers others of his best musketers. Aboute the dead time of the night they putt of into the harbers, whearein when they weare entred they weare præsentlie discried by the Spanish centronells ; for, as it shoulde seeme, the Spaniards the which wee had given chase unto not longe before had given notes all along the shore. The which our men perceavinge by theire unusuall and sundrie lights made retire ; the which our Generall was glad of, for that wee might discrie three great shipps plyinge downe upon us, the which wee judged then to be some of the Kings Armathases,[4] for that wee had bin informed that they

12 Dec.

---

[1] This and the following names represent Cascaes and Cape Espichel, on each side of the Tagus, the Sierra de Monchique (running down to Cape St. Vincent), Cape Sagres and the Bay of Lagos.

[2] MS. makinge.

[3] Capt. Benjamin Wood (*cf.* Dudley's narrative below). He took part in the voyage of Amadas and Barlow to Virginia in 1584 (Hakluyt, ed. 1809, iii, p. 307) and in the "Voyage made by two of Sir Walter Ralegh's pinasses . . . to the Azores" in 1586 (*Ibid.*, ii, p. 607). Ten years later, after returning from the present voyage, he commanded an expedition, chiefly fitted out by Dudley, to the Straits of Magellan and China, two of his three vessels being the *Bear* and the *Whelp*, perhaps the same which Dudley had on this occasion. T. Masham, in his account of the "third voyage set foorth by Sir W. Ralegh to Guiana" in 1596 (Hakl., iv, p. 189), says that he was spoken off the Barbary Coast on 28 January, 1596-7, but neither he nor any of his company ever returned home. All that was learnt of their fate is contained in a Spanish letter printed by Purchas (ed. 1625, i, bk. iii, p. 110).

[4] A queer plural form of Armada or Armatha, used in the sense of a single large ship of war.

weare abroade. Soe havinge taken in our men aborde, wee ourselves in readines for to fight plied up of all handes, givinge them a speedie chase, and by ten of the clock at night wee had fett them up. But findinge them to be all Englishmen, two great shipps of London marchandmen bounde for the straights and the thirde a man of war, and all of our familiar acquaintance, wee saluted each other after our sea manner, [they] giveinge our Generall a great peece (who commaunded they should be requited with the like kindenes), [and soe] wee parted, they for the straights and wee for the cost of Barbarie. The which course wee had not held that night but wee might the next morninge perceave a ship pack on all the saile they weare able to make after us, to follow us, the which wee hoped to have bin one of the Kings Armathases, beinge desirous to give us chase; and our Generall, to the intent they might with more ease fett us up, caused great draggs to be hanged over borde, oftentimes comminge on the staies, of purpose for them. Who when they weare com up with us, wee founde her to be a ship of Hampton, which had laine by us in Hampton rode and went forth some three weekes before us, the Captaine, one Mr. Daniell, shewinge himselfe a verie glad man to meet with our Generall at sea. And to signifie soe much unto him, [hee] gave him three peeces of great ordenance; the which kindenes our Generall requited with the like courtesies and soe departed, requestinge them withall that, if they did meet with our vice-admerall, they woulde hasten them forwarde towards the Canaries, wheare our Generall did meane to make some abode for them. Thus givinge to each other the *valeat*, wee helde on contrarie courses, they for the Cape St. Vincett and wee for the Canaries.

The which course wee had not continued longe, but within a day after wee had sight of a saile to leewarde; the which wee weare perswaded was one of our consorts,

for that wee might perceave a small pinness not far from her. Which pinness shee had sent to borde us and withall to give advertisement unto our Generall of a mishap which had hapened to one of our English men of war, beinge by two of the Kinges Armathases surprised and taken. And this beinge a shipp of a small burden woulde gladlie have consorted with us, the which our Generall was in some sorte content to accepte of, for that he was in some doubte of the meetinge of his two shipps which weare to com after him. But this consortship was hindered by our seperacion through a most vehement storme, with such soden gustes and monstrous raine that, unless theare shoulde have hapned a seconde enundacion of the whole worlde, wee coulde not have had the like accident. But as his force was most violent for the time, soe was his dainger less harmefull in vanishinge sodenlie, resemblinge the bullets who are noe sooner cast into the mouldes then they are made; this beinge our onlie comfort that, by how much the more his force was great in the highest degree of his extremitie, by soe much the less was his power available to continew the vehemencie of that extremitie. For it is a common sayinge, but more commonlie falleth out true, that *nullum violentum est perpetuum.* But after this storme the seas began to wax calme and the skies became perfect and cleare, and soe sailinge with a bare and scant winde towards the Ilands wee might perceave a small saile to stande with us, and standinge in for the ilands as wee did, [and] wee weare perswaded that shee was either her with whom wee shoulde have consorted or some other bownde for the Canaries. But meetinge togeather, wee weare given to understande shee was a bark of Waymouth, which in the monstrous stormes before had bin in some perilous dainger, beinge forst to cast overborde all theire great ordenance [and] theire fish and to stave theire caske in the which theire fresh water was, and havinge loste theire bote requested succour. The which our Generall afforded by sendinge them his bote and withall some fresh water, of the which they had none before. Thus after great bordinge and rebordinge each other, one the morrow wee solemnlie feasted[1] one another, for it was then Christmas day, and [it] beinge a verie hott day and [wee] withall 25 Dec. becalmed by reason of the high peeke of Tenerife, from of (*sc.* off) the which wee weare not far, our men swimminge from ship to ship made greate cheare each to other. And to congratulate them for the kindnes the which they had shewed our men, our Generall, havinge before verie bountefullie feasted them, went himselfe aborde them, wheare hee had a verie fyne banquet. After which repast returninge aborde, [hee] brought with him divers of them to supp with him [and] after supper sent them with his bote aborde theire shipp, determininge on the next morrow to conclude of some articles for a consortshipp. The which was not the next day, beinge St. Steevens 26 Dec. daie, concluded of, because they did defer it untell they came unto the Grande Canaries, wheare wee might both water afresh and must of necessitie anker theare, for to stay by our appointment for our vice-admerall. But all this was frustrated by the contrarietie of the winde, for neither might wee plie up unto that iland, the winde was soe contrarie for our course, neither was hee able to beare or keepe us companie, the weather growinge into such a monstrous outragiousnes.

Soe loseinge them wee weare driven ourselves under the ile of Tenerife, wheare [wee weare] beatinge up and downe untell the Sondaie followinge, beinge the xxix[th] 29 Dec. of December, on which daie it pleased God that wee sett sight of a carvell, the which wee coulde not reach with our shipp, for that it was such a calme, and the carvell

---

[1] MS. feastinge.

beinge neare the lande plied up to run her selfe a grownde rather then shee woulde willinglie be taken. Our Generall, to prevent all theire determinacions, caused his bote to be manned forth, committinge the chardge unto Cap. Jobson,[1] who verie resolutelie peroformed the takinge of her, beinge harde aborde the shore, notwithstandinge the lande forces, præsentinge themselves in the vew of our men, made a stande of some 500 pikes, havinge theire battles interlased with musketers answearable to the nomber of the pikes, who plied theire shott soe thick that our men weare forced to place all the Spanish prisoners between themselves and the shott; the which when the enimie saw, they forbare, sufferinge the prize to com from the shore without further resistance. But Cap. Jobson, by whose directions this exploite was accomplished, beinge well experiensed with such services, for that he had bin with Sir Francis Drake, and havinge chardge both at the sackinge of St. Domingoe in the West Indies and at the burninge of the Groyne in the Portingall action,[2] sent our admeralls bote aborde him with some six of the chiefest of the prisoners to know the Generalls further pleasure concerninge both prize and prisoners. Whose

---

[1] Further on styled a kinsman of Dudley, and addressed by him as his cousin. He was probably therefore a son of Sir Francis Jobson (d. 1573), Lieutenant of the Tower, who married Elizabeth, daughter of Arthur, Viscount Lisle (natural son of Edward IV), and Elizabeth his wife, sister of John Grey, Viscount Lisle, and widow of Edmund Dudley. Lady Jobson was thus half-sister to John Dudley, Duke of Northumberland, Robert Dudley's grandfather. Her two eldest sons, John and Edward, married heiresses, and were less likely to have sought fortune in adventure than their brothers, Henry and Thomas. As the last-named took his degree at Oxford, 12 February, 1578-9, and appears to have been a member of the Inner Temple (Foster, *Alumni Oxon.*), Henry was, perhaps, Dudley's Captain Jobson. A Richard Jobson commanded an expedition to explore the Gambia in 1620, and wrote an account of it entitled *The Golden Trade*, 1623, but he does not speak as if he had had previous experience.

[2] No one of the name of Jobson figures in the accounts of the taking of San Domingo on 1 January, 1586, or the attack on Coruña on 24 April, 1589.

direction was that the prize[1] shoulde be committed unto
Cap. Wood and the prisoners should be all broughte
aborde him ; with whom he delt soe honorablie, causinge
them to be sett ashore unrifeled of the sailers and
souldiers, they gave him the greatest commendacions of
any, protestinge to doe him all the service they might,
theire true dutifull obediance unto theire naturall Prince
onlie reserved. Thus, after he had given God thanks,
hee appointed Cap. Wood to goe on the one side of the
ilande and wee on the other, soe compassinge the ile
wee might happelie meet with some one driven into
that harber by reason of the last stormes bownde for
the Indies.

The next daie, beinge Monday the xxx[th] of December, 30 Dec.
in the morninge by breake of daie, our Generall beinge
in his gallerie discried another carvell at anker under the
shore side of Palma, the which he commaunded that wee
shoulde plie for ; who perceavinge our intent made out
into the sea, not doubtinge but to escape our dainger by
her swift sailinge. In the which they weare mightelie
deceaved, for our admerall beinge most singuler for her
saylinge fett her up within the dainger of our great shott,
and by that they had some 3 peeces bestowed on them
they stroke saile, yealdinge themselves unto the mercie
of our Generall, who delt as charitablie with thease ·as
he had done honorablie with the former [and] caused
them to be safelie sett on shore, unspoiled of theire
apparell or wealth. Afterwards, makinge one of his
gentlemen, one Mr. Wentworth,[2] captaine of her, appointinge Mr. Lister master, wee plied up and downe to finde

---

[1] Dudley calls her the *Intent*, the other, captured later, being the *Regard*. See also below, p. 28.

[2] Probably a relation of Margaret Cavendish, Dudley's wife, whose mother was a daughter of Thomas, first Lord Wentworth of Nettlested (Brit. Mus. Add. MS. 19,122, f. 350).

the other carvell; the which came unto us not long after without doinge of anie thinge worth the notinge.

That night the winde began to shew his force on us, drivinge us back againe to Palma, wheare I thinke wee weare haunted with some divelish witches, or at least with some sea divells; for beinge theare wee weare brought into such a laborynth of surpassinge troubles that to shew the horrors thearof I shall rather want wordes of effecasie then matters defective. Such they weare that those which had bin seamen some 30, some 40 yeares, did neaver see the like; such they weare that those ilanders which weare fowrescore yeares of age did neaver heare of the like; and such weare they that I beseech Christ wee neaver indure the like. Neither doe I thinke that eaver anie suffred the like withowt either detriment of goods, spoile of tacklings, loss of men or overwhelminge of all, somtimes havinge such dredfull flashes of fire that, allthoughe wee might account it midnight by the computacion of the time, yeat might wee compare it to midday for the brightnes of the ayre by the lighteninge, which seemed to fire the verie seas rownde aboute us, somtimes terrible thunders, other times both darke and durtie foggs, stinckinge and noysome mistes, continuinge thus some viijth daies togeather, that nomberless weare the stormes wee suffred, innumerable weare the daingers wee feared, but most infinite weare the calamities wee weare subject unto. The which our master[1] foreseinge, havinge a most perfect and singuler judgement into thease causes (for beinge a good naturall philosopher he was able rightlie to censure of supernaturall causes by theire unnaturall effects) and perceavinge thease things by findinge the heavens to

---

[1] "My master Abraham Kendall" (Dudley). He accompanied Drake and Hawkins on their last voyage, and died on the same day as Drake himself, 28 January, 1596, off Porto Bello (Hakluyt, ed. 1809, iv, p. 73). His own account of Dudley's voyage is the third of those here printed.

be troubled by theire extrordinarie courses, [hee] came unto our Generall, shewinge him *non est bellare cum diis*, theare is noe resistance of the divine powers. "Wee have," saith hee, "laine heare this 10 or 11 daies, a longe time for soe short a cutt, stringe to plie up for the ilands of the Grande Canaries for the accomplishment of your appointment unto your vice-admerall; the which how impossible a thinge it is, your honorable selfe (unto the great perill of your owne person and the hazarde of your shippinge) hath bin made an eie wittnes. Whearefore of necessitie wee must beare hence for Cape Blanke.[1] Lett it thearefore soe stande with your honorable likinge that yow rightlie censure of this determinacion." The which our Generall easilie condiscended unto, not a little notinge the instabilitie of mans determinacion.

The same day, beinge Satterday the fowrth of Januarie, wee sailed forwarde alonge within the sight of the ilande of Ferra,[2] making for Cape Blanke; and comminge within two daies saile of the Cape, our Generall sent away his two carvells before, that they shoulde not be mistrusted of the canters,[3] of whome hee determined to replenish his victuall a fresh, if possible hee might. Soe, bearinge a slacke saile, wee bore in for the shore, and the first lande wee fell withall was the maine continent of Affrica, the place Riodore, parte of the kingedome of Asanaga. The next was Cape Cyprian, parte of the kingdome of Gualata,

4 Jan.

---

[1] Cape Blanco, on the mainland of Africa.
[2] Ferro, one of the smaller Canary Islands.
[3] "Canthers, which are Portugal fishermen" (Dudley). A canter, however, was properly a fishing-boat, as in Drake's voyage round the world, 1577, "In this place (*i.e.*, off Cape Blanco) we tooke of the fishermen such necessaries as wee wanted and they could yeeld us, and leaving heere one of our litle barkes . . . . wee tooke with us one of theirs, which they called 'Canters,' being of the burden of 40 tunnes or thereabouts" (Hakluyt, ed. 1809, iv, p. 233). The word is no doubt connected with the Spanish and Portuguese *cántaro*, a widebellied pitcher, and this with the Greek Κάνθαρος, which is itself used by Aristophanes, *Pax*, 143, for a kind of boat.

then Cape Barbis, and soe to Cape Blanke; both which capes lie scituated within the limmetts of the desarts of Lybia. On the viii[th] day of Januarie, lyinge at this cape in the morninge, wee might discrie our two carvells comminge towards us, the which ankored not far from us. At which time likewyse, some fowre leagues of, wee sawe a saile to weather on us; the sight wheareof caused our Generall to send his bote aborde the carvells, commaundinge them that they shoulde plie up unto the shipps, to see what they weare, havinge with himselfe determined to lande. The which he did præsentlie upon the returne of his bote, and beinge landed with some twelve persons marched up in good order, determininge a further search of the place; and findinge theare nothinge worth the discoverie made his returne the speedier, not marveilinge that he founde noe inhabitante manuringe[1] in that uninhabitable desarte, abowndinge in nothinge but with huge mountaines of windedriven sandes, steipe piles of craggie rocks, and a few scattred bones, beinge the left rellicks of dead carkases slawtred by some more ravinous beastes then they themselves weare. And as wee made our retire, wee saw divers lyssards, the swiftnes of whose flight gave great delight unto our men in givinge them speedie chases. And beinge com unto the shore syde wee harde a great peece shoote of out from our admerall, which caused us to make more hast to com aborde. Thus leavinge behinde us certaine letters inclosed in a thinge of wood provided of purpose for the same, which weare directions for our vice-admerall to follow us accordinge unto the advertisement sent them from Plimworth to Famouth, wee came aborde. And by that time our

8 Jan.

---

[1] To manure (= manœuvre) properly means to work with the hand, hence to till or cultivate, in a more general sense than in its modern restricted usage. "Manuringe" here is almost equivalent to "dwelling."

Generall had supped it was night; soe the watch beinge sett everie one was commaunded unto theire rest. But before two glasses[1] were cleane run out of the first watch, our carvells weare perceaved to be in fight with the sailes unto the which they weare in the morninge commaunded to plie up for. The beginninge of whose quarrell[2] began first in this sorte. The carvells beinge com soe neare that they might trulie judge of them what they weare, perceavinge them to be French men of war, [they] determined to anker by them, not fullie resolved what to doe untell the next morninge. But the Frenchmen seinge two Spanish carvells, for as yeat they weare not altered, toke them to be some Spanish fishermen, præsentlie gave them chase and had taken them, had not our men verie resolutelie by force repelled theire forces; for in the exchainge of some halfe thowsande of bullets they then coulde not onlie perceave them to be Englishmen, but felt them likewyse to be English men of war, which caused them to devide theire forces, theire admerall, beinge a shipp of vii. score, givinge chase to one of the carvells, and her other consortes, beinge pinnesses of 30 tun a peece with a shallop of viij[th] tun, settinge upon the other of our carvells. Who havinge before beaten them back from bordinge them still [went on] plyinge[3] him soe hott with his small shott that in the end the Frenchmen weare as willinge to forgoe the chase as before they weare desirous to give the chase. And by this time had theire admerall brought his chase aborde us; but our Generall, beinge before advertised of theire fight and perceavinge by the light of the fireinge of theire peeces that they and wee weare in dainger of our great

---

[1] The nautical sand-glass was a half-hour glass, so that, the first watch beginning at 8, this would make the time nearly 9 o'clock.

[2] Dudley omits all mention of this action, perhaps because England and France were at peace.

[3] MS. and still plyinge.

C

ordenance, made a light to be hanged forth that they might see wheare wee weare and might, if they durste, com unto us, for they might com to us, but wee coulde not com to them to receave our carvell. Which when they refused, our Generall caused the master gunner to give them a great peece of ordenance, which was soe warme a wellcome unto them that with speed they soe sodenlie retired that in the morninge wee coulde not allmost perceave they had at all disankored. But that our men had them allwaies in sight, wee coulde not else have beleeved it.

Our Generall, as one doubtfull of the success of his other carvell, sent his bote abord the carvell that was com, who beinge before seperated by the French admerall coulde deliver noe certaintie of her, but sent worde shee was in some harde fight with two pinnesses and a shallop of the Frenchmen; and for that they coulde not see her this morninge they feared shee was surprised. The returne of which answear bred some discontentmente unto our Generall, who vowed the death of the rest, if his men weare perished. Thus commaundinge everie officer to see theire chardge in readines for to fight, [hee] gave commaundement that the carvell shoulde plie up into the weather, for that wee did discrie a saile makinge from the shore unto the French admerall, who laie aloofe of some six leagues to weather. Our carvell plyinge up into the winde weathered the saile which came from the shore and gave them soe sharpe a chase with the help of the great shott that came from aborde our admerall that hee caused them to hange owt a flagg of truce, cryinge "all freinds, freinds"; the which wordes gave us some hope that our other carvell was in safetie. And by this time wee might discrie another saile to make from the shore, after the which wee had noe soener cast abowte but wee did perceave her collers to be the collers of the carvell which wee wanted; which was the cause that the French chase was given over, who weare more joyous of theire freedome then wee gladsome of theire thraldome. Thus rejoycinge of all handes, they as free from the subversion which was likelie to be inflicted upon them, wee for the returne of our supposed lost carvell, givinge whole vallews of shott at our meetinge and likewise some great ordenance, our Generall now as this daie beinge the ixth of Januarie, beinge Thursedaie, having, God be thanked, all his men sownde without sicknes and his carvell safe without dainger, gave directions to proceed on his viage for one of the ilands of Cape Diverde called the ilande of St. Antonie, wheare our men had well hoped to have watred afresh. The which they had done, had not the master perswaded our Generall to the contrarie, for that this ilande beinge soe poisensome a place, by reason of the infectious ayre, might breed some contagious infection amonge our men. It was thearefore concluded secretlie betweene them, that in the night they shoulde overslip them[1]; the which was performed soe cunninglie that none coulde perceave it, but that it was rather done by ignorance then anie way by consent. After which time wee weare commaunded to beare hence away for the Indies, and for that our Generall woulde have noe occasion of rebordinge each other, the which might be some occasion of stay, untell wee recovered the aforenamed cost, hee sent the carvells victuall sufficient aborde to serve them. 9 Jan.

Soe the xiijth of Januarie wee sett forwarde, not alteringe our determinacion untell wee might safelie arive at Trinidado, havinge nothinge worth the notinge or remembrance, savinge that oftentimes wee might see a great multitude of thease flyinge fishes flie togeather, beinge 13 Jan.

---

[1] Dudley gives the same reason for making straight for Trinidad, but as if it was of his own initiative.

pursued by some other fishes, as if theare had bin some flock of larkes dared by the hobbie. Wee have had in a watch in the night a fish flie into a little scuttle of a cabbin, noe bigger then the hande of a man, a thinge that to some might seeme strainge, and yeat not soe strainge as true. The fish that doth most often give this fish chase is the dolphin, which is soe swifte that he coulde not escape him, had not nature provided him this remedie. But, as his safetie is wrought by his flight, soe is hee not voyde likewyse of dainger usinge that benifitt of nature ; for he hath noe sooner mounted on winge but præsentlie the gannet, a great fowle, lyeth hoveringe alofte and maketh ceasure of him like the fallcon, that pointinge it alofte and the fowle noe sooner is putt of from the ryver for the servinge of her, but præsentlie shee falleth and killeth her praie at sowce.[1] Soe doth this gannet lie watchinge alofte ; the dolphin, he pursueth in the sea and forceth her to take the benifitt of her winges, which noe sooner appeareth above water but [s]hee is made a praie of the aforenamed bird, the gannet.

Thus sailinge through the maine ocean, [wee] had[2] winde and weather most prosperous and faire for some xx. daies togeather before wee founde the alteringe of the coller of the water, which then began to forshew wee weare not far from some cost, fallinge most rightlie owt unto the computacion and reckninge of our Generall, who from time to time foretolde me by the reckninge of his carde, when he had taken the hight under whatsoemeaver meridian wee then hapned to be in, " wee shall," saith hee, " if

---

[1] *Sc.* at a plunge or swoop. "Dead, as a fowl at souse, *i.e.*, at the stroke of another bird descending violently on it" (Dyce, *Beaumont and Fletcher*, vii, p. 278). Halliwell, *Archaic Dict.*, also quotes Florio, 1611, p. 48, " To leape or seaze greedily upon, to souze doune as a hauke." Skeat, *Etym. Dict.*, connects the word with " sauce" and " souse," to pickle, plunge into brine.

[2] MS. havinge.

God prosper our proceedings, see land such a daie by
the prick of this my carde." And this was not done
once nor twise, but still from the first cape after wee weare
departed from our English cost, which was the North
Cape of Spaine, untell wee came to Trinidado. And when
all those that had bin masters, of the which some of them
have bin thought to be as good as anie in England, beinge
the masters mates and theire consortes, did faile in theire
reckninge, yeat fell it owt just with his reckninge. The
which how difficulte a thinge it is rightlie to censure of it,
lett those who have bin seamen all daies of theire lives
judge. For if a man doe but note how manie things doe
necessarilie concur unto the true perfection of the arte,
wee may justlie judge it not onlie the admirablest worke
in the worlde but one of the wonders of the worlde. But
leavinge this intricate arte, as not able to sett forth her
perfection, lett me returne unto that honorable and excellent practiser of the arte, that I may with admiracion
admire in silence to my unspeakable joye at those his
wonderfull actions, which heareafter will prove to be the
worlds wonder. I meane our vertuous and carefull, honorable and provident Generall, who seinge the water in the
night time to wax soe soedenlie white called unto the
master, who had noted it before, as both watchfull and
most carefull of his chardge, and havinge caused one to
heave owt a lead and sowndinge founde it to be but xv.
feadome water. Perceavinge wee weare not far of the
cost and the night withall darke, hee commaunded that wee
shoulde cast aboute, the which wee did and came unto 50,
wheare wee laie at hull untell Fridaie morninge, beinge
the last of Januarie.

And within two owers after the breake of day wee 31 Jan.
discried lande, which was the maine continent betweene
Brazeile and India; and within some two owers after our
good Generall himselfe discried the ilande of Trinidado,

for the which wee had allwaies borne. And forthwith he called unto the carvells, commaundinge them that they shoulde goe before and see if they might discover anie manner of shippinge within the baies before our admerall might be discried, and withall enjoyned them that they shoulde not pass belowe the pointe called Curiapan,[1] the which if they had performed, wee had withowt all peradventures loded ourselves with the richest ore of the worlde. This night wee ankored on the south west parte of the ilande in a baie the which our Generall called Baie Pellican, for the great abooundance of pellicans that wee see theare, and wheare wee founde our two carvells. This caveninge our Generall sent of (*sc.* off) his bote with Cap. Jobson with divers gentlemen, as M^r. Wright, M^r. Comley and divers others, both shott and pike, to the intent that they might if possible, by anie meanes they coulde, gett anie of the salvages or at least have conference with them. The which they did soe well accomplish as they did traffique with them, and they promised to com aborde the next

1 Feb. daie. It was Satterdaie night late eare our bote returned, our carvells havinge past not onlie the pointe but went soe far within the baie that it gave occasion to us to goe downe soe far to seeke them that wee passed downe soe far that it was impossible for us to recover those places wheare wee shoulde have done ourselves most good.

2 Feb. The daie followinge, beinge Sondaie, in the morninge came the salvages with two canowes aborde us, as they had promised our men, bringinge such commodities with them as theire ilande did afforde, savinge they brought

---

[1] "Point Curiapan, which the Spanyards call Punto de Gallo" (Ralegh's *Discoverie of Guiana*, ed. Schomburgk, Hakluyt Soc., 1848, p. 1); the southwestern extremity of Trinidad, now Point Icacos or Icacque. Pelican Bay is identified by Kingsley (*At Last*, 1872, p. 69) with Cedros Bay, still "very full of pelicans" (*cf.* Dudley), and this is confirmed by Kendall's narrative below, and by the position of the "Minera di Calcuri" in Dudley's map.

neither golde nor pearle, of the which theare are great store within the ilande, but tobacco, nutes and such kinde of fruites, the which they exchainged for knives, bugles,[1] beades, fishinge hookes and hatchetts. Our Generall, findinge one of them that coulde speake Spanish, inquired of him of a golde myne of ore, demaundinge if he coulde or woulde bringe us thither. The which he profered of his owne voluntarie will and, if wee woulde, he woulde goe with us thither. Wheareupon our Generall sent Cap. Jobson, repræsentinge his person with his authoritie, as his Leiftenante Generall, commaundinge all his other captaines to give attendance on him, and withall our master accompanied him. And soe wee marched some viii[th] miles alonge the cost eare wee founde the place and, findinge it to abounde with that kinde of ore,[2] each of us brought some of it unto our Generall, and soe returned that night aborde.

The next daie, beinge Mondaie, the thirde of February, our Generall gave directions for the landinge of all his lande forces, wheareupon [hee] commaunded his carvells to plie as neare unto the shore as they possible coulde and to lande theire men ; the which they did, the one of them before our Generall toke lande, who gave him a vallew of small shott upon his landinge, reanswearinge the great ordenance, which was some ten peeces, at his comminge from abord. The other carvell, by reason hee had taken all the souldiers aborde him out of the admerall, coulde not soe sone take lande, but præsentlie after landed all his forces. And soe our Generall appointed[3] certaine both for

3 Feb.

---

[1] Bugle, "a tube-shaped glass bead, usually black, used to ornament wearing apparel" (*New Engl. Dict.*). From its derivation as given by Skeat (*Etym. Dict.*), it may mean any ring-shaped ornament.

[2] It proved to be merely Marcasite (*cf.* Dudley), or iron pyrites of a bronze-yellow colour. No gold appears to be found in Trinidad (Wall and Sawkins, *Geology of Trinidad*, 1860, p. 68).

[3] MS. appointinge.

the marshallinge of his troopes and the leadinge of them,
as Cap. Wood and Cap. Wentworth for the'vawarde, Wyatt
and Canter for the maine battle of pike, and Vincent for
the rearewarde. And thus beinge marshalled in good order,
hee himselfe led[1] the march, accompanied onlie with his
Leiftenant Generall Cap. Jobson, who somtimes made his
retire unto the rearwarde, somtimes into the maine battle,
as occasion served, givinge speciall commaunde unto us,
both Wyatt and Vincent, who had the marshallinge of the
whole troopes as the two corporalls of the feilde, that wee
shoulde have a special care of the marchinge of our men
in good order. Which was soe well performed of all
handes in such good sorte as, if wee had bin charged with
ten thowsande Indians, they coulde not have harmed us.
Thus havinge marched viij[th] longe miles[2] through the deepe
sandes and in a most extreame hott daie, our Generall,
unaccustomed, God he knowes, to walke one (*sc.* on) foote,
leadinge the march, wee at length came unto the place
wheare this ore was, and havinge placed our courte of
garde in a convenient place and sett forth our centronells,
all the rest weare appointed to the geatheringe of ore.
And havinge allmost in a moment geathered such a quan-
titie that after everie one was equallie lodende yeat wee
left allmost a quarter of a hogsehead behinde us, that our
men weare not able to carrie, by this time it flowed soe fast
that wee weare forced to staie untell midnight, at which
time the full sea was past. In the meane while our
Generall, perceavinge a most filthie miste to fall, caused
an armefull of boughes to be cutt and laide on the grownde,
wheareon he himselfe lay downe; over whome Ancient[3]
Barrow helde his collers and Wyatt, chusinge some of the
best of our men, made his stande rownde about him. Thus

---

[1] MS. leadinge.
[2] "About three leagues to the eastwards" (Dudley); "six miles or seven to the east" (Kendall).
[3] A corruption of Ensign, immortalized by Ancient Pistol.

havinge reposed himselfe some ower hee awaked, and not longe pawsinge after, wee had alarum given us, which I rather impute to the ignorance of our centronells then anie way unto the chardginge of the enimie. For theare is a certaine flie which in the night time appeareth like unto a fire, and I have seene at the least two or three score togeather in the woods, the which make resemblance as if they weare soe manie light matches, the which I perswade myselfe gave occasion of some soden feare unto the centronells which gave the alarum. And our men beinge præsentlie in armes, the Generall toke Cap. Jobson and Wyatt with xx. shott and marched from the battle to discover what the cause shoulde bee; but, findinge all places free from dainger, wee made our retire, willinge that everie one shoulde be in a readines if the like occasion shoulde be offred. Thus after our men had rested themselves and the sea began for to ebb, our Generall gave commandement for our marchinge back againe; the which beinge signified both by his noyse of trumpetts and drome, wee of all handes marched alonge. And for that the waters weare deepe up unto the girdlesteid[1] of our men, our Generall himselfe first led through the water up unto the verie twiste, an unusuall thinge for him, beinge a courtier, but not unfitt for him, beinge our Generall in India, caryinge soe great a majestic in his march with such unremovable resolucions in his proceedings that wee all that followed him concluded in the idea of our consaites hee without all doubte woulde prove the onlie mirrour of knighthood. For when hee determined of anie thinge, he sett it downe with the great consideracion and advice of the masters, and, beinge concluded what shoulde be done, he woulde have it accomplished with such expedition that he might saie

---

[1] The waist, place for the girdle. The twist of the body is where the thighs part, the fork. "Twist" is used in Old English for "twig," where a branch forks or divides into two.

with Cæsar, *veni, vidi, vici*. Thus by two or three of the clock in the morninge wee had recovered our shipp and weare in a short space all safelie sett aborde.

4 Feb. This morninge, beinge Twsedaie, our Generall caused our Queenes armes to be drawne on a peece of lead and this inscription written underneath, the which was sett upon a tree neare adjoyninge unto the place wheare this myne of golde ore was discovered: *Robertus Duddeleius, Anglus, filius illustrissimi Comitis Leicestrencis, 3°*[1] *die Februarii, anno Domini 1594, cum suis copiis in hanc insulam descendit eamque cœpit ad usum serenissimæ principis Reginæ Elizabethæ Angliæ, Franciæ et Hiberniæ, fidei defensoris, etc., atque hunc locum divinæ Mariæ promontorium*[2] *appellari iussit, sibi omnia iura regalia vendicans, dum in hoc negotio aliquid a regina sibi in mandato habebit*. And for the accomplishment of it, he committed the doinge of it unto Wyatt and delivered unto him his sworde, joyninge with him in commission M[r]. Wright and M[r]. Vincent. Soe havinge assured them a sufficient power, wee landed and, beinge verie late before wee departed from our ship, wee coulde not recover the place before it was night, but weare inforced to intrenche ourselves that night in the woode; and havinge gotten a convenient place both for the releevinge of our men for fresh water and wood (two greate necessaries for all souldiers marching to anie service), as allsoe for the strength of the place, the which was soe fortified by nature that with one owers labour wee made it vnvincible, [wee there remained].[3] Thus lyinge in safegarde all that night, havinge our centronells forth for the discoverie of anie thinge that might

5 Feb. happen, in the morninge Wyatt was[4] informed by one

---

[1] MS. 30. The year was, of course, 1594-5.
[2] Interlined, over *insulam*.
[3] Some such words as these seem to be wanted in order to make sense. [4] MS. beinge.

of the centronells that in the night hee harde a dogg barke once, and the rest had[1] discovered a fire divers times in the night, the which gave some suspition of the enimies scowtes. Wheareupon takinge some two or three good shott [wee] cutt owt some 100 paces into the wood and marched as secret as wee coulde and at last founde the place wheare the enimie had sett his scowte to discover our forces of what strength wee weare of; and wee discried the track of theire feet in the woodes by the impression of the sandes. And havinge followed them up into the woodes as far as I[2] possible might, I retired unto our men, wheare wee had the night before incamped ourselves.

And soe marchinge forth in good order, wee came unto the place wheare this our service was to be accomplished, the which wee finished after this sorte: first wee caused the trumpetts to sownde solemlie three severall times, our companie troopinge rownde; in the midst marched Wyatt, bearinge the Queenes armes wrapped in a white silke scarfe edged with a deepe silver lace, accompanied with Mr. Wright and Mr. Vincent, each of us with our armes, havinge the Generalls collers displaid, both with the trumpetts and the drome before us, after the chiefest of the troopes, then the whole troope, thus marchinge up unto the top of the mounte unto a tree the which grew from all the rest, wheare wee made a stande. And after a generall silence Wyatt red it unto the troope, first as it was written in Lattin, then in English; after kissinge it [hee] fixed it on the tree appointed to bear it and, havinge a carpender placed alofte with hammer and nailes readie to make it fast, fastned it unto the tree. After wee pronounced thease wordes that "the Honorable Robert Duddeley, sonn and heyre unto the Right Honorable

---

[1] MS. havinge.
[2] The author here forgets himself, as elsewhere further on, and enables us to identify him with Captain Wyatt.

Robert, Earle of Leicester, Leiftenante of all Her Majesties fortes and forces beyonde the seas, Lord High Stewarde of her Majesties Howseholde, Knight of the most honorable order of the Garter, hath sent us heather and in his name to accomplish this honorable acte dedicated unto the service of his most gratious soveraigne and benifitt of his countrey, and this with his sworde, God favoringe his intent, doth hee sweare to make good against anie knight in the whole worlde." This beinge ended, the trumpetts and dromę sownded, the whole troope cryed "God save our Queene Elizabeth"; and havinge thus, as solemlie as wee coulde, accomplishte this committed unto our chardge, wee marched downe the mounte, and havinge equallie ladende our men with that ore with the which the place did abownde, wee sett forwarde towards our shippinge. And by foure of the clock wee had recovered the same, and beinge sett aborde wee gave an accounte unto our honorable Generall what wee had done.

6 Feb. The next daie wee waied our anker and doubled the points and ankored in a harber not far from Paracowe,[1] the which our Generall called Porte Peregrine. The day

7 Feb. followinge, beinge Fridaie the vijth of Februarie, he sent all his landmen aborde his carvell called the *Regarde*, commaundinge them to plie as neare the shore as possible [s]he coulde, havinge before commaunded the other carvell called the *Intent* to draw unto the crick, wheare shee might both grave, triine and wash her, and to stopp a great leak the which shee had receaved in the takinge of her; the which shee did. In the meane while our Generall landed himselfe the seconde time, havinge in his companie but six men (wheareof Cap. Jobson was one) when he tooke lande, for his forces weare then to

---

[1] "From Curiapan I came to a port and seat of Indians called 'Parico,' where we found a fresh-water river" (Ralegh, *Discoverie of Guiana*, p. 2).

be landed out of the carvell called the *Regard*. Who seinge the Generall ashore made the more hast to land us, beinge three owers before the first companie was landed; and beinge com unto our Generall, wee founde him usinge the salvages with all the kindnes he could devise. The which toke soe good effect that two or three voluntarie went aborde with him and lodged theare all night, wheare he made them great cheare and gave them such thinges as he saw did most delight them. At his goinge aborde he committed the chardge of those forces the which he left on land unto Cap. Wentworth, Wyatt and Vincent. And that night wee fortified ourselves as time and place did permitt us; but the next day wee 8 Feb. receaved worde from our Generall that it was his pleasure that wee should lie some viij^{th} or ix. daies ashore, for that he determined to water, balliss and trim our admerall. Which caused us to raise downe that fortification which wee had that daie before builded in haste and to begin another sconce as neare the fresh water as wee coulde, which wee intrenched and fortified like unto a halfe moone, havinge the other side soe strengthned with wood that it was impossible to be assaultid. That night, beinge Satterdaie night, our Generall sent Cap. Jobson unto us to take vew of our sconce and withall to send Cap. Wentworth abord his carvell, commaundinge him that they shoulde with as much speed as they coulde turne downe unto the other carvell, wheare shee was a gravinge, and theare for to wash and trime her, that wee might be all in a readines to sett forwarde when our admerall was trimmed. This beinge done our Generall sent for Cap. Jobson aborde, who left the chardge unto Wyatt and Vincent for that night.

The next daie, beinge Sondaie, our Generall sent our 9 Feb. victuall ashore, and withall came Cap. Jobson; upon whose comminge, wee that had the goverment ashore surrendred it up unto his handes, who laie ashore with us all that day and night untell Mondaie night. At which time, makinge choyse of some speciall musketers and pikemen for a convoy, [hee] marched up some fowre miles by lande unto our carvells, to impose certaine services upon them by the Generalls commaunde, leavinge the other forces with Wyatt untell his returne. The which he made that night by midnight, and at his returne [he] commaunded Wyatt to make choyse of a sufficient gard for himselfe and to march up wheare he had bin and fetch both the carpenders and the rest of such things which wee weare to have from the carvells for the speedie dispatchinge of our admeralls trimminge. The which wee did by Twsedaie dinner, and that night laie insconsed, makinge readie our caske and fittinge our necessaries.

The next daie Cap. Jobson was determined to march to Parracow and to have taken the towne, but as he had commanded Wyatt to make readie a companie to march alonge withall wee might discrie to com from the cliffs out of the wood two or three with a flagg of truce, wavinge unto us that it might be lawfull to com and speake with us.[1] The which Cap. Jobson did præsentlie grawnte, and, beinge come in presence of him, he uttred thease wordes, "*Vinie en pais ou con gero?*", which is as much to saie in our languish, "Come yow in peace or with war?", and withall [he] delivered him a letter, the which he toke and soe caryed both him and his letter aborde unto our Generall, leavinge direction with Wyatt and Vincent that our men shoulde remaine in armes untell his returne. The which was that night by midnight, bringinge ashore with him the one of the Indians and withall a letter to signifie his pleasure, how that little he did either regarde or respect the Spanish

---

[1] The Spanish Governor of Trinidad at this time was Don Antonio de Berreo. Ralegh, who took him prisoner soon after, has much to say of him in his *Discoverie of Guiana*.

forces, usinge them as most bitter foes unto God and his countrey and vilde enimies unto his Prince and her subjects. And for that it may be knowne unto the worlde, I have sett downe in writinge his lettre *verbatim*, as written unto his kinseman Cap. Jobson, who was then Lieftenante Generall to commaunde both us and his forces :—

"Cossen Jobson,

"It may be that Mr. Ben Wood will bringe some Spaniards, beinge gone to parlie with them that weare sent to me upon parlie, because I meane to stande upon my garde and have noe dealinge with Spaniards, but to take them, as it is my parte, as enimies unto our most gratious Soveraigne and State. Therefore I saie that, if it fortune that Mr. Wood bringe anie Spaniards, you may understande theire mindes, but in such sorte as they may not see your courtes of garde ; neither in anie case, I praie you, suffer them to com aborde, because I woulde not have anie Spaniards either to see my shipp within or my companies ashore, to discover my force. But lett them know I soe much disdaine the Spaniarde and his courtesies in respect of my dutifull services unto her Majestie as I woulde they knew I neither trust them nor care for theire force, be it neaver so great. By this and my courses all Spaniards shall know Englishmen of worth will neaver dishonour theire Prince, countrey and selves by fainthartninge unto theire curtesie, that villanouslie have sought the life of our most gratious Queene,[1] whom in dwtifull alegance wee are bounde to defende, and withall the overthrow of our countrey and selves, for whom in equitie wee weare borne to dye for. It weare not amiss yf you putt this into the mindes of my companies, the more to hate and disdaine the force of anie Spaniarde, and withall signifie unto them that whensoeaver they think themselves in anie dainger I will lie ashore and venter my life with them for companie. Soe fare you well.

"Your assured cossen,
ROBERT DUDDELEY."

---

[1] He probably alludes to the alleged plot to poison Elizabeth, for which her physician, Dr. Lopez, suffered death at Tyburn, 7 June, 1594, a few months before Dudley started on his voyage.

This letter beinge red unto the companie gave them more occasion of hatred unto the Spaniarde and better respect unto themselves for the strengthninge of our fortification in the which wee laie insconsed, and wheare wee refreshed ourselves with such supplies as the countrey did afforde us.

14 Feb. Upon Fridaie, beinge the xiiijth of Februarie, our Generall victualled his carvells with some three moneths victuall a peece and sent [them] before into the Indies, determininge not to meet them againe before wee returned into Englande. All this while wee harde nothinge of the Spaniarde untell
16 Feb. Sondaie towardes night, at what time wee had two Indians brought unto us by the centronells, which brought a lettre unto our Generall with certaine presents; the which our Generall did soe contemne that he refused to speake with them, much less to accept of theire presents. After this time we hard nothinge of the Spaniard, but the next day,
17 Feb. beinge Monday the xviith of Februarie, wee made our preprative to goe aborde. And that day, our Generall havinge two East Indians the which he had of M^r. Candish[1], the one of them, while wee weare everie one of us busie, spyinge oportunitie, he stole privilie awaie and, as wee suppose, ran unto the Spaniard. The which made us make noe great hast abord that night, to see if the Spaniarde, beinge trulie inforemed of the departure of our strengths, woulde give us anie bravado. And for the better fortificacion of ourselves our Generall sent his bote with a companie [of] musketers, to lie of (*sc.* off) the shore to chardge on the backs of those the which should give anie assaulte unto the baraskado.

18 Feb. The next morninge, beinge Twseday morninge, Cap.

---

[1] Thomas Cavendish, Dudley's brother-in-law (see Preface), who sailed round the world in 1586-1588. He sailed again for the South Seas, 26 August, 1591; but the voyage was disastrous, and he died at sea in May or June, 1592.

Jobson sent our bote aborde to know our Generalls pleasure for our comminge aborde. Shee was returned back againe, and withall theare was delivered by them unto Cap. Jobson another plate of lead with her Majesties armes drawne on it and with the like inscription as the former had, willinge that it shoulde likewyse theare be sett up, partlie for that wee had soe longe theare remained withowt resistance, neaver incountred with the Spaniarde nor disturbed by the countrey, and yeat doinge whatsoaver it pleased our Generall to commaunde and liked ourselves best, and partlie for that manie of the people of the ilande had theire habitacion not far from the place. Both the which beinge rightlie considered, it was thought good by our Generall to adorne the place with the like honorable service ; and for the better perforemance of it he sent directions unto Captaine Jobson, who performed it in his owne person with more solemnitie then the former was. The which beinge accomplished unto the good likinge of our noble Generall, wee weare sent for aborde, the Captaine himselfe being the last man that came from the shore aborde.

THE INSCRIPTION DRAWNE UPON THE PLATE OF LEADE.

"*Robertus Duddeleius, Anglus, filius illustrissimi Comitis Leicestrencis, decimo septimo die Februarii,* 1595, *cum suis navibus in anchoris stetit coram ista hujus insulæ parte, quam Portum Peregrinæ appellavit : deinde in terram cum suis copiis descendit, ubi diu commoratus est et sine ulla interruptione quæ voluit fecit et peregit. Præterea insulam hanc Serenissimæ Reginæ suæ Angliæ, Franciæ et Hyberniæ Majestatis licentiæ dicavit, propterea quod sibi videtur copiis necessariisque maxime abundare.*"

All this time our Generall overslipt noe opportunitie, but dalie delt with the Indian he had aborde to disclose wheare theire rich mines of gold weare, and, if he woulde discover them unto him, he woulde not onelie bountefullie rewarde him, but enlardge him at his owne pleasure. This

Indian at the first would discover nothinge, but at the last, beinge threatned unto death, promised to disclose a most rich myne of golde on the maine lande, soe that after hee might be enlardged and sett free, and what hee promised to doe, if he perforemed it not, hee woulde willinglie dye for it; and withall [he] discried the place [and] the ryver unto our Generall soe perfect that hee not onlie learned the richnes of the place but saw the entrance of the ryver. The which after he had bin soe sufficientlie instructed as this Indian might informe him, he toke others and by fayre meanes soe gott theire love that one of them voluntarie profered to goe with him into Englande or wheare soeaver he woulde. And of this Indian he not onlie learned that those rich mines of gold weare delivered of a truth, but [he] discried how the salvages theare hanged rich peeces of gold aboute theire necks in the steed of brestplates, and a most common thinge usuallie used amonge them. Wee have had at divers times at the least an hundred Indians com aborde us, and theare was not one but by signes confirmed the richnes of this myne.

Whearefore when our worthie Generall had to the uttermost learned what they might informe him, findinge[1] [them] by all theire demonstracions to agree in this for the admired riches of the place, he generallie purposed the sendinge of his bote thither and withall much desired that some attempte shoulde be made for the true discoverie theareof, whereby he might the better satisfie either her Majestie or such at home as are meet to be advertised of such designes. The worthy and valarous younge gentleman was verie desirous to goe himselfe, notwithstandinge the manifolde daingers delivered by our master, Abraham Kendall, which had before sene a disastrous experience theareof by the loss of some shippinge in the place, growinge by a current and

---

[1] MS. and findinge.

indraught neare to a rock which they call Diabolo;[1] the which dainger or anie thinge else pertaininge to matters of navigation our Generall, beyonde ordinarie practise havinge a very speciall perseverance or rather perfect knowledge, did well understande, and withall founde a meanes and course, which beinge well perceaved and dulie observed, it was possible, yf to pass forwarde, to make as safe a returne againe. Howbeit, it was generallie thought verie unfitt that the person of soe worthie and hopefull a gallant, as an unfeathered shafte, should be hazarded in soe small and simple a vessell, whearein coulde not be thrust anie sufficient guarde for his safetie or defence. To which proceedings above all others Captain Jobson, his Leif-tenante and deare kinseman, was much contradictorie and repugnante, desiringe and earnestlie beseechinge the Generall that it woulde please him to committ the seide service unto him, whose earnest thirste and desire eaver was to make sacrifice of his dearest blood and life for the service of him whom he honoured under his Soveraigne above all the worlde beside. The Generall gave place to his earnest suite, shewinge in few wordes his good acceptance of that his kindenes with friendlie thanks, proposed unto him the daingers and carefullie instructed him what course to take for his safetie, givinge him withall free choyse through all the companie of his shipp, to take such as hee thought meetest for his purpose in such an enterprize.

The good Captaine, puttinge on a verie willinge resolution to this service (notwithstandinge, as I hard him say, in his dreame the night before he did senciblie

---

[1] See Dudley's map and Kendall's narrative. "The Devil's Island" is marked on Capt. Edw. Thompson's map of *The Coast of Guyana*, 1783, and on Tho. Jefferys' map of *The Coast of Caracas, Cumana*, etc., 1794, to the west of Point Icacque. It does not appear in Chimmo's *Admiralty Chart of Trinidad and the Gulf of Paria*, 1866-8. It is probably the rock now commonly called the Soldado.

perceave himselfe drowneninge), toke unto him for his g[o]inge the two masters mates, the boatswaine, the gunners mate, the corporall and his mate, the armerer, a carpender, two proper younkers sailers, and two painfull and able Dutchmen. Thus havinge the daie before the bote sufficientlie trimmed and with sufficient preparacion of municion and victuall for some few daies, upon Thurse-

20 Feb. daie, beinge the xxth of Februarie, at the seconde watch in the night, [he] losed from the shipp side, havinge the weather fayre and caryinge with him the hartie praiers and well wishinge of us all for his faire condicions and good cariadge of himselfe towardes us all. The night beinge verie calme, his companie willinglie plied theire

21 Feb. owers, and soe by daie, when the winde began to fresh more then enoughe upon them, they came to an anker before a place called Sorama.[1] Yt blew soe much all the daie that it neither was saileworthy, nor coulde they possiblie use theire owers, soe that they continued all the daie at an anker, wheare they rid verie unquietlie, some of his companie beginninge to dispaire that they should hardlie gett passage over to the maine. But the Captaine, desiringe to performe the service to the uttermost of his power soe far forth as by anie reason he might be guided to the contentment of his deare and noble Generall, tolde his whole companie plainlie that hee woulde pro- ceed; and soe at night it pleased God somwhat to mittigate the raginge of the seas and to give them a faire gale to putt them over to the maine. In his passage he caused the lead to bee much and often goinge and observed diligentlie the tides, the currents, the indraughts, the highte of the lande with which they fell, [and] toke such markes as he coulde of the place whence he came

---

[1] Apparently on the south-west coast of Trinidad, and near Point Icacos. Dudley does not mention it, and it is not on his map.

and [did] all such other thinges as the Generall had verie
providentlie, wyselie and carefullie foretolde, forewarned
and commaunded him before. He allsoe receaved by
way of commission a whole sheet of paper written with
the Generalls owne hande, contayninge his minde and
pleasure in all matters; which the Captaine did not loke
into himselfe, neither did he participate the same unto
his companie, untell they drew neare to the place wheare
the thinges weare to be putt in execution, wheare he
was not a little carefull to see all things diligentlie performed and the service promoted to the uttermost that
hee might possiblie.

Upon Satterdaie, the xxii[th] of Februarie, by the dawn- 22 Feb.
inge of the daie or somwhat before, they aryved on the
maine, wheare they ankored for a while till daylight
appeared and then founde themselves by the informacion
of theire Spanish Indian, named Baltizar, to be at the
mouth of a great ryver called Capulia.[1] They disankor-
inge sett saile and had the winde with a tide to sett
them inwarde, for it was upon the flood. I have harde
Captaine Jobson gladlie and with pleasure make relacion
of the wonderfull pleasauntnes for manie respects and
most delectable varieties of manie thinges that was præsented to his eies, as well in that ryver of Capulia as
the rest, which weare verie manie; and, thus in generall

---

[1] Perhaps the Capure in the delta of the Orinoco (Ralegh, *Discoverie of Guiana*, p. 43, note 1). According to Schomburgk, Ralegh's Capuri was a different branch, now the Macareo. Dudley gives Capulio as the name of the foreland, S. by W., " wanting a fourth part," from Curiapan, at 4 leagues distance, and says they entered by a small river called Cabota, in the land of the Veriotaus. By the latter he probably means the Uaraus or Waraus (Ralegh, p. 49, note 1), and Cabota should perhaps more properly be Cabora, Capora in Arawak, signifying a small river (*ib.*, p. 101, note 1). In the list of names at the end of this narrative it appears, however, as Sabiota. It is not given in the map, where the Dudleano (*cf.* Kendall) represents the Capure. From the Cabota, according to Dudley, they passed, no doubt by one of the numerous lateral connections, into the Mana, Ralegh's Amana and the present Manamo.

receavinge it from his owne mouth-reporte, soe much as
I can well remember I will sett downe. But withall I
must confess that the Captaine did not make anie publike
declaracion how hee fownde the sowndings, either in
the cutt over to the maine or in the rivers hee passed
theare, nor of theire names nor of the traffique he had
or other conference with the people; but such things
he did observe and did in private deliver unto our
Generall accordinge as he had in chardge to doe. But
thus he saith of those ryvers,[1] that they weare faire,
spatious and broade, the water after one daies journey
verie fresh, sweet and pleasaunte and navigable for small
vessells, the banks munited naturallie with such uniforme
and beawtifull exornacions, the trees and herbs growinge
soe even and soe statelie high and tall as neather had
he ever seene or doth thinke it possible eaver to see in
anie walke, gardaine or arbour by mans witt, pollecie or
arte soe cunningelie framed and sett forth, and oftentimes
allsoe yealdinge a pleasante savoure when they passed
neare the shore. The rivers weare frequented with store
of fowle of divers strainge and pleasante collers, speciallie
some all pure white, others of all vermilian red and manie
of a perfect blew, infinite store of parratts, parakities and
other great birds of most fine and well mixed collers,
in sandie banks great store of tortoyses,[2] manie fine
marmasites of strainge collers friskinge in the trees,
wonderfull store of fish, but of noe great bignes.

---

[1] "I neuer saw a more beawtiful countrey, nor more liuely prospectes, hils so raised heere and there ouer the vallies, the riuer winding into diuers braunches, the plaines adioyning without bush or stubble, all faire greene grasse, the ground of hard sand easy to march on, eyther for horse or foote, the deare crossing in euery path, the birds towardes the euening singing on euery tree with a thousand seuerall tunes, cranes and herons of white, crimson and carnation pearching on the riuers side," etc. (Ralegh, *Discoverie of Guiana*, p. 82).

[2] On the freshwater turtles of the Orinoco, see Ralegh, *op. cit.*, p. 63, note 2.

After that the Captaine had passed with his bote fowre daies, havinge gone some fourescore leagues by the true computacion of our best maryners, and had passed sundrye places habited, yeat the people differinge in language, at the last they came to a place wheare theare was much people of men, woemen and children. And they weare a makinge certaine veric great canowes, the cheifest carpender beinge an aged olde creature, to whom the rest of the people gave great respect and reverence. The Captaine præsentinge him with a trifle from our Generall, hee did præsentlie dispatche a canowe with some five or six Indians to the mine of Calcurie.[1] The commaunder of that place, returninge our messingers the next daie with a servante of his owne, promised to accomplish our desire and to com and traffique with our Captaine and his companie, which the daie followinge was performed. And towards night with a great noyse, havinge som 70 or odd persons in certaine canowes, he approched our bote in the night, which our Captaine would in noe wyse permitt, but willed that they shoulde resorte unto him the next daie, which they obeyed. This people præsented manie thinges, speciallie victuall, for traffique, but weare unwillinge to discover other things which our Captain most desired. Yeat in some things

---

[1] In the glossary at the end given as the native name for gold. It no doubt represents *Carucuri* or *Carucuru*, which, according to Schomburgk, "in the Tamanac and Carib dialects signifies gold" (Ralegh, p. 100, note 2). There is, however, a curious entry about it in Père Raymond Breton's *Dict. Caraibe-Français*, 1665 (ed. Platzmann, 1892, p. 106), under *Calloucouli*, in which it is distinguished from gold: "c'est un metail qu'on a envoyé en France pour le cognoistre et contrefaire, mais inutillement, nos Sauuages ont toûjours discerné la fraude. L'argent, l'or mesme ne les touche pas à son égard. Ce metail a cét aduantage que la roüille, ne le vert-de-gris, ne l'attaque point, ny l'huile, ny le rocou, ny l'ordure mesme ne le salit pas tant qu'en passant la main dessus vous ne le nettoyez. Ils en font des croissans, qu'ils pendent à leur cols, et c'est le plus riche de leur bijous. Ils en font des pailles larges comme le doigt qu'ils attachent à leur nez percé," etc.

contented [he] hastned to returne, havinge hyred another Indian for a nearer passage in our returne, and had such favour with the Calcurian captaine that he sent allsoe one of his small canowes to attende our bote, takinge his leave of our Captaine with to much the Spanish grace. Most of his people weare tall of stature and of verie manlike visage, caryinge Indian bowes an[d] swordes, and most of them havinge some little tast of the Spanish tounge.

Our Spanish Indian guide Baltizar at the first incounter with the Calcurian commaunder semed verie unwillinge to be seen unto him or to have anie conference with him, but was afterwards content to talke with him and, as I feare, more then enoughe; for all theire conference was in the Indian tounge, which our Captaine nor anie of his companie did understande. And albeit the sayd Baltizar had not throughlie satisfied the expectacion of our Captaine, yet did hee wiselie dissemble his conceipte, that neither by word nor countenance the sayd Indian might perceave anie other then good acceptaunce of all his doings and proceedings. But the subtell villaine, who desired nothinge more then his libertie and knew within himselfe how weaklie hee had answeared our reposed trust and his owne promise, devised meanes for his escape, and soe, by a collour of bringinge us the nearest waie, brought them into a verie narrow ryver, beinge little more then twise the botes length, incombred with great branches and whole armes of trees lyinge across. And withall the weather provinge hasey and wett and all our provision of victuall consumed, savinge that which was bought of the Indians, the companie went on shore to make readie theire victuall, leavinge allwaies a sufficient watch upon the Indians, that they shoulde not gett awaie. Our Captaine had a great desire to have made the said Baltizar fast, but, in as much as he had receaved him withowt bonds of the

General, hee stood doubtfull what to doe in that behalfe, not knowinge in soe great a straight what ambuskado might be laide or practise of those Indians in theire owne countreis to the damage of him and his companie. The canowe which the Calcurian sent with us kept asterne for the most parte, somtime neare at hand, and [they] weare releeved by us for theire victuall. Beside Baltizar theare was two other Indians in our bote, the one our hyred guide, the other of the canowes companie. All the night wee held them safe in the bote. Our companie, makinge great hast to the shipp and finding theire labour with the ower yrksome in the heat of the daie, weare desirous to be stirringe in the night, and soe wee disankored about two of the clock in the night, most of the companie havinge taken little rest, the weather fowle and drowsie, the passage verie troublesome by reason of whole trunckes and bodies of trees lyinge cross the mouth of that narrow ryver, over which men weare forced to carrie the bote upon theire shoulders by maine strength. And whilst wee weare theare pusled, before daylight appeared, Baltizar, like a trecherous villaine, dropped overborde with his companion and sodenlie gott into the thicketts, wheare theare was noe possibilitie to recover them. The companie much amazed called the Captaine, beinge a little before sett downe to take some repose, who findinge noe remedie makes the best of the matter and caused præsentlie hands to be laide on the other Indian guide and him to be fast bownde with cordes and ropes; of whome they had little comforte, in respect none understood his language.

Heare will I leave our Captaine and his companie pusled in the bote and returne to speake of our conceipts aborde the shipp. For theire longe absence eaverie private person gave his censure as his fancie led him, bemoninge the loss of theire mate and companion. The master

Abraham Kendall, of whom wee weare to receave our cheifest light, did give the bote and companie lost. Onlie the Generall retayned good hope and assurance in his minde to see his kinseman, whom hee much favoured for his longe and faithfull love, togeather with his companie and bote, to be safelie returned to him againe. Wee did dailie aborde make sacrifice to God, in great devotion callinge upon Him in hartie prayer for them.

Now returne I againe to our Captaine, who, as it is reported, greatlie encouraged his companie, which willinglie did undertake great travaile and theareby in short time had gott themselves out of that straite and uncomfortable place to a more spacious ryver,[1] wheare wee toke direction from our Indian pilott by the motion and wryinge of his mouth, hee neaver sayinge anie other thinge then *Paracoa*.[2] And this wretch, when wee thought him most safelie bownde, much aboute the same season in another night made escape overborde, but, the river beinge bigger, wee gave him chase and had thearein good sporte; but I thinke he hardlie eaver returned to his countrey, for that hee was stricken with a browne bill. Thus weare they left unto themselves, havinge not bin in anie parte of thease rivers before; but, findinge by the course of the tide that they had theire returne into the sea, they founde a passage and recovered the seaside againe. But imagininge that they had bin to the eastwarde, when they weare indeed verie much to the westward, they weare put to leewarde and, insteed of goinge to the ilande of

---

[1] Dudley calls it the Braha, and in his map he gives this name to a branch connecting the Capure (Dudleano) with the Amana. Perhaps it was the branch now known as the Vagre, which would bring them out on the western side of the Bay of Guanipa. See also the list of names below, p. 65.

[2] Probably he meant that they were nearing the sea, *bara* in Arawak meaning the sea, and *koan* to be there (*cf.* Brinton, *The Arawack Language of Guiana*, 1871, p. 14). In Caribbee, *Paragua*, according to Humboldt (*Personal Narrative*, 1821, v, p. 785), means the sea.

Trinidado, putt into a bay of the maine; which they at
length perceaved, and with unspeakable dainger and
infinite travaile, theire victuall spent and fresh water
consumed, they susteyned a great temptacion. At which
time, and all other times of theire greatest extremities,
it is reported generallie that they receaved great comforte
and consolacion by the vertuous exhortacion and speeches
of theire Captaine, layinge before them the mightie providence of God, which in mans greatest weaknes and
infirmitie sheweth Himselfe stronge and of most force
and puissance. At length with much labour, both in
rowinge, towinge and caryinge the bote, they recovered
over the indraughts and currents and gott to the windward of the rock called Diabolo and soe putt over and
seyced the iland. But not findinge theire shipp at the
place wheare they left her at theire departure, most of
the company weare verie much discomforted and dismaide,
not knowinge what to doe. But our Captaine wishinge
them eaver with patience to attend the pleasure of God,
which eaver worketh for the best to them that feare Him,
etc., shortlie after they discried our shipp at an anker
before Paracow, called by our Generall Porte Perigrine.
And soe beinge recovered aborde, wheare they weare
with great joye and tryumph receaved both by the
Generall and the whole companie, the which was signified
by the shootinge of the great ordenance and small shott
for the space of a whole ower both owt of the admerall
and allsoe Captain Pophames[1] shipp, all togeather answear-
ing each other, this night wee spent with great joy and
gladnes, giving God thanks for the safe returne of
our men.

---

[1] He had arrived with a pinnace of Plymouth while the boat was
absent (*cf.* Dudley, p. 75). No doubt he was the Capt. George Popham
who took at sea, in 1594, "certaine Spanyardes letters concerning
Guiana," an abstract of which was printed by Ralegh as an appendix
to his *Discoverie of Guiana*.

Soe the next day, Wyatt beinge appointed by our Generall to goe ashore with som 30 men lay theare untell Satterday, providinge such things as was directed him by the master Abraham Kendall. Thus after it had pleased God to restore safe to our Generall those companie I spake of now before, which by his owne directions he sent to the maine, noe otherwyse knowne but to be a continent joyninge to Brazeile, and by him called the continent of Calcurie, in the Indian language the worde for golde—in the meane time, whilst this enterprize was in execution, our Generall had 7 or 8 of the cheife Indians of Trinidado, that voluntarilie wear content to yeald theire dwtie and allegiance to her Majestie and withall desirous to see the gallant florishinge kingdome of Englande, havinge by some Christians hard both of it and the admirable fame of our most gratious soveraigne, who is[1] a Queene milde and gentle and the onlie Christian prince that doth withstande the crueltie of the tyranous Spaniarde, the which maketh her gratiousnes to be more then admired throughout all the face of the earth, not onlie by Christians but allsoe by pagans, infidles and salvages, who continuallie unto theire great greife feele the smarte of the others rigor. By the reporte, I saie, of thease Indians that yealded themselves unto our Generall, [he] had notes given him of the towne wheare this *calcurie* was melted into mettall. Whearupon our Generall, havinge all his men safe returned and desirous to see the triall of this mettall, gave directions for his marchinge up into the countrey for the discoverie of this towne and people, the which made this *calcurie*, that is, golde, of the mettall which they gett out of this ore. The which is gotten out of this myne that was discovered before by our Generall, who beinge wonderfull desirous to see the end of this

---

[1] MS. beinge.

discoverie, both as well for the service of her Majestie as allsoe for the good of his countrey, upon Satterday, being the viij^th day of March, landed some 30 men and one Captaine Popham some ten men, who came unto the ilande some five daies before. Wyatt, lyinge then ashore with 30 men more, receaved his Generall with a vallew of small shott; after the which, directions beinge given from our Generall unto his Leiftenant Generall Captaine Jobson, who signified what his pleasure was unto Wyatt and Vincent, wee marshalled our men in beinge in good order, our good Generall leadinge the march, Captaine Jobson the vawarde, Wyatt the battle of pike, and Vincent in the rearward. Thus marchinge unto the wood side, wee weare then inforced, for the more easie passage of our men, to march one after one. The woods weare soe thick that wee had all our longe march but a footpath to pass through, the which how laboursome a thinge it was they onlie can judge of, which weare partakers of the travailes or performers of the like in the same countreis, which differ from all the worlde beside with the strainge growth of theire woodes.

 Thus with much toile and extreame travaile wee marched on towards this place I first spake of, named Carowa;[1] and by the way wee went to a towne called Paracow, hopinge to have taken one Braio, an Indian which is reported by the Indians to be verie expert in meltinge of this discovered ore into the mettall of *calcurie*, which wee call golde, whose howse was not far from the sea side wheare wee weare used to lie insconsed, and, beinge accostomed unto our sounde of trumpetts and shootinge of our peeces at the settinge and dischardginge of caverie watch, never mistrusted us untell wee weare come upon

---

[1] Neither this place, nor Loweco below, is mentioned by Ralegh. It appears in Dudley's map as "Carao."

him; who soe hardlie escaped us that he was driven to leave his victualls seethinge on the fyre readie to be eaten, of the which labour our men eased him, hee onlie with his famulie escapinge into the woods and soe saved themselves. Soe not makinge anie staie theare, for our Generall woulde suffer none of theire howses to be rifeled or towched, wee passed one our march unto another towne called Loweco, wheare our souldiers weare not permitted to take anie thinge neither, by reason our Generall was desirous to bringe the Indians to convers with us in all kinde of familiaritie.

Thus [wee] passed[1] forwardes, somtimes through dertie and comfortles vallies, somtimes over high and unpleasinge mountaines, other times through deep and daingerous ryvers, at noe time free from troublesome and combersome woodes, in the marchinge of som xx. English miles unto the towne Carowa, unto the which towne wee came by night, albeit it was somthinge late. And beinge com thither wee founde the people fled, the howses dispossessed of all theire wealth, onlie some of the ore the which our Generall had discovered with theire meltinge potts and some of the dross;[2] the which contented our Generall, for that it was a confirmacion of thease reportes the which the Indians had made before unto our Generall. The cause that made thease people flie from us, as it should seem, was the sowndinge of our trumpetts and drome with the continuall noyse of shootinge of our peeces, the which wee did of purpose that wee might still give notes unto the Spaniard which way wee marched, with our collers displaide in honour of Englande and maugre the Spaniards berd, albeit wee had true

---

[1] MS. passinge.
[2] So Ralegh: "I saw an Indian basket hidden, which was the refiners basket, for I found in it his quicksilver, saltpeter . . . . . and also the dust of such ore as he had refined" (p. 59).

informacion that hee was at the least some 200 stronge of fightinge men, beside the huge nomber of the Indians subject unto his yoke, the which have a kinde of order amonge them for theire alarumes by the sowndinge of a great pipe, the which they performe with such arte as that on a soden yow shall have all quarters up in armes, as if they had bin instructed with the greatest discipline of the best men of war in the worlde.

But to my purpose. Beinge com unto the towne and our companies quartred, our cowrtes of gard placed and centronells sett, wee might senciblie heare the noyse of theire pipes in everie quarter ; the which gave us occasion to perswade ourselves that wee shoulde be incountred by the enimie. And that night the Generall givinge the chardge of his Indians to severall men, it hapned one of them to be committed unto one of those which had bin in the performance of that service on the which our bote was sent, and seeinge much villanie practised by thease in his companie he[1] not onlie piniond them with tying their handes fast behinde them, but with his naked dagger threatned theire throates, if anie trecherie weare plaied by them against us. The which hard usage when our Generall hard [he] forbad, and the Indians beinge suffred to sitt afterwarde at libertie, beinge fearfull of his hard usage, in the night one of them stole awaie, and soe our Generall, perceavinge theire feare, toke the less care of keepinge them perforce, judginge that actioma to be authenticall *quod diuturnitatis malus est custos timor.*

The next morninge, beinge Sonday, in the morninge 9 Mar. betimes wee sett forwarde with as great care as possible wee coulde, not imagininge but that wee should be incountred by the way home, our Generall unto the great joye and comfort of his followers leadinge the march,

---

[1] MS. and.

givinge such comfortable speec[h]es unto his companies that, allthough the waies weare daingerous, troublesome and comfortles, yeat wee marched it with great pleasure and cam that night unto our shippinge.

10, 11 Mar. The next daie, beinge Mondaie, wee fitted ourselves, and the next day, beinge Twseday, the xi[th] of March, betweene twelve of the clock and one, wee disankored from the ilande of Trinidado and sett saile, bearinge north and by east, and came within some 3 leagues of the mouth of the current called the straights of Calcurie,[1] between the maine continent of the West Indies, parte of the cost of Cracos, called the high land of Paria, one of the fruitfullest places in the worlde for excellent good tobacco, which is called for his worthines cane tobacco,[2] and the other part bordringe over against beinge the north west partes of the ilande of Trynidado.

12 Mar. The next day, allthough with some dainger by the reason of the difficultnes of the straightnes of the current, yeat with safetie, God be thanked, wee passed and, bearinge as close by the winde as possible wee coulde, made[3] for the iland of Granado; but the current was soe stronge that it caryed us soe far to leewarde that it was impossible for us to reach it. Whearefore our Generall determined to make for St. John,[4] and in passinge thitherwarde it pleased God to bless him soe that on the xij[th] day of March at
13 Mar. foure of the clock at night, beinge Thurseday, wee had sight of a Spanish shipp, the which wee gave chase unto and by midnight brought her within the dainger of our

---

[1] As they had entered the Gulf of Paria through the Serpent's Mouth, round the south-western extremity of Trinidad, they left it by the Dragon's Mouth, between the north-western extremity and the promontory of Paria. "Cracos" apparently represents Carácas.

[2] Murray's *New English Dictionary* quotes Harington's *Epigrams*, 1612, iv, p. 34: "Then of tobacco he a pype doth lack Of Trinidade in cane, in leaf or ball."

[3] MS. makinge.

[4] The island of San Juan de Puerto Rico (see below).

great shott, notwithstandinge when shee appeared first in
sight shee was some fowre leagues to weather of us, a
thinge most strainge to be accomplished in soe shorte a
space. And wee had not made three great shott at them
but they submitted themselves unto our Generalls mercie,
signifyinge theire submission by strikinge theire sailes, and
cam under our lee. Upon theire submission our Generall
sent Captain Jobson and the master to take sight of such
commodities as they weare ladend withall, and they
findinge them to be ladend with wine, iron, linnen, hatts
and such commodities as weare fittinge for the Indians
decreed the next morninge to putt in for Margarita and
theare to make the best of her; but after altringe theire
determinacion they made for the same porte they first
determined, beinge St John de Porte Recho. The Spanish
prisoners which weare aborde with us confessed that the
next moneth, beinge Aprill, the Indies fleet determined for
Spaine, the nomber some 150 saile, the richest fleet that
eaver cam out of the West Indies, the great *Phillipp of
Spaine* beinge theare to wafte them home as theire chiefe
admerall, with a great companie of the best armathoes the
Kinge of Spaine hath.

Thus continuinge on for the iland aforenamed, wee sailed
untell Monday night till twelve of clock at night, at what 17 Mar.
time wee discried land, and runninge in to make the same
wee founde it to be the iland of St de Cruce.[1] Soe,
runninge all alongst the side of it, wee bare away for
St John de Porte Recho, the which wee discried by
Twseday dinner. Soe, passinge alongst this iland this 18 Mar.
night, wee stroke saile and lay at hull untell morninge,
beinge most mightelie troubled for halfe the night with
a most tempestuous gust, afterwardes continuinge our

---

[1] Santa Cruz, a small island lying between Puerto Rico and St.
Christopher's.

E

20 Mar course untell Thursday, somtimes lyinge at hull stayinge for our prize; the which beinge com up, by Thursday three or foure of the clock wee came to an anker on the south west parte of the ilande of St John de Porte Recho.

21 Mar. The next day, beinge Friday, all the prisoners by the commaunde of our Generall weare delivered unto Wyatt, who, causinge a bote to be manned forth, went with them ashore, givinge them some victuall to finde them untell they might com to the partes of the ilande the which was inhabited. Who upon theire departure after theire Spanish fastion vayled theire bonnetts in the honour of our Generall, but thought verie hardlie of Wyatt for dealinge soe stricklie with them; for, by the meanes our Generall used them soe kindelie, they forgott that they weare prisoners, but beinge from the Generalls sight they then did learne that, beinge captives, they weare to suffer with patience the fortune of the warrs. And yeat I[1] protest before God I used them in such sorte as, if my fortune weare to be towched with the like miserie or punnishment (as theare is noe calamitie but wee are all subject unto) I would wish to be soe delt withall. By this time that I was returned our prize began to drive, and they stringe to tack aboute to gett the

22 Mar. winde weare driven soe far to leeward that it was Satterday morninge before shee coulde recover us againe.

After which time our men wrought dalie to hoyse aborde all such goodes that shee had bestowed in her, and upon

23 Mar. Sondaie, by that time wee had dined, wee might discrie on shore a flagg of truce and waved to parlle with us. Wheareupon our Generall commaunded a bote to be manned forth [and] committed the commaunde of her unto Wyatt, givinge him in chardge that he should have a speciall regarde unto the men he had with him, and that

---

[1] The writer here, as also a little further on, again identifies himself with Captain Wyatt.

he shoulde not in anie case trust the Spaniard, but stand
allwaies on his owne guarde; the which in everie respect
I performed. For beinge com unto the shore side, I
suffred none of my companie to goe on shore, but caused
the Spaniard the which was the captaine of the Spaniards
of the prize to com from his companie and com himselfe
unto the water side and theare to deliver unto mee his
minde, havinge an interpriter to shew me his request.
The which was that one of our companie should make as
thoughe hee woulde shoote at him and soe overshoote him
that it may seme unto the other Spaniards that wee toke
him perforce, for that hee came without his flagg of truce
with him. The which was no sooner executed, but the
Spanish captain fell downe and the other ran awaie, fearinge
least the like might happen unto him. And soe havinge him
alone, his request was that hee might be brought aborde,
for hee desired to have some conference with our Generall,
whose request wee[1] graunted and soe brought him abord
with us. Beinge com unto our Generall, his request was
unto him that he would bestow the hull on him with some
old saile; but it was thought good he should be denied it,
least, havinge her, hee might goe into other harbers and
give notes of our Generalls lyinge theare of and on, which
might be a greate hindrance unto the makinge of our
viage.

The next morninge, beinge Mondaye morninge, the 24 Mar.
master caused her to be towed up unto the admerall,
layinge her side by side, and by one or two of the clock
the same day our men had soe laboured that shee had
nothinge left in her but such substance as was fitt to burn
with her for companie; and beinge sett on fyre shee
continued burninge all that day and most parte of the
night. Whearat the Spaniarde toke noe great pleasure,

---

[1] MS. beinge.

but besought the Generall that he might be sett on shore and that hee woulde send some one with him that might have such commaunde that hee might be kept from beinge rifeled of those that weare to sett him on shore. The which our Generall graunted and, calling unto Wyatt, gave commaundment unto him to make choyse of sufficient men to man the bote and sett him on shore; the which was done.

25 Mar. And upon our returne præsentlie [wee] wayed anker and sett saile this daie, between one and two of the clock, beinge Twsedaie the xxvth of March, passing that night most difficultlie and daingerouslie between St John de Porte Recho and the ilande Zechea,[1] and havinge somtimes most soden gustes and againe in a moment beinge starke becalmed, soe that between soden gustes, dertie foggs, flatt calmes, and the settinge of head seas in soe darke a night within soe straight and daingerous a passage, it gave occasion of little sleep unto our watchfull Generall and less rest unto our carefull and provident master; whom I must not onlie commende for his singuler perfection in this arte of navigation, excellinge all others in his profession as a rare scholler, a most selldome thinge in a maryner, but the good cariadge allsoe for the good preservacion of the health of all those being under his chardge. But passinge the straighte wee bare awaie north and by east for some two daies as the winde woulde suffer us, but after altered that course and bare for the coste of Florida, a more westernlie course, to lie in the wake of the fleet of the West Indies bownde for Spaine.

11 Apr. Soe sailinge alonge by the coste of Virginia wee came by the xith of Aprill, beinge Friday, soe far to the northwarde that wee fell with the hight of the Bermudes, a

---

[1] About midway between Puerto Rico and Hispaniola or San Domingo.

climett soe far differinge from the nature of all others
from under the which wee had allreadie passed that wee
might then thinke ourselves most happie when wee weare
most farthest from it. For had I as manie tounges as
hath my head heares, and everie one the use of the pens
of readie writers, yeat might I com to short of the true
description of the extremitie of this outragious weather
which this place continuallie affordeth without anie inter-
mission of times. For often before wee have had daingerous gustes, and they not soe sodenlie hapninge but
as sodenlie vanishinge; but thease [were] ever ordinarie
and theire daingers still extrordinarie, theire dreadfull
flashinge of lightninge, the horrible claps of thunder, the
monstrous raginge of the swellinge seas forced up into the
ayre by the outragious windes, all togeather conspiringe in
a moment our destruction and breathinge owt, as it wear,
in one breath the verie last blast of our confusion, soe that
—this beinge a generall actioma of all seafaringe men
delivered for a veritie, both of our English and the Spanish,
French and Portingall, that hell is noe hell in comparison
of this, or that this itselfe is hell withowt anie comparison—
all this[1] togeather did betoken greater greife to us then
can be spoken. But thease weare but præpratives to
further daingers. After wee weare past the meridian of
the Bermudes our courses brought us not far from the cost
of Labradore or Nova Francia, which wee knew by the
great aboundance of whalles. Between this and New
Found Land, not 60 leagues from the daingerous iland of
Sabels,[2] wheare Sir Humfrey Gilbartes admerall was cast
awaie, and much about that place himselfe in a pinnes

---

[1] MS. which.
[2] Sable Island, in the Atlantic, 44° N., 60° W. Sir Humphrey Gilbert himself went down in the little *Squirrel* at midnight of 9 September, 1583, near the Azores. The *Delight*, however, his largest vessel, had previously been lost on a shoal between St. John's and Sable Island (Hakluyt, iii, p. 197).

with the outragiousnes of one of the most terrible stormes that eaver was seen was suncke and swallowed in the merciles occian—not above 60 leagues, I say, of this daingerous place thus weare our sorrowes agravated. Wee had the winde for our course favowrable, but disfavowringe for our safetie, for soe continuallie weare his threats intollerable that everie ower thundred hee forth his storme, and everie storme threatned unto us noe less then death. And allthough, Right Honorable,[1] the remembrance of our forepassed sorrowes wil be little less then a present death to our dawnted spiritts, the which wee not without great anguish of soule did then indure, neither without bitternes of passion can I resist nor your honour pittiless can heare. For this was our onlie comforte that, beinge mortified and resolved to dye, of sinfull and earthlie creatures wee weare, by yealdinge nature her dwe dett, to be made saintes for God, verilie beleevinge then to be made partakers of His heavenlie happines and everie one givinge his last farewell to his best and most dearest freinds, desirous to see the last end of this sorrowfull stratagem. But at last, when, through the foggs that ryss out of the seas, the blacknes of the skie coulde not be seen for the darcknes of the ayre, when wee expected nothing less then splittinge of sailes, breakinge of shrowdes, spendinge of mastes, springinge of plankes—in a worde the dreadfull devouringe of us all by some sea swallowinge wherlepole—wee weare most myraculouslie delivered. For this fogg beinge converted into soe monstrous a shower of rayne that it shoulde seme the verie windowes of heaven weare sett open that it might with the more speed worke our deliverance fell with such vehemencie that it not onlie alaied the ragings of the fearefull seas growne and sowlne up into an incredible bignes, but brake the hart of that most bitter storme.

---

[1] There is nothing to show who is thus addressed : probably Sir Robert Cecil.

Thus whilst wee weare all soe mated[1] and mased that, neither hearinge what the master say'd for the whistlinge and bussing of the windes, nor knowinge for feare what to amende, yeat, to to well [wee] knew that all things weare amiss, wee weare most myraculously by the mightie hand of God, past mans capacitie and alltogeather unlooked for of ourselves, safelie delivered.

And before it pleased God to inflict upon us this punnishment, hee foretolde us by his warninge messinger a most rare accident; for the eaveninge before theare fell a fyre,[2] the which of the maryners is called Santelmo or Corposantie; the which appeareth before anie tempestuous weather as a presagement of a most dainegerous storme. And for that the opinion[s] of all wryters are variable as concerninge the true essence of it, I am perswaded theare can be noe certaine truth delivered of it. The Greeks they call it Poliduces, the Lattins call it Castor and Pollux; Plynie wryteth that it is as well seene at land in a great armie of men as at sea amonge the maryners; Virgill in his second of Æneidos semeth to confirme it, sayinge that such appeared on the head of Julius Ascanius; and Titus Lyvius affirmeth that such a like thinge appeared upon the head of Servius Tullius, the sixt Kinge of the Romaines.[3] But howsoeaver it seemeth to be variablie censured of sundrie writers, thys is

---

[1] So the Doctor in *Macbeth*, v, i: "My mind she has mated and amazed my sight." The metaphor is, of course, taken from chess.

[2] The Corpo Santo or St. Elmo's Fire, names given to the balls of electric light seen on the masts and yard-arms of a ship in stormy weather. Thus, in the account of Sir H. Gilbert's voyage, just before his foundering: "We had also upon our main-yard an apparition of a little fire by night, which seamen doe call Castor and Pollux. But we had onely one, which they take an euill signe of more tempest. The same is usuall in stormes" (Hakluyt, iii, p. 202). There is a good note on the subject in *The Voyages and Works of John Davis*, ed. A. H. Markham, Hakluyt Soc., 1880, p. 164.

[3] The references are to Pliny, *Hist. Nat.*, ii, cap. 37; Virgil, *Æn.*, ii, ll, 681-4; and Livy, i, cap. 39.

for a certaintie agreed upon, that it foretelleth some great thinge to com, and if it appeare in two lights, then goodnes, and yf but one, then some eminent dainger at hand to enshue, and especiallie at sea; for, if but one fyre is sene, it presageth a most cruell, daingerous and tempestuous storme, hazardinge both shipp, goodes and the lives of all such as happen to be in it. This is not onlie confirmed by all sortes of nations which are navigators, as Spaniards, French, Portingalls, Turkes, Mores, yea all kinde of seafaringe men, but wee unto our great perill weare made *oculati testes*, which in my opinion unto us was and is more authenticall then if wee weare delivered by the reportes of thowsands. It is a fearefull tale to tell and a discourse dreadfull unto the hearer to have delivered for a truth, that in the night a substance of fyre resemblinge the shape of a fierie dragon should fall into our sailes and theare remaine some quarter of an ower, after fallinge upon the deck passinge from place to place, readie to sett all on fyre, for that fyre moste commonlie converteth all things into the same substance that hee himselfe is of, which is fyre, being the true confirmacion of that actioma of Aristotle that *omne tale efficit majus tale*. This, I say, might seme dreadfull to the hearer, but much more dreadfull unto us that with our eies beheld it. This was strainge, but the event much more strainge, for this fyerie dragon, havinge continued some halfe ower unto the astonishment of us all, vanished without anie harme done either unto our shippinge or anie of our companie, but the sequell most strainge, as you have allreadie hard in the description of this last storme, and yeat not soe strainge as true.

Thus as men prepared for God, allwaies leadinge our lives as if wee should dye owerlie, we passed on forwarde of our course towards the ilands of Flowers and Corves[1]

---

[1] Flores and the smaller island Corvo, the most western of the Azores.

with a most forseable gale of winde, saylinge between
the Bermudes and thease ilands with such an incredible
swiftnes that not onlie our masters mates in theire
rckninge weare overseen som hundred leagues, but the
master himselfe was deceaved in the swifte gate of our
shipp and caused our Generall to reduce his reckninge
back som 50 leagues. Whose owne observacion if he
had lett stood had brought him directlie with the fall of
the ilands, whose meridian wee fell withall by the xxviij[th]
day of Aprill, beinge Twsedaie ; and runninge in between 28 Apr.
them wee wear discried by the ilanders, the which toke
us to be some of the fleet com from the Indies and came
forth with a carvell stored, as it should seem, with victuall.
The which came directlie with us, but, at last descryinge
what wee weare, cast abowt and stood againe into the
shore, soe that by noe meanes wee might doe anie harme
unto her.

After which day wee sett forwarde for Englande and
sayled with a reasonable gale of winde homwarde for
some fowre daies, and then the winde came up unto the
north east contrarie unto our course and held some two
daies, [but] after came aboute fayre for us for Englande.
Soe, takinge our opportunitie, wee shaped our course
for our cost untell the vi[th] of May, beinge Twsedaie ; on 6 May.
which day at three of the clock in the afternoone our
Generall beinge on the quarter deck in lookinge abroade
was the first that scryed a sayle, unto which by all the
meanes wee coulde, workinge warelie to keep the winde,
wee gladlie gave chase. And in short time wee fett her
up and haylinge her required amaine[1] for the Queene of
Englande ; but she verie stoutlie keepinge her loofe bare
with us [and] neaver budged for anie thinge that coulde

---

[1] To amain, from the French *amener*, was to lower the topsail as a
sign of yielding, or in salute to a superior.

be done, notwithstandinge that wee had franklie bestowed upon her verie rownde and sownde vollies of shott, both small and great, continuinge and warmelie maintayninge the same for the space of five or six owers. They verie proudlie ever and anon resaluted us againe with such as they had, givinge us thearebie to know that they weare otherwyse provided then wee expected or wished them to be. In the meane space wee had the opportunitie well to vew and survey her, and made her a shipp of three hundred tun,[1] beinge indeed a verie fine snugg long shipp, havinge on each side vi. portes open, beside her chase and her sterne peeces. Her ordinance lyinge well to pass, shee went as upright as a church, havinge fine contryved close fightes[2] with nettings and graplings in as warlike manner as anie armatho of the kings that was presented in the narrow seas, when wee had the memorable conflict with the Spanish forces. Our olde seamen gave theire sundry censures of her, some one thinge, some another, but all agreed in this that shee was a man of war and a wafter either to theire Byskin[3] fleet of fishermen for Newfoundlande or bounde to meet theire Indian fleet now comminge home. But whatsoeaver shee might be, the resolucion of our worthy younge Generall was to have a further sayinge unto her, and theareforc [hee] caused his leiftenant Captaine Jobson to commaunde the gunners to make readie all such great peeces of ordinance as weare not allreadie dismounted and stowed, as allsoe to make good store of cartrages against the morninge, to give this our prowde consorte a warme breakfast, keepinge them wakinge in the night now and

---

[1] Dudley says she was of 600 tons, while Kendall contents himself with describing her as "a very great galleon."

[2] Screens, or protections, along the bulwarks for the combatants.

[3] Biscayan. A "wafter" is used in the sense of a convoy, like the verb "to waft" on p. 49.

then with a cross-bar shott. And to saie the truth, they weare not idle, neither did theire light goe owt all the night, but still rummidginge, as it seemeth, provided well for theire defence. Captaine Jobson, most carefull and diligent to have the Generalls will, pleasure and service througlie performed, caused the boteswaine to stow downe in howlde all truncks, chests and other things alofte, makinge the decks afore and afte fayre platformes cleare of anie pesteringe or impediments. And to prevent all wants [hee] toke out of the rome good store of powlder of rownde shott, of langrell[1] shot, gadds of steele for dice shott and cross-barrs, with provision of lead for bullets and match for our musketers, givinge order to Mr Wyatt and to Mr Vincent, two ould and discreet souldiers, to see that the corporalls should have all thinges in a readines that pertayned to theire chardge and everie souldier his furniture as yare and fine as might be; the which beinge before in great forwardnes was sone accomplished.

Soe in the morninge by breake of day, our good shipp beinge putt in her best trym and all things in a perfect readines, Captaine Jobson caused the collers of our countrey and of our Generall to be advansed in the topps, poope and shrowdes of our shipp. And givinge worde unto the Generall, hee came forth unarmed, havinge onlie his leadinge staff in his hand, [and] saluted and incouraged his people, placinge them in this sort: himselfe toke his standinge on the open deck, wheare hee might best see and be seen of his enimies and might allsoe have an eye upon his gunners and small shott and an care to the master and conduct of his shipp, [and hee] willed Captain

---

[1] Langrel or langrage shot were "fragments of iron bound together, so as to fit the bore of the cannon" (Smyth, *Sailor's Word Book*). A gad was properly a spike of metal, but also means a bar, as in this case, when it seems to have been cut into short lengths so as to make the small cubical bullets known as die or dice shot.

Jobson to take some few small shott upon the poope, placinge the trumpetts on the topp of the masters cabbin, Mr Wyatt and Mr Vincent placinge the corporalls and the rest of the musketers in the forecastle, in the boughes and other places of the shipp, themselves and the Generalls servants, beinge all fine and readie shott, neare abowte the Generall. Amonge which companie Mr Thomas Comley, owt of a manlie courage and a wonderfull resolucion, performed this day with his muskett incredible good service. Eaverie gunner standinge by his peece, eaverie souldier and sayler, with our manlie boteswaine, our quarter-masters and other officers of our shipp knowinge theire due places, wee bare up the helme to our prowde consorte, that was as readie as ourselves, stuck not to wave us to leewarde and made the first shott upon us. Unto whom wee gave as sownde a replie, and with as great furie as hath bin seen at anie time in thease affayres and, to say truly, well answeared of the enimie with a more desperate and divelish resolucion to indure soe great a chardge then is ordinarie with the Spaniardes. They made manie and daingerous shott upon us, especiallie exceedinge neare the verie face and head of our Generall, and had soe well taken theire aime at that place, from which indeed they receaved most damage and hurte, that at length with a fayre saker[1] shott they strake the verie blade of his leadinge staff into manie peeces, goeinge within a handfull of his head, havinge before torne the sayles, cutt the shrowdes and pearced the shipp verie neare the place of his

---

[1] From a table of English ordnance given in an interesting Appendix on "Guns and Gunnery in the Tudor Navy" in *Papers relating to the Navy during the Spanish War*, 1585-1587, ed. J. S. Corbett, Navy Records Soc., 1898, p. 322, it appears that the "saker" was a piece of 9 feet in length, with a calibre of $3\frac{1}{4}$-4 inches, and weight of shot of 5-5½ lbs. "Saker" was properly the name of a hawk (*falco sacer*), and is said to be derived through the Port. *sacre* from the Arabic. As applied to a cannon, it represented a heavier piece than the similarly named "falcon" and "falconet."

standinge; and yeat would hee not budge or remove by
anie meanes. The enimie allsoe strake the formaste with
a great shott and cutt the shrowdes and the maine sheate
abafte whear Captaine Jobson standinge somtimes played
upon them with his muskett and somtimes waved them
with his sworde amaine. One of the masters mates
standinge in the poope next to Captaine Jobson was hurte
in the face with the splinter of a great shott strikinge the
missen maste. But it pleased God in all this sharpe
encounter mightelie to defend us both against the furie
of our malicious enimie and against the fearefull mis-
chaunce of fyre in our owne shipp, which either by over-
heatinge our ordinaunce or other occasion once hapened
amongst us, but was most hapelie and speedilie extin-
guished. And in all this conflict and sundry skirmishes
none miscaried or was pearsed with the bullet but onelie
a man of Captaine Jobsons called Thomas Gillingham,
who, standinge not farr from our Generall, receaved a
dangerous shott through his left legg; which our Generall
perceavinge caused him to be sent downe to our surgion
and did afterwardes most honorablie comfort him with his
promise of an almes mans roome in his hospitall of Warwick[1] for that hee receaved that hurte in his service.

I will heare be boulde to sett downe a good conceipte of
our captaine, havinge observed the fine spirite, painfull
indevowres and valiant courage of our Generalls page
Mr William Bradshew, whom Captaine Jobson eaver called
his sonn. The youth in thease hott skirmisses by often
chardginge and rechardginge his peece brake the same
abowte his eares. The captain suddenlie stepped downe
from the poope, brought him by the arme unto our
Generall with his broken peece and rowndlie recytes those

---

[1] The Leicester Hospital, still in existence, founded by Dudley's father, Robert, Earl of Leicester, for a master and twelve brethren.

verses of olde Hieronimo in the Spanish Tragedie[1] in this sorte :

> " This is my sonn, gratious Generall,
> Of whom though from his tender infancie
> My lovinge thoughts did neaver hope but well,
> He neaver pleased his fathers eies till now,
> Nor fild my hart with overcloyinge joye.
> Longe may hee live to serve my Generall,
> And soone decaie unless hee still doe serve my Generall."

The noble gentleman honorablie acknowledged the moste praisworthy forwardnes of his towardlie page, havinge bin an eiewitnes thearof himselfe, and thanked his kinseman for that fine conceipt and fitt applicacion and gave unto his page a dellicate furniture[2] of his owne, for his better incouragement and well doinge and valiancie.

Thus after wee had fought with this great armatho of the Kinge of Spaines some five or six owers upon Twsedaie and from morninge till night the next day with most parte of Twseday at night, givinge this prowde Spaniard remembraunce that wee wear neare him, wee gave him seaven sownde canvasadoes,[3] whearin, as I saide before, our Generall escaped often most narrowly both great and small shott and, thanks be given to God, but one hurte with the bullet, which was most strainge, seeinge theare

---

[1] *The Spanish Tragedie, containing the lamentable end of Don Horatio and Belimperia, with the pitiful death of old Hieronimo,* etc., London, [1594?], 4to. This play, full of horrors, and one of the most popular of the time, was by Thomas Kidd, and was licensed for the press in Oct. 1592. The earliest extant copy is, however, as above. The quotation is from Act i, where young Horatio enters with the Prince of Portugal, his prisoner, and is presented by his father to the King of Spain. The last two lines are not in the printed play, and in the first, " generall" is substituted for " soveraigne."

[2] A suit of armour or any warlike equipment ; here perhaps merely a gun.

[3] A canvasado is explained in the *New Engl. Dict.* as " a sudden attack". The word is connected with the verb " to canvass," in the sense of beating, battering or pounding, and " canvasadoes" has some such meaning here.

was noe one man in the shipp but stood in the face of the
enimie without either fights or nettings. And after our
foure peeces of ordinance (which was all wee coulde use,
the rest beinge stowed in howlde) and xv. small shott had
spent all the good powlder wee had, which was ix. barrells,
for the rest that was left was soe wett with the water that
came in at her boughes that it woulde rather flie owt at
the touch hole then carry forth the bullet, and after wee
had soe beaten her with great and small shott as by our
seamen the like was neaver scene, for wee thought it
allmost impossible for him to swyme above water, and
borde her without loss of all wee coulde nott, which they
desired much more then our shott, for it was impossible a
shipp soe farr greater and higher then ours and soe manned
in respect of us, not havinge twentie men that had weapons
to enter, but pikes to defend, without the ruine of us all,
which must needs have bin if they had but ten fightinge
men within—wee for wante of powlder left our enimie to
the mercie of the occeon. Whearof yf wee had had but
two barrells, wee undoubtedly should have seen theire
miserable end in short time. But, indeed, I must commende in this the Spanish men of war, especiallie those of
Biskye, whearof this shipp was one, that havinge once
taken a vowe to dye rather then to be taken they will
willinglie sinke in the sea before they will breake theire
vowe; which in my opinion this Byskaine hath trwlie
performed. For wee sawe, beinge continuallie allmost
borde and borde, his shotts soe many under water, in
caverie place soe torne, and perceavinge his soe often
lyinge by the lee to stopp them, as wee coulde all judge
noe less but that either hee was sunck in yt or at least
neaver able to gett home without some divine providence.[1]

---

[1] Dudley says that after his return he learnt that she actually had sunk.

Thease things thus performed as you heare, and findinge it bootelesse to strive against the streame, wee betooke ourselves to our course for Englande, takinge that the greatest calamitie that eaver happened to anie, the want of powder, havinge taken soe much paines, and coulde neyther receave the sweet of our paines nor see the end of itt. Our Generall by this fight being disfurnished of many of his necessary provisions was constrained to beare roome for his countrey, having before privately determined to spend som time upp and downe betwene the ilande of Treceraz[1] and the cost of Spaine, to meete with the fleete which my Generall knew by the Spaniardes he tooke the time certaine of their comming from the Havana and their welth, which was 50 millions of duckettes of the King, 60 millions of his subjectes. The oportunity of which fortune we overslipped by a storme that brought us into 44 degrees, where an honorable fight [was] performed, only pursued by our Generall to do her Majestie service. [For] disdaining much to disgrace his countrey or dishonour himself, [he] chose rather, occasion being offered, to venter the loss of his voiage and the expectation of a fleet so rich then basely to leave of fighting with the enemy of God, oure Queene and countrey; whose fraught pillage and purchas was nothing but thundring of shott both greate and small, the treasure presaging death with honoure.

This enemy, as you hard, so left and we for waunte of meanes to fight constrained to retyre, we hoysed the most of our sayles for England, where we fell by reason of most extreame mistie weather with a fisher towne called St Jiues in Cornwall uppon Severine,[2] the fyrst land we saw being hard abord the shore, and comming betwene Syllie and the Landes End without sight of either. Thus it pleased God

---

[1] Terceira, one of the Azores, and the seat of government.
[2] If this means "upon [the estuary of the] Severn," it is a strange description of the position of St. Ives.

our Generall did land in his country in saffety and health both of himself and all his company.

Aroaca,[1] Sermo Indianus.

Burgo, comertium.	*Casaca*, nubes.
Calcurey, aurum.	*Taiourah*, corda.
Chipperarey, argentum.	*Adda*, lignum.
Dacabo, manus.	*Eduólah*, cultellum.
Dabárroh, crines.	*Arkekano*, forceps.
Dabádoh, unguis.	*Weeuah*, cœlum.
Ticorah, lapis viridis.	*Dacy*, caput.
Colperey, lapis albus.	*Dacasi*, oculus.
Uree, tobaco.	*Dary*, dens.
Arara, aurum vulgare.	*Dadica*, auris.
Bara, aqua.	*Daciboh*, facies.
Hadaley, sol.	*Da la rócoh*, labrum.
Basya, ventus.	*Dacirey*, nasus.

[1] This word seems to represent the name of the people, the Arawaks of Trinidad and Guiana, whose language can be recognized without difficulty both in this vocabulary and in that given by Dudley himself; the two together being apparently the earliest known. Another, dating from 1598, is printed by De Laet, in his *Novus Orbis*, 1633, p. 642, and is compared with one of 1800 by Dr. D. G. Brinton in *The Arawack Language of Guiana*, Philadelphia, 1871, p. 9, thus :—

	Ar. 1598.	Ar. 1800.
Caput	*wassijehe*	*waseye*
Auris	*wadycke*	*wadihy*
Oculus	*wackosije*	*wakusi*
Nasus	*wassyerii*	*wasiri*
Os	*dalerocke*	*daliroko*
Dentes	*darii*	*dari*
Crura	*dadane*	*dadaanah*
Pedes	*dackosye*	*dakuty*
Arbor	*hada*	*adda*
Arcus	*semarape*	*semaara-haaba*
Sagittæ	*symare*	*semaara*
Luna	*cattehel*	*katsi*
Sol	*adaly*	*hadalli*

The difference in the initial syllable in words otherwise alike is due to the fact that the prefixes *wa* and *da* respectively mean "our" and "my." Another vocabulary, French-Arawak, is that of Dr. Sagot (*Bibliothèque Linguistique Américaine*, viii, Paris, 1882, p. 61). It furnishes for comparison with that in the text, main, *dákabi, dakkabou*; cheveux, *dabara*; mer, *bara*; soleil, *hadali*; arbre, *adda*; couteau, *iadoala, iadolle*; œil, *dakouchi*; dent, *dari*. For *calcurey* see above, p. 39, note. As for *chipperarey*, according to Schomburgk (p. 100), "the Indians of Guiana have no word for silver in their language. They have adopted the Spanish and Portuguese *plata* and *prata*". Hence probably the *perota* in Dudley's vocabulary, below, pp. 73, 78.

Places and people of the mayne.

Capulio, the eastermost poynte.

Werinóca,[1] the entring in of the ryver.

Moroca,[2] the men-eaters.

Caribia be also man-eaters.

Sabiota[3] is a small ryver; the people of the river are called *Veriotaus*, of whom we weare well intreat[ed].

Mana, the ryver of Carpembres.

Maria, the ryver wheare the myne of *calcurey* is.

Armaio, captaine of the sayd myne.

Bradha is a small ryver by the which wee did com back, and yt did putt us too leeward of the ship.

---

[1] Apparently the same as Orinoco. Worinoque is, in fact, one of the names given by Schomburgk (p. lxx) as applied to the river, and it is so called also by Kendall, below.

[2] These must be the people of Dudley's "Kingdom of Morucca" (p. 72). The Caribs (*cf.* p. 73) are better known as being cannibals, their very name, Caribales or Canibales, having become since the discovery of the West Indies a generic term for man-eaters.

[3] Dudley's Cabota (*cf.* p. 37, note). He also mentions the Mana (p. 72) and the Braha (p. 73), but not the Maria, nor does he give any help for the meaning of Wyatt's "Carpembres."

ROBERT DUDLEY'S
VOYAGE TO THE WEST INDIES,
1594-1595.
NARRATED BY HIMSELF.

A voyage[1] of the honourable Gentleman M. Robert Duddeley, now Knight,[2] to the Isle of Trinidad, and the coast of Paria: with his returne home by the Isles of Granata, Santa Cruz, Sant Iuan de Puerto Rico, Mona, Zacheo, the shoalds called Abreojos,[3] and the isle of Bermuda. In which voyage he and his company tooke and sunke nine Spanish ships, wherof one was an armada of 600 tunnes. Written at the request of M. Richard Hakluyt.

AUING euer since I could conceiue of any thing bene delighted with the discoueries of nauigation, I fostered in my selfe that disposition till I was of more yeres and better ability to vndertake such a matter. To this purpose I called to me the aduise of sufficient seamen, and principally vndertooke a voyage for the South Seas; but, by reason that many

---

[1] Reprinted from Hakluyt's *Voyages*, iii, 1600, p. 574.
[2] He was knighted by the Earl of Essex during the expedition to Cadiz, June, 1596.
[3] The Abrolhos (in modern maps the Natividad) bank off the north-eastern coast of San Domingo. The name, which means in Portuguese "Open your eyes," is applied for obvious reasons to other reefs, off Bahia in Brazil and off the west coast of Australia.

before had miscaried in the same enterprise, I could not be suffered to hazard more of her Maiesties subiects vpon so vncerteine a ground as my desire, which made me by constraint (great charges already by me defrayed) to prepare another course for the West Indies, without hope there to doe any thing woorth note, and so common is it indeed to many as it is not woorth the registring. Neuerthelesse, I haue yeelded to your former importunity, and sent you this my iournall to supply a vacant roome amongst your more important discourses.

Nowe being prouided for this last enterprize, rather to see some practise and experience then any wonders or profite, I weighed ancker from Southampton road the sixth of Nouember, 1594. But the winde falling scant, it was the 17 day of the same moneth before I could put into the sea. Upon this day my selfe in the *Beare*, a shippe of 200 tunnes, my admirall, and Captaine Munck in the *Beares Whelpe* vice-admirall, with two small pinnesses called the *Frisking* and the *Earewig*, passed through the Needles, and within two dayes after bare in with Plimmouth. My busines at this port-towne dispatched, I set saile; whither againe by contrary winds to my great misfortune I was inforced to returne backe. I might call it misfortune, for by this meanes I vtterly (for all the voyage) lost my vice-admirall; which was the cause likewise of loosing mine owne pinnesse, which three[1] were the principall stay of my voyage. For at this last leauing of England in a storme I lost mine owne pinnesse, as is beforesaid. Notwithstanding all these crosses, all alone I went wandering on my voyage, sailing along the coast of Spaine within view of Cape Finister and Cape S. Vincent, the North and South capes of Spaine In which space

---

[1] See p. 5; the third was the vice-admiral's pinnace. Out of the four vessels only the *Bear* or *Peregrine* made the voyage.

hauing many chases, I could meet with none but my countreymen or countreys friends.

Leauing these Spanish shores I directed my course the 14 of December towards the isles of the Canaries. Here I lingered 12 dayes for two reasons: the one, in hope to meete my vice-admiral; the other, to get some vessel to remoue my pestered men into, who being 140 almost in a ship of 200 tunnes, there grew many sicke. The first hope was frustrated, because my vice-admiral was returned into England with two prizes. The second expectation fell out to our great comfort; for I tooke two very fine carauels under the calmes of Tenerif and Palma, which both refreshed and amended my company and made me a fleete of 3 sailes. In the one carauel called *The Intent* I made Beniamin Wood captaine, in the other one Captaine Wentworth.

Thus cheared as a desolate traveller with the company of my small and newe erected fleete, I continued my purpose for the West Indies, and first for Cape Blanco in Africa vpon the deserts of Libya. My last hope was to meete my lost ship, and withall to renue my victuals vpon the Canthers, which are Portugal fishermen; but the Canthers had bene so frighted by Frenchmen as I could get none. Riding under this White Cape two daies, and walking on shore to view the countrey, I found it a waste, desolate, barren, and sandie place, the sand running in drifts like snow and being very stony; for so is all the countrey, sand vpon stone (like Arabia deserta, and Petrea) and full of blacke venemous lizards, with some wilde beasts and people which be tawny Moores, so wilde as they would but call to my carauels from the shore, who road very neere it. But not desirous to make any longer aboad in this place, by reason of the most infectious *serenas* or

This[1] M. Beniamin Wood was in the end of the yeere 1596 sent forth with two ships and certaine pinnesses vpon a voyage for the South seas and for China, at the charges of this honourable gentleman Sir Robert Dudley.

A description of Cape Blanco in Africa.

---

[1] See p. 8, note 3. The marginal notes were added by Hakluyt.

dewes that fall along these coasts of Africa, I caused my
Master Abraham Kendall to shape his course directly for
the isle of Trinidad in the West Indies; which after 22
dayes we descried, and the first of February came to an
anker vnder a point thereof called Curiapan, in a bay
which was very full of pelicans, and I called it Pelicans
bay. About 3 leagues to the eastwards of this place we
found a mine of Marcazites, which glister like golde; but
all is not gold that glistereth, for so we found the same
nothing worth, though the Indians did assure vs it was
Caluori,[1] which signifieth gold with them. These Indians
are a fine shaped and a gentle people, al naked and painted
red,[2] their commanders wearing crownes of feathers. These
people did often resort vnto my ship, and brought vs
hennes, hogs, plantans, potatos, pinos, tabacco, and many
other pretie commodities, which they exchanged with vs
for hatchets, kniues, hookes, belles, and glasse buttons.

From this bay I fell downe lower to a place called
Paracoa,[3] where I desired rather to ride, because it was a
conuenient place to water, balast, ground, and graue my
carauels. Then I commanded all my men to lye on shore,
after I had caused to be made for them a little skonce,
like an halfe moone, for their defence, being iealous of the
Spaniards, of whose estate I could gather no certaintie, till
from Margarita Antonie Berreo for his defence had gotten
some 300 souldiers, a greater number then I was able to
encounter withall, hauing then but 50 men, because my
carauels before their comming were sent away. The

---

[1] So in Hakluyt, but it is probably a printer's error for *Calcuri*, the word elsewhere given as the native name for gold.

[2] With *roucou*, the pulp which coats the seed of the shrub *Bixa Orellana*, the source of the well-known Arnotto dye. "The Indian of the Orinoco prefers paint to clothes; and when he has 'roucoued' himself from head to foot, considers himself in full dress" (Kingsley, *At Last*, p. 179).

[3] For the position of Paracoa, see Kendall's narrative below.

Simerones[1] of the yland traded with me stil in like sort.
And the Spaniards, now prouided for me, began to send
messengers to me in kindnesse. Notwithstanding, though I *A treason-*
had no reason to assault them, because they were both poore *tize of the*
and strong, yet for my experience and pleasure I marched *Spaniards*
4 long marches vpon the yland, and the last from one side *They*
of the yland to the other, which was some 50 miles,[2] *one side of*
going and comming through a most monstrous thicke wood *to the*
(for so is most part of the yland) and lodging my selfe in *other.*
Indian townes. The country is fertile, and ful of fruits,
strange beasts and foules, whereof munkeis,[3] babions and
parats were in great abundance.

Being much delighted with this yland, and meaning to
stay here some time, [I set][4] about discouering the maine
right against the same (the entrance into the empire of
Guiana), being shewed the discouery thereof by Captaine
Popham, who receiued the discouery of the saide empire

---

[1] From Spanish and Portuguese *cimárron*, properly "living in the mountains" (*cima* = a mountain-top), and hence "wild" or "savage;" especially applied to runaway slaves who had taken to a wild life in the woods and mountains. The English verb "to maroon," meaning "to set ashore on a desert island," is from the same source, as also the French *marron*.

[2] The greatest length of the island, north to south, is 50 miles, with an average of 48 miles; the greatest width is 65 miles, with an average of 35 miles (De Verteuil, *Trinidad*, 1884, p. 36). According to Wyatt (above, p. 45), they started on the 8th March, and came back to their ships again on the night of the 9th. It is very doubtful, therefore, whether they really marched from one side to the other. Taking the position of Carao in Dudley's map (Wyatt's Carowa) to be roughly correct, the course of the march would probably be along what is called in De Verteuil's map the "Mayaro Trace," from San Fernando on the west to Point Mayaro on the east, or about 30 miles across.

[3] "His 'munkeis' were, of course, the little Sapajous; his 'babions' no true Baboons, for America disdains that degraded and dog-like form, but the great red Howlers" (Kingsley, *At Last*, p. 69).

[4] The words in brackets are here added to Hakluyt's text in order to make the sentence intelligible. Captain Harper's report is not included among the matter supplied by Popham to Ralegh, and printed in his *Discouerie* (see above, p. 43), nor is it otherwise known. The reference to Ralegh's work shows that Dudley's narrative was not written until after its publication in 1596.

from one Captaine Harper, which, being a prisoner, [he] learned of the Spaniards at the Canaries in the selfe same maner almost as Sir Walter Ralegh very discreetly hath written. The intelligence of Harper I conceiue the Captaine hath yet to shew in Spanish. This discouery of Guiana I greatly desired; yet least I should aduenture all occasions vpon it onely, I sent my two carauels from me the 17 day of February, to try their fortunes in the Indies, not appointing any other place to meet but England, furnishing them with all the prouision that I could spare and diuiding my victuals equally with them, knowing they were able to do more good in the Indies then greater ships.

The carauels being gone, I began to enquire priuately of the sauages concerning the maine ouer against vs, and learned that the names of the kingdomes ioyning to the sea-coast were in order these:[1] the kingdom of Morucca, the kingdome of Seawano, the kingdome of Waliame, the kingdom of Caribes, the kingdome of Yguirie, and right against the northermost part of Trinidad the maine was called the high land of Paria, the rest a very lowe land. Morucco I learned to bee full of a greene stone called *Tacarao*,[2] which is good for the stone. In Seawano I heard

---

[1] With the exception of Waliame, all these names are given in Dudley's map, but the positions of Morucca and Seawano (with Wakeren, as it is there spelt) are reversed, the latter being on the east of the Essequibo. The Morooca river in modern maps debouches just north of Cape Nassau. Though Ralegh speaks of the Ciawani, it is only as one of the two castes into which the Tivitavas were divided (*Discoverie*, pp. 48, 108). Dudley's Waliame is perhaps the same as the Waliana of his map, an alternative name for Guiana. Orocoa, mentioned below as a town belonging to it, is at the head or the delta of the Orinoco, and is no doubt Ralegh's Arriacoa, "where Orenoque deuideth it selfe into three great braunches" (p. 100).

[2] These "greene stones which the Spaniards call *Piedras hijadas*' are also mentioned by Ralegh (p. 28), and his editor has a long note on the subject. They are known as Amazon Stones, and are of a green colour, generally cylindrical in shape and perforated, being worn as amulets against diseases of the liver (*higado*) and kidneys, fever and snake-bites. Père Breton writes of them in his *Dict. Caraïbe-Française*, 1665 (ed. 1892, p. 445): *tácaoüa*, pierre verte, *tacoúlaoüa*, celle cy est plus blaffastre : elles servent pour la gravelle, pour faire

of a mine of gold to be in a towne called Wackerew, the the Captaines name Semaracon. Of Waliame I will speake last, because therein I made most discouery. The Caribes I learned to be man-eaters or Canibals, and great enemies to the Islanders of Trinidad. The kingdome of Yguiri I heard to be full of a metall called by the Indians *Arara*,[1] which is either copper (as I could learne) or very base gold. In the high land of Paria I was informed by diuers of these Indians that there was some *Perota*, which with them is siluer, and great store of most excellent Canetabacco. But lastly to come to Waliame, it is the first kingdome of the empire of Guiana. The great wealth which I vnderstood to be therein, and the assurance that I had by an Indian, mine interpreter, of a golden mine in a towne of this kingdome called Orocoa, in the river (as he called it) of Owrinoicke, was much to be esteemed. This Indian spake Spanish, and whatsoeuer he knew, he reueiled it to my selfe onely by a priuate interpreter, not in words alone, but offered vpon paine of life to be guide himselfe to any place that he spake of. This discouery of the mine I mentioned to my company, who altogether mutined against my going, because they something feared the villany of Abraham Kendal, who would by no meanes go. I then wanted my lost pinnesse, and was constrained to send 14 men[2] in my ship-boat for this discouery, with most of the discreetest men in my ship, and gaue them their directions to follow, written vnder mine owne hand.

They went from me, and entred into one of the mouthes

This Indians na was Balthasar, who afte. ward ga our men the slip o their greatest need.

---

accoucher les femmes et pour le mal caduc. Les femmes des sauuages les pendent à leur col, comme vn de leur plus pretieux bijous," etc. There are numerous specimens, of green felspar, in the Ethnographical Department of the British Museum.

[1] This word is not included, as a metal, in available vocabularies. Possibly it is for *ororo*, a lengthened corruption of *oro*, just as *perota* below represents *plata*.

[2] Counting Capt. Jobson, Wyatt only enumerates thirteen (p. 36).

by the broken lands, which riuer goeth vnder the name of the great Riuer Orenoque, the foreland wherof was called Capulio, bearing South and by West, wanting a fourth part, from the point of Curiapan aforesaid, being 4 leags distant. They found the maine (as China is reported) full of fresh riuers running one into another, abounding with fish, and a land al woody, seeming to haue great store of strange beasts and foules, and very populous. They entred into a small riuer called Cabota,[1] the people named Veriotaus, a courteous people. The next riuer they passed was called Mana in the kingdome of Tiuitiuas, where the king offered to bring a Canoa full of this golden oare, and to this purpose sent a Canoa, which returned and brought my men this answere, that Armago, Captaine of the towne of Orocoa and the mine, refused them, but if they would come thither, hee himselfe would make them answere. Upon this my boat went, and at his appointed place hee met them with some 100 men in Canoas, and tolde them that by force they should haue nothing but blowes, yet if they would bring him hatchets, kniues, and Jewes-harps, he bid them assure me he had a mine of gold, and could refine it, and would trade with me; for token whereof he sent me 3, or 4, Croissants or halfe moones of gold, weighing a noble apiece or more, and two bracelets of siluer. Also he told them of another rich nation, that sprinkled their bodies with the poulder of golde and seemed to be guilt,[2] and farre beyond them a great towne

---

[1] See above, p. 37, note.

[2] Ralegh's story (p. 20) is as follows: "All those that pledge him [the emperor] are first stripped naked and their bodies annoynted al ouer with a kinde of white *Balsamum*. . . When they are annointed all ouer, certaine seruants of the Emperor hauing prepared gold made into fine powder blow it thorow hollow canes vpon their naked bodies, vntill they be al shining from the foote to the head, and in this sort they sit drinking by twenties and hundreds and continue in drunkennes sometimes sixe or seuen daies togither: the same is also confirmed by a letter written into Spaine which was intercepted, which

called El Dorado, with many other things. My men being satisfied, and thinking their company too fewe to stay among these sauages, and their victuall spent, returned. This Balthazar, my Indian, their guide ranne from them; which distresse caused them to borrow of Armago newe guides, who brought them home another way through a riuer called Braha by the high land of Paria, and so to my ship. They accompted Orocoa 150 miles distant, so they rowed in my boate aboue 250 miles. Their absence from me was 16 dayes, making but one nights aboad any where. The report of this made mee attempt my company to goe with them againe. But nowe they were worse then before; for vnlesse I would haue gone my selfe alone, not one man would goe with me (no, albeit I had had commission to hang or kill them), for my men came home in very pitifull case, almost dead for famine; and indeed such was their misery as they dranke not in three dayes, for so long they were out of the fresh riuers before they recouered the shippe, and yet the boat was filled with as much victuall as it could holde.

In this time of my boates absence there came to me a pinnesse of Plimmouth, of which Captaine Popham before named was chiefe, who gaue vs great comfort. And if I had not lost my pinnesses, wherein I might haue carried victuals and some men, we had discouered further the secrets of those places. Also this Captaine and I stayed some sixe or eight dayes longer for Sir Walter Ralegh (who, as wee surmized, had some purpose for this discouery) to the ende that by our intelligence and his boates we might haue done some good; but it seemed he came not, in sixe or eight weekes after.[1] So Captaine Popham and I helde it not conuenient to stay any longer; therefore

Captain Popham arrival

Master *Robert Dudley* told me he had seen." On El Dorado, see Sir R. Schomburgk's Introduction to Ralegh's *Discouerie*.

[1] He arrived on 22 March, only ten days after Dudley had left.

new watering our selues at Paracoa, we set saile to see further of the Indies, leauing the yle of Trinidad the 12 day of March.¹ The 13, I tooke a small prize of sackes² 25 leagues to the northward of an yland which I sailed by, called Granata. This prize refreshed vs well; yet meaning to sel her at the yle of Sant Iuan de Puerto Rico, and shaping our course thither by the ylands of Santa Cruz³ and Infierno, I coasted all the south side of the said yle of S. John, till I came to an ancker at Cape Roxo,⁴ where riding 14 dayes to expect S. Domingo men, which oftentimes fall with the yland of Mona, and finding none (neither would the Spaniards of S. Iuan de Puerto Rico buy my prize), I vnladed her, tooke in the goods, and after burned her.

This ended, I disemboqued⁵ (where fewe Englishmen had done before, by reason of the great dangers betweene this yland of S. Iuan de Puerto Rico and Hispaniola) by a little yland called Zacheo. And after carefully doubling the shoulders of Abreojos,⁶ I caused the Master (hearing by a Pilote that the Spanish fleete ment now to put out or Hauana) to beare for the meridian of the yle of Bermuda, hoping there to finde the fleete dispersed. The fleete I found not, but foule weather enough to scatter many fleetes, which companion left mee not in greatest extrem-

---

¹ This agrees with Wyatt's account, but Kendall says he set sail on 5 March.

² The wine so called; *cf.* Wyatt, "Wine, iron, linnen, hatts," etc., and Kendall, "vino di Spagna, confezzioni," etc.

³ A small island to the south-east of Puerto Rico (see p. 49). By Infierno he must mean the Bocca de Infierno, west of Point Pozuelo on the south coast of Puerto Rico.

⁴ Cape Rojo, the south-western extremity of Puerto Rico. Mona island lies midway in the channel between Puerto Rico and San Domingo, Zacheo, or Desecheo, being to the north-east of it.

⁵ Disembogue, to come out of the mouth of a river, strait, etc., into the open sea (*New Engl. Dict.*).

⁶ See above, p. 67, note 3. Dudley, in his map xi of America, in the *Arcano del Mare*, calls the bank "Baxos de Babucca o Abrolhos."

itie till I came to the yles of Flores and Cueruo; whither *Flores a Cueruo.* I made the more haste, hoping to meete some great fleete of her Maiestie my souereigne, as I had intelligence, and to giue them aduise of this rich Spanish fleet, but finding none, and my victuals almost spent, I directed my course for England.

Returning alone, and worse manned by halfe then I *A fight two day* went foorth, my fortune was to meete a great Armada of *with a Spanish* this fleete of some 600 tunnes well appointed, with whom I *Armad.* fought board and board for two dayes, being no way able *600 tun.* in all possibilitie with fiftie men to board a man of warre of sixe hundreth tunnes. And hauing spent all my powder I was constrained to leaue her, yet in such distresse without sailes and mastes, and hull so often shot through with my great ordinance betweene winde and water, that, being three hundred leagues from land, I dare say it was impossible for her to escape sinking. Thus leauing her by *They* necessitie in this miserable estate, I made for England, *arriue S. Iues* where I arriued at S. Iues in Cornewall about the latter ende *Cornwa in May* of May, 1595, scaping most dangerously in a great fogge *1595.* the rocks of Silly.

Thus by the prouidence of God landing safely, I was kindely intertained by all my friends, and after a short time learned more certaintie of the sinking of that great shippe, being also reputed rich by diuers intelligences out of Spaine; which we then supposed not, and were doubtfull whether she had bin of Biscay or S. John de Luz in France, laden with fish onely from Newfoundland.

In this voyage I and my fleete tooke, sunke and burnt nine Spanish ships;[1] which was losse to them, though I got nothing.

---

[1] Kendall gives the same total, but only six are mentioned in the three narratives, viz., the two carvels, the ship taken near Granada, the great galleon, and the two prizes made by the vice-admiral.

Here follow certaine wordes of the language of Trinidad[1] which I obserued at my being there:

Gvttemock, a man.
Tabairo, *Dabarah*, or *Dabarra*, the heare of ones head.
Dessie, the forehead.
Dasereth, or *Dacosi*, an eye. *(is be-in this age ed worle.)*
Dalacoack, the mouth.
Archeh, the teeth.
Daria, the gummes.
Desire, the lips.
Dill, the tongue.
Dudica, the eares.
Dacan, a hand.
Dacabbo, the palme of the hand.
Dadena, the wrist.
Dacurle, a knee.
Daddano, the calfe of the legge.
Dabodda, the toes.
Dacutti, the feete.
Cattie, the moone.
Tauraroth, a rope.
Arkeano, a paire of cizers.
Weeuah, the heauen.
Harowa, a stone good for the head ache. *(ie name 'e riuer noque)*
Mointiman, yron or steele. *(seeme de-d from word.)*
Howa, munkeis in generall.
Carotta, a thing like pappe.
Sakel, it is well, or I am well.

Techir, a bracelet.
Bodad, a boxe or chest.
Mentinic, a tree.
Addehegaeno, a glasse.
*Calcouri, gold.
Perota, siluer.
Tacorao, a green stone.
Arrara, copper.
Caulpiri, a white stone.
Casparo, a sword.
Tibetebe, cockles.
Marrahabo, a bow.
Semaro, an arrow.
Huculle, a bow-string.
Halete, a potato roote.
Caerwoda, a sweete root.
Maurisse, wheat.
Queca, a basket.
Yeddola, a knife.
Sambolers, a hat.
Beyou, a pipe.
Callit, bread.
†Oronuie, water.
Arguecona, a paire of cizzers.
Heldaro, a spoone.
Hemachugh, a bread which they eate.
Hicket, fire.

---

[1] See above, p. 65. This longer vocabulary includes many words not given by Brinton or Sagot, or in the "Arawakisch-Deutsches Wörterbuch" printed in the *Bibliothèque Linguistique Americaine*, viii, p. 69. Some equivalents, however, may be added, chiefly from the last-named work, to those in the earlier note, as *katti*, the moon; *wijua*, the Pleiades; *hoa*, ape; *ikii*, *hikkihi*, fire; *ballida*, comb; *kassipara*, sword; *simara*, arrow; *tchimalaabo* (*simarahabu*, Sagot), bow; *halti*, *halit* (*aletchi*, Sagot), potato; *sambuleru* (*cf.* Span. *sombrero*), hat; *kalli*, cassava; *siba* (*tchiba*, Sagot), stone; *buhiri*, bat (perhaps the same as Dudley's *bohery*, a flying-fish). Practically the same vocabulary is given by Dudley in his *Arcano del Mare*, pt. iv, bk. vi, ch. xxxvi, after the description of map XIV. Sometimes, however, he is a little more explicit, as "Callit o Hemachug, pane che essi fanno come biscotto di una radice nominata da loro Indiani Cassava."

Walrowa, a parrot.
Vreit, tabacco.
Barudda, a combe.
Addioth, a sticke.
Barrennaire, a button, or beads.
Curaballa and *Sibath*, for 2 sundry stones: but *Sibath* in general signifieth a stone.
Tolletillero, bels.
Vllasso, a tuny-fish.

Bohery, a flying-fish.
Bara, water.
Haddalle, the sunne.
Babage-Canoaseen, the maner of the Indians hailing of a ship, calling it after the name of their *Canoas*.
Non quo, or *Non quapa*, I know not, or I cannot tell.

ROBERT DUDLEY'S VOYAGE TO THE WEST INDIES,

1594-1595,

NARRATED BY ABRAM KENDALL, MASTER.

Ruttier[1] *by the learned mariner Abram Kendal, Englishman, in the voyage which he navigated, as chief pilot, to the West Indies with the author himself, who was then General, counting the longitude from the island of Pico in the Azores.*[2]

THE General made sail for the Indies in his admiral named the *Great Bear*,[3] of about 300 tons, from the port of Plimouth in England on the 1st December, 1594, having with him other vessels of war, the vice-admiral of his fleet being called the *Little*

---

[1] Translated (see at the end) from the Italian version printed in Dudley's *Arcano del Mare*, Florence, 1646-47, Bk. II, ch. v, p. 12. The old English term, "Ruttier," from the French *route* and *routier*, is given as the rendering of the Italian "Portolano." It is used by Hakluyt and others (as in *The Safegard of Saylers, or Great Rutter*, 1590), and is defined by Cotgrave as "a directory for the knowledge or finding out of courses, whether by sea or land." It corresponds, therefore, with the modern "Sailing Directions," which, among less strictly nautical matter, contain "descriptions of ports and anchorages, with accounts of the winds, currents and tides, for various coasts and seas" (Raper, *Practice of Navigation*, ed. 1891, p. 347), and it may fairly be applied to Kendall's narrative.

[2] Dudley gives the reason for this in the description of his map of

[3] "*L'orsa maggiore,*" the *Bear's Whelp* being rendered "*l'orsa minore.*"

Bear. We went out of port with the wind N.E., blowing strong, which was in our favour; and we sailed by the quarter S.W. (the variation being 13 degrees N.E.) until we were free of the Ediston rock, and then we went a quarter more S., where the island of Ushant lay E.S.E., in long. 23° 10′ and lat. 48° 34′, distant about 16 leagues.[1] The said port of Plimouth lies in long. 24° 8′ and lat. 50° 21′. Then we kept on the quarter S.S.W. of the common compass through lat. 45°, and half a quarter more S. to lat. 44 20′, so as to follow the shorter way of the great circle.[2] And then we saw Cape Finisterre[3] in Galicia of Spain, to the S.S.W., about 20 leagues distant, that is, about a degree of the great circle, in long. 17° 40′

the Azores (Africa, map ii, in the *Arcano del Mare*, Bk. VI, Pt. II, p. 24), "the longitude of all these maps of the author is counted from the middle of the island Pico, because there the compass makes no point of variation" (see also below, p. 91). Pico lies in lat. 38 20′ N. and long. (from Greenwich) 28° 30′ W. Dudley gives the lat. as 38° 40′. In this narrative and in all his maps the longitude is reckoned, not E. and W. from Pico to 180°, but right round the world eastward to 360°.

[1] Ushant is in 48° 28′ N., 5° 3′ W. (= 23° 27′ from Pico), and Plymouth in 50° 22′ N., 4° 9′ W. (= 24° 21′ from Pico). In the number of leagues given, "16" is perhaps a misprint for "46," Ushant being distant from Plymouth about 140 miles.

[2] A great circle is a circle dividing the sphere of the world into two equal parts. Great circle sailing, grounded on the fact that the shortest distance between any two points on the earth's surface is along an arc of a great circle, is defined by John Davis in *The Seaman's Secrets*, first published in 1594 (the year of Dudley's voyage): "The third [part of navigation] is great circle navigation, which teacheth how vpon a great circle drawne betweene any two places assigned (being the onely shortest way betweene place and place) the ship may bee conducted, and is performed by the skilfull application of horizontall and paradoxall Navigation" (2nd ed., 1607, reprinted in *The Voyages and Works of John Davis*, ed. A. H. Markham, Hakluyt Soc. 1880, p. 239). Davis reckoned the longitude, not from Pico, but from St. Michael's, another of the Azores, "because that there the compasse hath no variety" (p. 284). As his editor remarks, this is not now the case, the variation being about 25° W. From Ptolemy's time to the end of the sixteenth century, the usual reckoning was from Ferro, the most westerly of the Canaries.

[3] Cape Finisterre is in 42° 53′ N., 9° 16′ W. (= 19° 14′ from Pico); Cape Roca in 38° 57′ N., 9° 30′ W. (= 19°); and Cape St. Vincent in 37° 4′ N., 9° W. (= 19° 30′).

and lat. 43 8', although the common chart makes it 43 19'. The meridian compass was 8 degrees N.E.; the current ran towards S.W.; the wind was N.N.E. Thence we travelled S. to lat. 40° 45', and we saw Cape Roxo, seven leagues distant S.S.W., in long. 17 50' and lat. 38 53'. The variation was 6 degrees N.E., and the wind was N.E.; and we sailed along in sight of the coast of Portugal as far as Cape St. Vincent, in long. 18 22' and lat. 36° 55'. The compass inclined to N.E. half a quarter.

From Cape St. Vincent, that is, from six leagues distance, we sailed S.W. by W.; and we saw the island of Salvages[1] on the 22nd December, 1594, in lat. 30 and long. 10 49'. And on the way, in lat. 31° 20', the meridian compass inclined N.E. 5 degrees. Then following (from the island Salvages) the quarter S. and half a quarter S.W., by the common compass, we saw Cape Navos[2] of the island of Teneriffe, in lat. 29° 9' and long. 10° 50'. The peak of that same island is a very high mountain, and it is seen, when the weather is clear, high above the horizon from the island of Salvages. Within these islands of the Canaries one finds calms and plenty of tempests, with winds variable and shifting; and therefore it is not well to go too close in to land, especially in those parts where one cannot find bottom to cast anchor.

From the island of Palma, from the west part of it, in lat. 29 and long. 8° 50', we kept on with the vessel S.S.W. half a quarter S. to lat. 26 24' towards Cape Blanco in Africa; the variation was 3 degrees N.E. Then we followed the rhumb[3] S.S.E., and in lat. 23 50' found

---

[1] Salvages, one of the Canary Islands, in 30 6' N., 16' W. (= 12 30' from Pico).

[2] C. de Nouos, the northern point of Teneriffe, in Dudley's map iii of Africa, corresponding either to Pt. Hidalgo or to Pt. Anaga.

[3] A rhumb or, as it is also spelt, rumb is primarily a meridian and then any point of the compass. To sail on a rhumb line is to keep

ourselves in 30 fathoms, without seeing the coast of Africa, which is low and sandy with a sandy bottom. And here we saw weeds carried down by the current of the river of Gold.[1] Then we kept on the same rhumb, or S.S.E., until the ship had a little passed the Tropic of Cancer, in lat. 23° 20'. The bottom was 10 fathoms, sandy; the winds are N.E. and steady, with good weather. Then we followed the coast within sight of land, four leagues distant, the which is low and sandy, and the bottom is also of sand, from 8 to 10 fathoms. On the way we saw Cape Barbas,[2] in lat. about 21° 30' and long. 9° 50'. The variation was 3 degrees N.E. Cape Blanco, or Bianco, is in lat. 20° 24' and long. 9° 58'. High tide at the Cape is at 9 hours and ¾. We anchored S.S.W. of the Cape, at three miles distance, in 6½ fathoms, on a sandy bottom like the coast. The winds are N.E. and steady, with good weather as far as the Indies.

On the 6th January, 1595, we took soundings in the said bay, and on entering the bottom was 13, 9, 10, 8, 7, and 6 fathoms, and 8, 7, and 6½ where we anchored; and farther within the bay the bottom was not more than 7 fathoms, nor less than 3.[3] The bank S.S.W. of the Cape is large, and it is distant about 2½ leagues; on the which the Portuguese catch great quantity of fish with certain vessels called Canters. There is no good water there, since the country is sandy and desert; nevertheless,

---

the ship's head constantly directed to the same point, her track therefore cutting all the meridians at the same angle (see Raper *Practice of Navigation*, ed. 1891, p. 129).

[1] The Rio do Ouro of the Portuguese, an inlet between Cape Bojador and Cape Blanco. It was erroneously supposed to be the mouth of a river, but this was finally disproved by a Spanish expedition in 1885-6 (Vivien de St. Martin, *Nouv. Dict. de Géographie*, iv. p. 465).

[2] Cape Barbas is in 22° 8' N., 16° 56' W. (= 11° 34' from Pico); Cape Blanco in 20° 37' N., 17° 4' W. (= 11° 26').

[3] These soundings are given in Dudley's map iv of Africa, together with the bank, "Secaia e Banca di Capo Bianco doue pescano."

by making wells in the sand near the sea, fresh water is found, and, although it is not very wholesome to drink, yet it serves in urgent need.

On the 9th January, 1595 (by the Calendar and old style), the General set sail with his other vessels for the island of Trinidad in the West Indies, to explore the main and the rich empire of Guiana, or Walliana, according as he had order to do from Queen Elizabeth of England then reigning. So we steered W.S.W. as far as 19° 35′,[1] and the variation was 2½ degrees N.E., keeping the same quarter to 18° 50′, the intersection of which with the latitude gave the longitude on the globe, following the same rhumb to 18° 50′. Here the island of St. Nicholas of Cape Verde, in lat. 18° 16′ and long. 3°, lay W.S.W. of the vessel.[2] The winds were N.E., steady; the current is W.S.W. And we kept the same rhumb through lat. 18° 22′ and 17° 8′, 190 leagues distance from Cape Blanco, and in 16° 22′[3] there were 226 leagues distance from the cape of the great circle, counting 20 leagues to a degree, although by the common chart there are at least 230 leagues, for the coast is nearer than the common chart makes it. The compass varied one degree N.E. only. And keeping the quarter W.S.W. to lat. 15° 49′, the distance from the cape was 278 leagues, and the compass varied a small matter N.W., and one judged the longitude to be 354 30′. And following the same quarter to lat. 11° 5′, we were distant from the Cape about 536 leagues, and in lat. 9° 56′ and long. 337° we were 640 leagues of the great circle (counting 20 leagues to a degree) distant from Cape Blanco.

---

[1] The Italian text has "gr. 29 e min. 35."

[2] The island of San Nicolao lies in 16° 30′ N., 24° 20′ W. (= 4° 10′ from Pico). In Dudley's map (Africa, iv) the latitude is rightly given as 16° 30′, and the longitude is about 3, as here.

[3] The Italian text has "gr. 76 e min. 22."

Here we began to see some birds of the Indies called by the Portuguese *Forcados*.[1] The meridian compass inclined somewhat to the N.W., that is, about one degree. We followed then the same rhumb to lat. 9° 30′, and the longitude was 335°, and we saw, as a sign we were nearing America, some great birds like crows, but white, with long tails. The water of the sea was not very clear. With this same quarter we found the vessel in lat. 9° 28′ and long. 333° 30′, about 22 leagues distance from the island of Trinidad; where some sea-birds settled by night within the vessel and the water began to whiten considerably. And these are manifest signs of the neighbourhood of the coast of the Indies. The winds are N.E. steady, and the variation is one degree N.W.

On the 30th January, 1595, we saw the island of Trinidad, from the south side, from Cape Carao[2] in lat. 9° 20′ and long. 332° 40′, distant about 752 leagues of the great circle from Cape Blanco. The water whitened considerably towards the shoal along the coast of Guiana, but we did not see the main of the Indies, the land being very low and full of rivers and woods; and although the coast was nigher the vessel than was the island of Trinidad, we plainly saw the island first, as it is a high land and more visible. The bottom was at 9 fathoms, rather muddy towards land. And then we turned to the N.W. at 9° 25′, to follow the channel of the island of Trinidad from three miles distance

---

[1] The well-known Frigate-bird (*Fregata aquila*) of tropical seas, so called by sailors from the swiftness of its flight, and from its habit of hovering round other birds with predatory intent. The Portuguese name for it is *rabiforcado* (forked-tail), its long forked tail, as it soars in mid-air on apparently motionless wings, being a conspicuous object, opening and shutting continually like a pair of scissors.

[2] This is now Point Galeota, the south-eastern extremity of Trinidad, 10° 9′ N., 61° W. (= 327° 30′ from Pico) (*cf.* Dudley's map). Ralegh's Point Carao is, however, identified by Schomburgk with Point Negro, further along the south coast (p. 2). About four miles east of the latter there is a Point Curao in the Admiralty Chart and in the map prefixed to De Verteuil's *Trinidad*, 1884.

to the west as far as Cape Curiapan,[1] called by the Spaniards the Punta de Gallo, lat. 9° 26′ and long. 330° 50′. There the current is very strong, so that one cannot return by that way, and it drives towards the little island called Diavolo, within danger of the shallows which are within three miles W.N.W. from Cape Curiapan. One gets near, however, to the said cape in 4 fathoms of depth at half a mile distance or a little more, so as to turn towards the bay, which is a good harbour, having a bottom at 4 fathoms, nigh to certain small islands. The winds are N.E., steady; though they change sometimes, but only for a short space, with torrents of rain, as one often sees in the Indies.

In the said bay or harbour is a small stream of good water and easy to get. There is found a certain black bitumen like mineral pitch,[2] good to patch vessels, near to Cape Curiapan; and six miles or seven miles to the east is found a mine of Marcasite, which supplies much gold to the Indians, who dig it out for the purpose of making certain half-moons which they wear on the neck for ornament, and they call it *Calcuri*, which in their tongue means gold. And of this mine a good quantity was dug out.

---

[1] See p. 22, and for the rock Diavolo, p. 35. Ralegh speaks of Cape Curiapan, or Point Icacos, as "situate in 8 degrees or thereabouts" (p. 2). This is less correct than Kendall's 9° 26′. Its actual position is 10° 3′ N., 61° 56′ W. (= 326° 34′ from Pico). The description that follows is in close agreement with the Admiralty Chart, and it is clear that they passed through the eastern channel round Point Icacos and anchored in Cedros Bay.

[2] The reference is to the famous pitch lake of La Brea on the south-west coast of Trinidad, covering an area of nearly 100 acres. A full account of it is given by Wall and Sawkins, *Geology of Trinidad*, 1860, p. 134, and by Kingsley, *At Last*, 1872, p. 173. Considering its remarkable character, it is curious that neither Wyatt nor Dudley mentions it. Ralegh was more observant: "At this point called *Tierra de Brea* or Piche there is that abundance of stone pitch that all the ships of the world may be therewith loden from thence, and wee made triall of it in trimming our ships to be most excellent good and melteth not with the sunne as the pitch of Norway, and therefore for ships trading the south partes very profitable" (p. 3).

From this port we turned N.N.E. to the Bay of Paracoa,[1] about three leagues distance, near the port and city of St. Joseph, held by the Spaniards for the purpose of exploring Guiana. There is bottom there at 4 and 5 fathoms; and there is a very good beach, where one can get water in lat. 9° 34′ and long. 331° 10′, distant from Cape Blanco aforesaid 758 leagues of the great circle. And from there one could see to the N.N.W. the cape and high land of Paria and the strait, in lat. 10° 10′ and long. 330° 27′. One could also see from there the harbour of Conquirabia in the island, fortified and garrisoned by the Spaniards, of the which place Don Antonio de Berco was Governor.

From Paracoa the General marched on land several times with 300 soldiers[2] and made himself absolute master of the island and fortified it with posts, from which he then explored the main over against him, being the empire of Guiana in the Indies. And by means of the utility of the rivers he entered at Cape Capuglio to the S. half a quarter S.W. from the Cape Curiapan, and the General named that river Rio Dudliano after his own name; and by this way he entered 300 miles within Guiana by a navigable river with small boats and frigates, and discovered the great river of Orinoche, in the map called by the

---

[1] From this description and Dudley's map it appears that his Paracoa lay to the north of Point La Brea, probably at or near San Fernando. It was therefore not the same as Ralegh's Parico, which Schomburgk no doubt rightly locates in Cedros Bay; but the meaning of Paragua (see p. 42, note 2) makes it likely that any place on the sea-shore might be so called. Judging from his map, Dudley supposed St. Joseph (taken and burnt by Ralegh) to be identified with Port of Spain, capital of the island, instead of being some miles inland to the east; while Conquerabia, described by Ralegh as "that place which the Spaniards cal *Puerto de los Hispanioles* and the inhabitants *Conquerabia*," is placed by him to the south of the Caroni.

[2] This, like other statements in the same paragraph, is an obvious exaggeration (*cf.* p. 45,; and it will be noticed that Kendall, or his editor, speaks as if Dudley himself had gone on the boat expedition up the Orinoco.

Indians Worinoche. He found the country very low and full of woods, but fertile and rich in gold, as the Indians of the country narrated. The chief city of the kingdom is great and very rich; it is named Manoa, and by the Spaniards El Dorado, for the great richness of it.

The said General returned with good success by the river Amana towards Paria, and having ended his exploring and done what pleased him as to the enterprise of Guiana, he set sail on the 5th[1] of March, 1595. And the day following he passed the Strait of Paria, called by him the Strait of Calcuri, that is, of Gold in the Indian tongue. This passed, we found the the wind N.E. steady, the current was towards the W, and we went by the sounding-line, and we saw the small islands of Testigos near the island of Margarita, where they fish for pearls in the Indies. And then we saw the island of Granata[2] to the N.E., in lat. 11° 20′ and long. 331° 10′, holding continually to the rhumb N.W. by N. And in seven or eight days[3] we saw towards the N.E. the island of Santa Cruz. And on the way the said General took a ship of the enemy laden with wine of Spain, confections and other rich merchandise, and having passengers of quality, who were going to the Indies; and our vice-admiral had already returned to England with two great and rich galleons, taken by our vessels at the outset of the voyage.

And after sighting the island of Santa Cruz, sailing N.W., we coasted along the south side all the length of the great island of San Juan de Porto Rico in the Indies, which is well peopled by Spaniards and very fertile; and we

---

[1] According to Wyatt and Dudley, they passed through the straits on 12 March (pp. 48, 76).

[2] Grenada, the southernmost of the Windward Islands, 12° 8′ N., 61° 42′ W. (= 326° 48′ from Pico).

[3] According to Wyatt, on 17 March (p. 49).

passed near to the island of Inferno, where the water is so
clear that one sees the bottom at 20 to 25 fathoms. Then
coasting along towards the W. we found bottom under
Cape Roxo,[1] where is a very good beach north of the cape,
in lat. 17° 54′ and long. 323° 20′, with five fathoms of
depth, towards the little island off the cape. The variation
was 3 degrees N.W.; the wind was steady and N.E.; the
current is towards N.W. And in the bay we found good
water. On this coast the General unladed the wares
from the ship he had taken and gave liberty to all the
Spaniards, among whom were sundry persons of quality,
putting them on land courteously in boats at a village
inhabited by Spaniards in the bay, seeing that with his
vessel he could not go near the shore because of the shoals;
and then he burnt the said ship.

And as the said General had notice from some Spaniards
whom he had taken that the silver fleet had parted from
Havana a few days before, he resolved to follow it up,
according to the instructions he had from Her Majesty of
England, to wit that he should find the fleet when it was
scattered by reason of the storms and bad weather which
are wont to prevail in those seas. Whereupon, on the
10th April[2] he made sail from Cape Roxo in the Indies
and navigated by the rhumb N.E. by N., so as to disembogue from the Indies in sight of land between the island
of Zecchio and the island of Mona (which is low-lying
land and near to the island of Hispaniola), and to avoid
also the bank of Abrolhos,[3] in lat. 21° and long. 320° 40′.
And following always the same rhumb N.E. by N. (the

---

[1] Cape Rojo (p. 76, note 4) lies in 17° 58′ N., 67° 12′ W. (= 321° 18′ from Pico).

[2] In Wyatt's narrative (p. 52) this was on 25 March. See also p. 76.

[3] The Abrolhos (or Natividad) bank is in 20° 8′ N., 68° 50′ W. (= 319° 48′ from Pico).

current being N.W., we ran as far as 23° 20' in rough weather; the variation was 6½° N.W. And from there we kept the rhumb or quarter N.W. by W. by reason of the winds to lat. 26°. The compass inclined N.W. eight degrees, and the intersection of the rhumb followed with the latitude observed gave the longitude. Thence we sailed by the quarter N.W. to lat. 29° 40', being distant from the island of Bermuda 140 leagues of the great circle, counting 20 leagues to a degree; and we kept the same rhumb to lat. 36° 4', where we passed the longitude and meridian of the island of Bermuda on the N.E., its latitude being 32° 30' and long. 328° 20'.[1] And we passed this meridian in great storms and tempests and horrible thunders and lightnings, which give clear tokens that one is passing the longitude of the island.

The winds of that part of the ocean are variable and tempestuous, but the greater part come from the main-land of America and from the great islands of the Indies towards the S.W.; and in lat. 38° 30' the island of Bermuda lay S.S.W. and the variation was 10 degrees N.W.; and in lat. 39° 4', following the rhumb as above, the island of Bermuda was distant 110 leagues of the great circle, and we saw frigate-birds and sea-mews. The current ran to N.E., and carried with it weeds from the rocks of the Indies. And when one no longer sees suchlike weeds, it is a sign that one passes the longitude of Cape Razo,[2] long. 344° 10' from Pico of the Azores. And in lat. 40° 10', driven by contrary winds, we were 160 leagues distant by the great circle from the island of Bermuda. Then we began to run before a great storm to lat. 38° 20', distant by the common chart from the islands of Flores or Corvo 120

---

[1] Bermuda lies in 32° 10' N, 64° 45' W. (= 323° 30' from Pico).

[2] Cape Race in Newfoundland, 46° 40' N., 53° 5' W. (= 335° 25' from Pico).

leagues. From which one learns how false the chart is, that it makes the distance too much by about 80 leagues, because the vessel was there not more distant from the island of Flores than 40 leagues of the great circle, and the compass, for greater confirmation of the truth, inclined to N.W. three degrees only. And it followed that the next day, early in the morning, we saw the island of Flores in the Azores, which is high land, near the island of Corvo, to the S., where the variation is not more than two degrees to the N.W. And then we passed the meridian of the island of Pico and the variation was imperceptible, and therefore we count the longitude from the same island of Pico.

Then we sailed by the rhumb N.E. and N.E. by N. towards England to lat. 45°. There our admiral found herself alone and discovered a very great galleon of the fleet of the Indies, exceeding rich, which was separated from the fleet by a storm. And our General fought the said galleon always to windward, within musket shot, two days together; and at the end, after very many cannon shot, he sent her to the bottom,[1] and the General's staff was carried away out of his hand by a cannon shot of the enemy. We followed then the rhumb N.E. by N. until we arrived at the port of St. Ives[2] in England at the end of May, in lat. 50° 15' and long. 22° 40'. And one finds that the common chart makes the distance about 25 leagues[3] of the great circle from the island of Pico to England, which is too far, and this is because of the equal degrees of the same chart, the which are in practice most false, and

---

[1] Neither Wyatt nor Dudley speaks so positively as this (pp. 63, 77).

[2] St. Ives in Cornwall, 50° 13' N., 5° 29' W. (=23° 1' from Pico).

[3] There is a great error here, due perhaps to a confusion between leagues and degrees. The real distance is about 28 degrees or 560 leagues.

cannot be made to agree well with the longitude treated in this Ruttier.

The General took in this voyage nine vessels of the enemy, rich enough, whereof one was sent to the bottom, war being then declared between England and Spain.

The original of this Ruttier was found in the English tongue among the writings of the same pilot, Abram Kendal, when he died at Porto Bello in the Indies with Drake, then General of an English fleet, in the year 1597.[1]

---

[1] This is an error, which is corrected in the second edition of the *Arcano del Mare*; the year should be 1596 (see p. 14, note).

APPENDIX.

Explanation by Sir Robert Dudley of maps xiii (here reproduced) and xiv of America in his " Arcano del Mare," vol. iii, pt. ii, the former containing the coast of South America from the island of Margarita to the river Seawano, east of the Surinam, and the latter the coast of Guiana and Brazil from the Seawano to Maranhão.

MAP XIII.

This chart [is] of Guiana, and part of the coast was discovered by the author, as appears in the first Portolano of the second Book, in the year 1595, which [chart] afterwards the said author caused to be printed at Florence in 1637,[1] with the explanation, and dedicated it to the Most Serene Ferdinand II, Grand Duke of Tuscany, who now happily reigns, and the printer was Francesco Onofri. And to the said explanation he refers, adding only what follows, namely that the said chart begins with the Island of St. Margarita, in long. 327 and lat. 10° 35' north, where they get more and better pearls than anywhere else in the Indies; and the same chart ends with the river Seawano on the coast of Guiana, in long. 337 and lat. 5° 50', of which coast the author writes of ocular knowledge, as by the said Portolano more plainly appears. And in this voyage the author made himself master of part of the Island of Trinidad towards Paracoa, in order to discover better the main of Guiana or Walliana (held then for a country and kingdom very rich in gold and in other commodities), especially by means of the great river of Orinoque, called by the Indians Worinock, although in its mouth, by reason of shoals, ships of any burden cannot enter, which prejudices much the enterprise of

---

[1] Nothing is known of this edition, which was evidently distinct from that in the *Arcano del Mare*, and was accompanied by more text. The Portolano is printed here (p. 80).

Guiana. And Guiana begins from the Cape of Paria and Strait of Calcuri (so named by the author, when he passed the same Strait), and the coast ends with the river Amazons, as one sees by chart xiv following.

And at the said Cape of Paria issues the river Amana or Braha, as one of the seven mouths of the river Orinoque, named the seven Mouths of the Dragon because of the violence of the said river in time of floods and of the heavy rains which fall almost continuously in the months of June, July, and August and inundate all the country, which is low land, marshy and full of woods and of small rivers, and these last shift their channels every year, except the seven principal mouths as above. The tide near to the Cape of Paria will be at two hours and a quarter after midday; and so through the Gulf of Caribes, in the which at Cape Curiapan, in the island of Trinidad, the current is strong, and it makes toward the gulf and by the small island called Diavolo, which is girt round by dangerous shoals. There vessels of high board pass the said Cape of Curiapan toward Paria, and they cannot return by the said Cape, but go out freely from the Gulf of Caribes by the Strait of Calcuri near the Cape of Paria, the beginning of the mainland of the Indies. This may be seen better in the same chart xiii of America, in which chart, as being of large scale, one will see minutely all the perils of the rocks, shoals, and currents, with other necessary observations as to the winds and the air, the which is most healthy because of steady winds, except in the months of June, July, and August, when it rains almost continuously and the winds are variable, and because of the excessive heat and the great humidity of the coast the air then is unhealthy and produces malignant fevers, which kill the sufferers in short time; and on that account they are called ephemeral, malignant, and pestilential fevers, and few survive them, letting blood being of no avail, but rather doing harm. And in that season the weather is very bad, because of tempests and great thunders and horrible storms at sea, called by the Indians *orocani* or *uracani*, which are very perilous in those seas in sinking vessels, although of high board and handy.

The variation of the compass in this chart is one degree north-west, although the chart by an error in engraving makes it half a degree only. The people of that country are very bad and treacherous, so that one can put no trust in their courtesies, especially those called Caribs, who eat human flesh and fight with the other Indians to that end, and they are commonly more robust than the rest.

MAP XIV

This chart begins with the river Seawano, in long. 337, and ends with Cape Palmas, about long. 347, where disembogues the great river Maranghan; and the coast there and the river Amazons are better revised in chart xv following. This chart, however, is to be trusted principally for the coast of Guiana, which begins with Seawano and ends with the Cape of the river Amazons, named Arowai[1]; into which river Amazons entered Captain Richard Thornton, Englishman, commanded to those parts by order and at the charges of the Most Serene Grand Duke Ferdinand [I] his lord.

The said Captain went and returned prosperously, and although he had never been in those parts before, nor yet in the West Indies in anywise, yet by means of the charts and instructions in the author's own hand he, by grace of God, achieved his voyage without loss except one man, who died of sickness. And he discovered the coast of Guiana more exactly than had ever before been done, and he discovered, moreover, the good port of Chiana,[2] which is a royal port and safe, the which was never before discovered by Christians in past times, and from there he brought with him five or six Indians to present them to their Highnesses in Florence, as he did, who were of those Caribs who eat human flesh. They died afterwards in Florence, the greater number of them of small-pox, which in them is more virulent than the plague itself, because in those countries they have no knowledge of a like disease. One alone of them survived, who served afterwards in the court for some years the Prince Cardinal Medici, and learned to speak the Italian tongue passably well.

---

[1] Cape Arowari, now called Cape do Norte.

[2] Cayenne, where the French, under Laravardière, had attempted to form a settlement in 1604, four years earlier (Mourié, *La Guyane Française*, 1874, p. 172). Captain Robert Harcourt, who followed Thornton very closely, leaving England March 23rd, 1605, reports of it: "At Caiane there is an excellent harbour for shipping of any burden, which heretofore by Captain Lawrence Keymis was called Port Howard" (*Relation*, 1613, p. 22).

This Indian of Chiana recounted ofttimes to the author and to others the fertility and richness of the kingdom of Guiana, and how he had been in the famous city of Manoa, metropolis of the kingdom, and where their king resides, called Emperor because he has divers kingdoms under his sway; and he said that the city was rich in gold and was situate nigh to a great lake, and that this city was eight days' journey distant from the port of Chiana, being that the Indians travel quickly afoot and make commonly fifty [Italian] miles a day and sometimes more.

The same Indian said moreover that nigh to Chiana (which is a country of hills) was a mine of silver, very rich, which they call *perota*, as also of base gold, called by them *calcuri*, with which they make certain images and half-moons for ornament. The above-named Captain Thornton said the same, and added thereto that the spiders of that country made silk, and that there was found rosewood (legno verzino) in good quantity, and wild sugar canes, white pepper, speckled wood (legno pardo), "pitta," balsam, cotton and many other kinds of commodities, abundant for commerce; and, if the country might be well planted by Christians, the air was most healthy, and the entry of the port was convenient to fortify for the command of the port; with other particulars of the country already printed by the author in 1637, as is said above, to which for brevity he may refer.

The said Captain moreover recounted that, when he had discovered the river Amazons or Orelliano, in entering it he found a bore (bornea), so called in English and by the Portuguese *macarea*, and it is a dreadful tide and perilous in the days of the new and full moon, noted here in the said chart by the author in these words: "Beware of a bore at six hours and a quarter" (Guardatevi da una Bornea à hore 6 e un quarto). And with these few words of warning the Captain saved his vessel, by grace of God, and the subjects of his Highness, as the same Captain testified to his Highness, and that without the warning inscribed in the chart he would have known nothing of such peril, there being few of such bores in the world; and that he would have been lost, if beforehand he had not been advised of the peril, and had not warped his vessel with cables in a safer position, so as to receive the bore with his prow, and thus the vessel did not founder but escaped that peril. From this example one may see how important are the warnings inscribed in the charts of the author for manifest perils, which in other common charts are not noted, seeing it was possible with three words of warning to save on divers occasions the vessel and her people.

From the said river Amazons the said Captain Thornton coasted Guiana, with the island of Trinidad, or the Trinity, and had great satisfaction in the truth and perfection of the author's chart, and above all in his instructions to begin his voyage in the best season, that thereby they might return all with good health, with good weather, and with favourable winds. He began his voyage from Leghorn about the month of September, 1608, and returned to the same port of Leghorn at the end of June following, 1609, or thereabout.

INDEX.

Abreojos or Abrolhos, shoal of, near San Domingo, 67, 76, 89
Amana, a branch of the Orinoco, 88, 94. *See also* Mana.
Amazons, river, 95
Arara, copper or base gold, 65, 73
Arawak language of Trinidad, vocabularies of the, xxvi, 65, 78
Arcano del Mare, L', work by R. Dudley, lx.
Armago, Armaio, chief of a gold mine, 66; chief of Orocoa, 74, 75
Armathases (*sc.* Armadas), 8, 9, 10
Armathoes (*sc.* Armadas), 49
Arowari, Cape, 95
Asanaga, kingdom of, in W. Africa, 15

Baboons (babions), 71
Baker, Matthew, shipwright, invited to Italy, lvii
Balthazar, Baltizar, an Indian interpreter, 37; treachery and escape of, 40, 75
Barbis or Barbas, Cape, in W. Africa, 16, 83
Barrow, ——, "Ancient" to R. Dudley, xx, 24
Bear, the, R. Dudley's admiral, xix, 3 *n*, 68, 80
Bear's Whelp, the, R. Dudley's vice-admiral, xix, 3, 5, 68, 69, 80, 88
Beauchamp, Lord. *See* Seymour, Edward.
Bermuda (the Bermudes), 52, 53, 76, 90
Berreo, or Berrio, Antonio de, Spanish Governor of Trinidad, xxiv, xxviii, 70, 87
Birds of the Orinoco, 38
Blanco (Blanke, etc.), Cape, in W. Africa, 15, 16, 69, 82, 83, 85, 87
Blount, Charles, Earl of Devonshire, xlix
Blount, Sir Christopher, ix
Bordeaux (Burteus), 4
Bore in the Amazons, 96
Bourgès, in Gascony, 5

Bradshew, William, page to R. Dudley, bravery of, in action, xxxiv, 61; presented by Dudley with a gun, 62
Braáha, Braha, a branch of the Orinoco, 66, 75, 94
Braio, an Indian of Trinidad, 45
Brest, English expedition to, in 1594, 4

Cabota, a branch of the Orinoco, 74
Cadiz, English expedition to, in 1596, xxxvii
Calcouri, Calcurey, Calcuric, the Indian name for gold, 39, 44, 45, 65, 78, 86, 88, 96
Calcurie, continent of, the "main" so called by R. Dudley, 44
Calcurie, straits of (*sc.* the Dragon's Mouth), between Trinidad and Paria, 48, 88, 94
Calshot Castle, 3
Caluori, Indian name for gold (?), 70
Caminha (Camena), in Portugal, 6
Canary Islands, 15, 69, 82
Cane-tobacco, in Paria, 48, 73
Canter, Capt., commands R. Dudley's pikemen, 24
Canters, canthers, Portuguese fishing-boats, 15, 69, 83
Capulia (*sc.* Capure ?), a branch of the Orinoco, 37
Capulio, a foreland at the mouth of the Orinoco, 66, 74, 87
Carácas (Cracos), 48
Carao, in Trinidad, xxxii. *See also* Carowa.
Carao, Cape, in Trinidad, 85
Caribes, kingdom of, 72; cannibals, and enemies to the natives of Trinidad, 73, 95
Caribia, people of, cannibals, 66
Carowa, an Indian town in Trinidad, xxxii, 45, 46
Carr, Robert, Earl of Somerset, lii; letter to, from R. Dudley, liii
Cascaes (Cascales), in Portugal, 8
Catwater, at Plymouth, 5

INDEX

Cavendish, ——, first wife of R. Dudley, x
Cavendish, Beatrice, wife of Thomas Denny, x
Cavendish, Douglas, first wife of R. Hakluyt, xi
Cavendish, Thomas, the circumnavigator, x, xi, 32
Cayenne (Chiana), in Guiana, 95, 96
Cecil, Sir Robert, letter to, from R. Dudley, xxxv; letter to, from Sir W. Ralegh, xxxvi; as Earl of Salisbury, xlvii
Chaloner, Sir Thomas, tutor to R. Dudley, viii; letter to R. Dudley, li
Checo, Mount. *See* Monchique.
Chiana. *See* Cayenne.
Chirk, lordship of, bequeathed to R. Dudley, ix
Clewer, or Cluer, William, evidence by, as to R. Dudley's birth, iv
Cockeyne, ——, at Florence, xlix
Combley, or Comley, Thomas, ix, 8, 22; bravery of, in action, 60
Conquirabia, in Trinidad, 87
Copper (*arara*), found in Yguiri, 73
Corpo Santo (Corposantic), or St. Elmo's Fire, 55
Coruña (the Groyne), 6
Corvo (Corves, Cuervo), island of, in the Azores, 56, 77, 90
Counter-galliass, a ship invented by R. Dudley, liii, lv
Crale, ——, one of R. Dudley's company, 8
Curiapan, Point, in Trinidad, 22, 70, 74, 87, 94; called Punta de Gallo, 86
Cyprian, Cape, in W. Africa, 15

Daniell, Capt., 9
Davis, Capt. John, eulogy of, by R. Dudley, xvi
Denbigh, lordship of, bequeathed to R. Dudley, ix
Denny, Thomas, married R. Dudley's wife's sister, x
Desecheo (Zacheo, etc.), island of, near Puerto Rico, 52, 76, 89
Devereux, Lettice, Countess of Essex, v. *See also* Dudley, Lettice.
Devereux, Walter, Earl of Essex, v
Devonshire, Earl of. *See* Blount, Charles.
Diabolo, a rock off Trinidad, 35, 43, 86, 94
Direttorio Marittimo, work by R. Dudley, viii, lxii; quoted, xii, xxxvii

Drake, Sir Francis, xvi, xix, 12, 92; A. Kendall's opinion of, xvii
Drury, Thomas, attempts to establish R. Dudley's legitimacy, xli; death of, *ib.*; convicted of fraud, xlvi
Dudley, Alice, Lady, second wife of R. Dudley, xxxviii; deserted by her husband, xlvii; created Duchess Dudley, li
Dudley, Ambrose, Earl of Warwick, iv, ix
Dudley, John, vii
Dudley, Lettice, Countess of Leicester, v-vii, ix; opposes R. Dudley's claim to legitimacy, xxxix
Dudley, Robert, Earl of Leicester, father of R. Dudley, ii-ix, xl-xlvi, 1, 26, 28
Dudley, Robert, life of, ii-lxvii; date of birth, iii; at Oxford, viii; contract of marriage with F. Vavasour, ix; marries —— Cavendish, x; administers T. Cavendish's estate, xi; portrait of, by N. Hilliard, xii; account of, by Sir W. Dugdale and A. Wood, xii; narratives of his voyage, xiii; relations of, with Sir W. Ralegh, xxi; letter to Sir R. Cecil, xxxv; serves at Cadiz, xxxvii; knighted, *ib.*; marries Alice Leigh, xxxviii; attempts to prove his legitimacy, *ib.*; loses his cause, xlvi; leaves England with Eliz. Southwell, xlvii; goes to Florence, xlviii; his license to travel revoked, *ib.*; letter to Earl of Northampton, *ib.*; his estates sequestrated, li; sells Kenilworth to Prince Henry, *ib.*; letter to, from Sir T. Chaloner, lii; proposition of, for the bridling of Parliament, *ib.*; paper by, on naval supremacy, *ib.*; ships invented by, liii; letter to the Earl of Somerset, liv; description of his "counter-galliass," lv; at Florence, lvii; builds ships for the Grand Duke, *ib.*; builds a mole at Leghorn, lviii; takes the title of Duke of Northumberland, lix; attempts reprisals on English merchants at Leghorn, lx; manuscripts, etc., of, at Florence, lxi; his *Direttorio Marittimo*, lxii; his *Arcano del Mare*, *ib.*; forbidden to go to the South Seas, 1, 68; prepares for the West Indies, 2, 68; sails from Southampton, 3, 68; leaves Plymouth, 5, 68, 80; loses his pinnace and reaches Finisterre, 6, 68;

INDEX

misses a Spanish prize, 7; reaches Lagos Bay, 8; meets four English ships, 9; meets a barque of Weymouth, 10; driven under Teneriffe, 11; takes two carvels, 12, 13, 69; driven back to Palma, 14; makes for Cape Blanco and comes to Riodore, 15, 69; lands on the mainland, 16, 69; his carvels fight with French ships, 17; passes the Cape Verde islands and makes for Trinidad, 19, 70, 84; skill of, in navigation, 21; reaches Trinidad, 22, 70, 85; enquires for a gold mine, 23; marches to the mine, 24; eulogy upon, 25; returns to his ships, 25; sets up the Queen's arms, etc., on plates of lead, 26, 33; removes to Paracowe, 28, 70, 87; his good treatment of the Indians, 29; makes a "sconce," 29, 70; letter of, to Capt. Jobson, 31; sends away his carvels, 32, 72; refuses Spanish presents, 32; dealings of, with the Indians as to gold-mines, 33; anxious to explore the Orinoco, 34, 71; is dissuaded, and sends Capt. Jobson, 35, 73; confident of Jobson's return, 42; joined by Capt. Popham, 43, 71, 75; treats with the Indians, 44; marches into the interior of Trinidad, 45, 71, 87; spares the native houses and goods, 46; returns to his ship and leaves Trinidad, 48, 76, 88; makes for Puerto Rico and takes a prize, 48, 76, 88; releases his prisoners and burns the prize, 50, 51; makes for Florida, 52; driven by storms, 53; reaches the Azores, 56, 77, 90; sails for England, and has a two days' fight with a Spanish galleon, 57, 77, 91; his "leading staff" broken in his hand, 60, 91; rewards the bravery of his page, 62; for want of powder leaves the enemy, 63, 77; lands at St. Ives, 64, 77, 91; took and burned nine Spanish ships, 77, 91; his own account of his voyage, 67-79; enumeration of the kingdoms on the main, 72; learns of a mine at Orocoa, 73; waits for Sir W. Ralegh, 75; Abram Kendall's account of his voyage, 80-92; makes himself absolute master of Trinidad, 87, 93; names a river "Dudliano," 87; enters 300 miles within Guiana, 87

Dudley, Robert, Lord Denbigh, death of, vii

Dudliano, Rio, a branch of the Orinoco, so called by R. Dudley, 87

Dugdale, Sir William, account of R. Dudley by, xii; on the attempt to prove R. Dudley's legitimacy, xxxviii

Earwig, the, a pinnace, xix, 68

Edward Bonadventure, the, xvii; at Trinidad, xxv

El Dorado, capital of Guiana, 75, 88

Elizabeth, Queen, iii, v, xlv; forbids R. Dudley's voyage to the South Seas, 1, 68; arms of, on plates of lead, set up in Trinidad, 26, 33; Dudley's account of, given to the Indians, 44; orders Dudley to explore Guiana, 84; orders Dudley to attack the plate fleet, 89

Erisa, Avice, godmother to R. Dudley, iv. *See also* Parker, Avice, Lady.

Espichel (Pitcher), Cape, in Portugal, 8

Essex, Countess of. *See* Devereux, Lettice.

Essex, Earl of. *See* Devereux, Walter.

Ferdinand II, Emperor, recognises R. Dudley as Duke of Northumberland, lix

Finisterre, Cape, 6, 81

Fire-flies in Trinidad, 25

Flores (Flowers, Flores), island of, in the Azores, 56, 77, 90

Florida, 52

Flyboat (flibote), 7

Flying-fish, 19

Foulis, Sir David, letters to, from R. Dudley, lii, liii

Frigate-birds (*Forcados*), 85, 90

Frisking, the, a pinnace, xix, 68

Frodsham, Henry, witness in the case as to R. Dudley's legitimacy, xli, xlvi

Frodsham, Magdalen. *See* Salisbury, Magdalen.

Galicia (Calitie), in Spain, 6

Galley-royal, a ship invented by R. Dudley, liii

Gallizabra, a ship invented by R. Dudley, liii

Gannet, pursues the flying-fish, 20

Gilbert, Sir Humphrey, ship of, wrecked on Sable Island, 53; lost at sea, 54

Gillingham, Thomas, wounded in action, 61

INDEX.

Gold, supposed mine of, in Trinidad, xxvi, 23, 24; mines of, reported by the Indians, 34; breastplates of, 34; *caleurie*, the Indian name for, 39, 44, 45, 65, 78, 86, 88, 96; ore and melting-pots found at Carowa, 46; *caluori*, the Indian name for (?), 70; mine of, at Wackerew in Seawano, 73; mine of, at Orocoa, 73; crescents of, 74, 86, 96; nation powdered with, 77
Granada (Granado, Granata), island of, 48, 76, 88
Groyne, the (*sc.* Coruña), in Spain, 6
Gualata, kingdom of, in W. Africa, 15
Guiana, empire of, xxix, 71, 84, 87; maps of, by R. Dudley, lxv, 93; voyage of Capt. R. Thornton to, lxv; different kingdoms of, 72; Waliame the first kingdom of, 73; called Walliana, 84, 93; low coast of, 85; description of, 88
Gurnard (Gurned) Bay, in the Isle of Wight, 4

Hakluyt, Richard, married Douglas Cavendish, xi; *Voyages* of, xiv, 67
Hampton (*sc.* Southampton), 2
Harper, Capt., information received from, as to Guiana, 72
Havana, 76, 89
Henry, Prince of Wales, buys Kenilworth from R. Dudley, li; paper on naval supremacy sent to, lii
Hilliard, Nicholas, portrait of R. Dudley by, xi
Hispaniola, or San Domingo, island of, 76, 89.
Horsey, Sir Edward, xli
Howard, Charles, Lord Howard of Effingham and Earl of Nottingham, vi, xliv
Howard, Douglas, ii. *See also* Sheffield, Douglas.
Howard, Frances, iii
Howard, Henry, Earl of Northampton, letter to, from R. Dudley, xlviii
Howard, Thomas, Duke of Norfolk, xliv
Howard, Lord Thomas, xxxvii
Hythe (Heeve), near Southampton. 2

Indians, trade with R. Dudley at Trinidad, 22; good treatment of, 29; dealings with, as to gold mines, 33, 44; sound alarms with a "great pipe," 47; description of, by Dudley.

70; use gold half-moons for neck ornaments, 86, 96. *See also* Armago, Balthazar, Braio.
Inferno, Infierno, island of, off Puerto Rico, 76, 188
Intent, the, a captured carvel, 69

James I, resentment of, against R. Dudley, xlviii, lii; design of a ship offered to, by Dudley, liii
Jobson, Capt. Thomas, ix; R. Dudley's lieutenant, xix, 22, 23, 24, 28, 29, 30, 49; with Sir F. Drake, 12; letter to, from Dudley, 31; sets up a plate of lead with the Queen's arms, etc., 33; sent to explore the Orinoco, 35, 73; crosses to the main, 36; description of the river, etc., 37; dealings of, with the Indians, 39; betrayed by his Indian interpreter, 40; difficulties of, on his return, 41, 42; reaches the ship, 43; commands the van in the march across Trinidad, 45; prepares the ship for action, 58; post of, in action, 61; quotes the *Spanish Tragedie*, 62
Jones, Owen, evidence of, as to R. Dudley's birth, vii, xlii, xlvi
Julio, Dr., physician to the Earl of Leicester, iv

Kendall, Abraham or Abram, teaches R. Dudley navigation, xiii; account of, xv-xviii; opinion by, of Sir F. Drake, xvii; invents the seven "symmetries", lxi; master of the *Bear*, 14, 44, 70, 76; opposes Dudley's exploring the Orinoco, 34; gives the boat expedition up for lost, 42; skill of, in navigation, 52; fear of his villany, 73; narrative by, of Dudley's voyage, xv, 80-92; death of, 92
Kenilworth castle, etc., bequeathed to R. Dudley, ix; sold to Prince Henry, li

Labrador, or Nova Francia, 53
Lagos (Lawgust), Bay of, in Portugal, 8
Lead, plates of, with the Queen's arms, set up in Trinidad, 26, 33
Lee, Sir Henry, iv
Leghorn, mole built by R. Dudley at, lviii; reprisals on English merchants at, lx
Leicester, Countess of. *See* Dudley, Lettice.
Leicester, Earl of. *See* Dudley, Robert; Sidney, Robert.

Leigh, Alice, second wife of R. Dudley, x, xxxviii. *See also* Dudley, Alice.
Leighton, Sir William, xlvi
Lister, ——, made master of a prize, 13
Lizards, in West Africa, 16, 69
Loweco, an Indian town in Trinidad, 46

Mana, a branch of the Orinoco, 65, 74. *See also* Amana.
Manoa, or El Dorado, capital of Guiana, xxix, 88, 96
Marcasite, mine of, in Trinidad, 23, 70, 86
Margarita, island of, 49, 70, 93; pearl fishery at, 88
Maria, a branch of the Orinoco, 66
Marmosets, 38
Merchant Royal, the, of London, xvi
Mermaid, the, R. Dudley's rear-admiral, 3
Mona, island of, near Puerto Rico, 76, 89
Monchique (Mounte Checo), Sierra de, in Portugal, 8
Monck, or Munck, Capt., commands the *Bear's Whelp*, vice-admiral, xix, 68; returns to England with two prizes, 69, 88
Mones, ——, English merchant at Florence, xlix
Moroca, people of, cannibals, 65
Morucca, kingdom of, 72
Mountjoye, Staggs of, on the coast of Spain, 6
Morris, ——, one of Dudley's company, 8

Navos, Cape, in Teneriffe, 82
Nevill, Edmund, self-styled Earl of Westmorland, xlix
Nonpareil, the, commanded by R. Dudley at Cadiz, xxxvii
Norfolk, Duke of. *See* Howard, Thomas.
Northampton, Earl of. *See* Howard, Henry.
Northumberland, Duke of, title of, assumed by R. Dudley, lix
Nottingham, Earl of. *See* Howard, Charles.
Nova Francia, or Labrador, 53

Offington, co. Sussex, R. Dudley at school at, vii
Orinoco (Orinoche, Orenoque, Owrinoicke, Werinoen, Worinoche) river, 66, 73, 74, 93; R. Dudley anxious to explore it, 34; boat expedition up, 35, 73, 87
Orocani, Indian name for storms, 94
Orocoa, on the Orinoco, gold mine at, xxix, 73; Armago, captain of, 74; distance of, from the coast, 75
Ouro, Rio do, in West Africa, 83

Palma, island of, 13, 14, 69, 82
Paracoa, Paracowe, Parracow, in Trinidad, xxviii, 28, 30, 43, 45, 70, 76, 87, 93
Parakeets, 38
Paria, famous for its tobacco, 48, 73; the high land of, 72, 75; *perota* or silver found in, 73
Paria, cape and strait of, 88, 94
Parker, Avice, Lady, evidence of, as to R. Dudley's birth, xlii, xliv. *See also* Erisa, Avice.
Parrots, 38, 71
Pelican Bay, in Trinidad, so named by R. Dudley, xxvi, 22, 70
Peregrine (al. *Bear*), the, R. Dudley's admiral, xix, 3
Perota, silver, in Paria, 73; in Guiana, 96
Philip of Spain, the, 49
Phillips, ——, one of R. Dudley's company, 8
Pico, island of, in the Azores, longitude reckoned from, 80, 90, 91
Pitch, lake of, in Trinidad, 86
Pitcher, Cape. *See* Espichel.
Plymouth (Plimworth, Plimmouth, etc.), 3, 4, 5, 75, 80, 81
Popham, Capt. George, joins Dudley at Trinidad, xxi, 43, 75; shows him the "discovery" of Guiana, 71
Port Peregrine, in Trinidad, so called by R. Dudley, 28, 43
Puerto Rico. *See* San Juan de Puerto Rico.

Race, Cape, in Newfoundland, 90
Ralegh, Sir Walter, reference to his *Discoverie of Guiana*, xiv, 72; relations of R. Dudley with, xxi; sends Capt. Whiddon to Trinidad, xxv; Dudley waits for him at Trinidad, 75
Ratcliffe, Thomas, Earl of Sussex, xlv
Regard, the, a carvel taken as prize, 28
Rich, Robert, Earl of Warwick, lix
Riodore, in West Africa, 15
Roca, Cape, in Portugal, 6, 82
Rooke, ——, at Florence, xlix
Roxo, Cape, in Puerto Rico, 76, 89

INDEX.

Sabiota, a river at the mouth of the Orinoco, 66. *See also* Cabota.
Sable (Sabels) island, 53
Sagres (Saker), Cape, in Portugal, 8
St. Elmo's Fire (Santelmo), or Corpo Santo, 54
St. Ives in Cornwall, R. Dudley lands at, 64, 77, 91
St. Vincent, Cape, 8, 82
Saker, a small cannon, lv, 60
Salisbury, Earl of. *See* Cecil, Sir Robert.
Salisbury, Magdalen, born Frodsham, witness in the case as to R. Dudley's legitimacy, xli, xliv, xlvi
Salvages, one of the Canary Islands, 82
Salvetti, Amerigo, Florentine Resident in England, lx
San Antonio or Sant' Antão, island of, Cape Verde, 19
San Domingo or Hispaniola, island of, 76, 89
San Giovanni Battista, ship built by R. Dudley in Italy, lvii
San José, town of, in Trinidad, xxiv, 87
San Juan de Puerto Rico, island of, 48, 49, 50, 76, 88
Santa Cruz, island of, near Puerto Rico, 49, 76, 88
Seawano, kingdom of, in Guiana, 72 ; a gold mine at Wackerew in, 73 ; river of, 93, 95
Seymour, Edward, Lord Beauchamp, l
Sheen House, co. Surrey, R. Dudley born at, iii
Sheffield, Douglas, Lady, mother of R. Dudley, ii-vi, xl-xlvi ; marries Sir Edw. Stafford, vi, xl
Sheffield, John, Lord Sheffield, ii
Sheffield, Robin, R. Dudley so called as a child, vi
Sherley, Thomas, x
Sidney, Robert, Lord Sidney of Penshurst, opposes R. Dudley's claim to legitimacy, xxxix ; made Earl of Leicester, lix
Silver (*perota*), in Paria, 73 ; in Guiana, 96
Simerones, of Trinidad, 71
Sisargas Islands (Sysarck), in Spain, 6
Somerset, Earl of. *See* Carr, Robert.
Southwell, Elizabeth, elopes with R. Dudley, xlvii ; her children by him, lix
Sorama, in or near Trinidad, 36
Southampton (Hampton), 2, 9

Spanish Tragedie, The, lines from, quoted during a sea-fight, 62
Stafford, Sir Edward, marries Lady Sheffield, vi, xl ; deposition of, as to R. Dudley's legitimacy, xlv
Star Chamber, case in the, as to R. Dudley's legitimacy, xxxix
Stoke Newington, co. Surrey, R. Dudley brought up at, vi
Stone, - , at Florence, xlix
Sussex, Earl of. *See* Ratcliffe, Thomas.

Tacarao, a green stone in Guiana, used for a charm, 72
Teneriffe (Tenerife), island of, 11, 82
Terceira, island of, in the Azores, 64
Testigos islands, 88
Thornton, Capt. Richard, voyage of, to Guiana, lxv, 95
Tivitivas, kingdom of, in Guiana, 74
Tobacco, 23 ; excellence of, in Paria, 48, 73
Tortoises on the Orinoco, 38
Trinidad, arrival of R. Dudley at, xxiv, 21, 70, 84 ; claimed by him for England, xxvi, 26, 33 ; map of, by Dudley, xxvi, lxv, 93 ; his dealings with the chief Indians, 44; his march across the island, 45, 71, 87; he leaves the island, 48, 76; vocabularies of the Arawaks of, 65, 78 ; description of, 71 ; the Caribs enemies to the natives of, 73; a high land, 85 ; currents, etc., on the S.W., 86
Tuscany, Cosmo II, Grand Duke of, lvii, lxi
Tuscany, Ferdinand I, Grand Duke of, receives R. Dudley at Florence, lvii ; sends an expedition to Guiana, lxv, 95
Tuscany, Ferdinand II, opposes reprisals on English merchants, lx ; R. Dudley's *Arcano del Mare*, etc., dedicated to, lxiii, 93

Ushant, island of, 81

Vavasour, Frances, contracted to R. Dudley, ix ; marries T. Sherley, x
Veriotaus (*sc.* Waraus?), a tribe at the mouth of the Orinoco, 74
Vincent, Capt., 24, 26, 29, 45 ; an "old and discreet soldier," 59 ; post of, in action at sea, 60

Wackerew, in Seawano, gold mine at, 73

INDEX.

Waliame, kingdom of, in Guiana, 72; great wealth of, **73**; gold mine at Orocoa in, 73
Walliana, a name of Guiana, 84, 93
Ward, Thomas, proctor, witness in the case as to R. Dudley's legitimacy, xli, xlii
Warwick, Earl of. *See* Dudley Ambrose; Rich, Robert.
Warwick, Leicester Hospital at, 61
Wentworth, Capt., 13, 24, 29, 69
Werinóca, the Indian name of the Orinoco, 66
Westmorland, Earl of. *See* Nevill, Edmund.
Weymouth (Waymouth), 10
Whales, abundance of, on the coast of Labrador, 53
Whiddon, Capt. Jacob, sent to Trinidad by Sir W. Ralegh, xxv
Windebank, (Winnebancke), [Francis], at Florence, xlix
Wood, Anthony, account of R. Dudley by, xii, lviii
Wood, Capt. Benjamin, xx, xxxvii, 8, 24, 31; made captain of a prize, 13, 69

Worinoche, Worinock, the Indian name for the Orinoco, 88, 93
Wotton, Sir Henry, ambassador at Venice, xlviii; character of, xlix
Wright, ——, one of R. Dudley's company, 22, 26
Wright, Edward, his *Certaine Errors in Navigation* quoted, xvii
Wyatt, Capt., narrative of R. Dudley's voyage, xiv, 1-66; commands the "maine battle of pike," 24, 45; sets up the royal arms, etc., on a plate of lead, xxvii, 26; in charge of the forces on land, 29, 44; strictness of, to Spanish prisoners, 50; sets the Spanish captain on shore, 52; an "old and discreet soldier," 59; post of, in action at sea, 60

Yguirie, kingdom of, 72; full of the metal *arara*, 73
Yorke, Capt., at Florence, xlix

Zacheo, Zechea, Zecchio (*sc.* Desecheo), island of, near Puerto Rico, 52, 76, 89

LONDON:
PRINTED AT THE BEDFORD PRESS, 20 AND 21, BEDFORDBURY, W.C.

THE HAKLUYT SOCIETY.

1900.

President.
Sir CLEMENTS MARKHAM, K.C.B., F.R.S., Pres. R.G.S.

Vice-Presidents.
The Right Hon. The Lord STANLEY of ALDERLEY.
Rear-Admiral Sir WILLIAM WHARTON, K.C.B., F.R.S.

Council.

C. RAYMOND BEAZLEY, M.A.	F. W. LUCAS.
Colonel G. EARL CHURCH.	A. P. MAUDSLAY.
Sir W. MARTIN CONWAY.	MAJOR M. NATHAN, C.M.G., R.E.
ALBERT GRAY.	E. J. PAYNE, M.A.
F. H. H. GUILLEMARD, M.A., M.D.	E. G. RAVENSTEIN.
EDWARD HEAWOOD, M.A.	HOWARD SAUNDERS.
DUDLEY F. A. HERVEY, C.M.G.	H. W. TRINDER.
Admiral Sir A. H. HOSKINS, G.C.B.	CHARLES WELCH, F.S.A.
J. SCOTT KELTIE, LL.D.	

Hon. Secretary and (*pro tem.*) Treasurer.
WILLIAM FOSTER, B.A., BORDEAN, HOLLY ROAD, WANSTEAD, N.E.

Bankers in London.
MESSRS. BARCLAY & Co., 1, PALL MALL EAST, S.W.

Bankers in New York.
THE MORTON TRUST CO., CORNER OF CEDAR AND NASSAU STREETS.

Agent for distribution, &c., of Volumes.
MR. B. QUARITCH, 15, PICCADILLY, W.

Annual Subscription.—One Guinea (in America five dollars

THE HAKLUYT SOCIETY, established in 1846, has for its object the printing of rare or unpublished Voyages and Travels. Books of this class are of the highest interest and value to students of history, geography, navigation, and ethnology; and many of them, especially the original narratives and translations of the Elizabethan and Stuart periods, are admirable examples of English prose at the stage of its most robust development.

The Society has not confined its selection to the books of English travellers, to a particular age, or to particular regions. Where the original is foreign, the work is given in English, fresh translations being made, except where it is possible to utilise the spirited renderings of the sixteenth or seventeenth century.

A hundred volumes have now been issued by the Society. The majority of these illustrate the history of the great age of discovery which forms the foundation of modern history. The discovery of AMERICA, and of particular portions of the two great western continents, is represented by the writings of COLUMBUS, AMERIGO VESPUCCI, CORTES and CHAMPLAIN, and by several of the early narratives from HAKLUYT'S collection. The works relating to the conquest of PERU, and to the condition of that country under the Incas, are numerous and of the highest value; similar interest attaches to STRACHEY'S *Virginia Britannia*, DE SOTO'S *Discovery of Florida*, and SIR ROBERT SCHOMBURGK'S edition of RALEIGH'S *Discoverie of Guiana*. The works relating to AFRICA already published comprise BARBOSA'S *Coasts of East Africa*, the *Portuguese Embassy to Abyssinia* of ALVAREZ, and *The Travels of Leo the Moor*. Notices of AUSTRALIA, INDIA, PERSIA, CHINA, JAPAN, etc., as they appeared in early times to European eyes, both before and after the discovery of the Cape route, are also included in the series, a well-known example being the work on *Cathay and the Way Thither*, contributed by a former President, SIR HENRY YULE. The search for the North-west and North-east Passages is recorded in the narratives of JENKINSON, DE VEER, FROBISHER, DAVIS, HUDSON, BAFFIN, etc.; whilst more extensive voyages are signalised by the great names of MAGELLAN, DRAKE, and HAWKINS.

The works selected by the Council for reproduction are printed (with rare exceptions) at full length. Each volume is placed in the charge of an editor especially competent—in many cases from personal acquaintance with the countries described—to give the reader such assistance as he needs for the elucidation of the text. Whenever possible, the interest of the volumes is increased by the addition of reproductions of contemporary portraits, maps, and other illustrations.

As these editorial services are rendered gratuitously, *the whole of the amount received from subscribers is expended in the preparation of the Society's publications*.

The subscription should be paid to the Society's Bankers on the 1st January in each year. This entitles the subscriber to receive, free of charge, the current publications of the Society. Usually two volumes are issued each year; but it is hoped to add from time to time a third volume, whenever the state of the funds will permit. Members have the sole privilege of purchasing sets of the previous publications; and the more recent of the Society's volumes are also reserved exclusively for its subscribers. In addition, they are allowed a special discount of 15 per cent. on the volumes permitted to be sold to the public. It may be mentioned that the publications of the Society tend to rise in value, and those which are out of print are now only to be obtained at high prices.

The present scale of charges for back volumes is as follows:—

To MEMBERS.—*Sets of the* FIRST SERIES, omitting Nos. 1-10, 12, 19, 25, 36, 37, to be sold for . . . . *net* **£30.**

 N.B.—*Most of the out-of-print volumes have been, or are being, reprinted as later volumes of the series.*
 Nos. 82-87, 90-100, at . . . . *net* **10s.**
 Nos. 88, 89, at . . . . *net* **15s**

To THE PUBLIC GENERALLY.—*A limited number of single copies* as follows:—
 Nos. 23, 26, 29, 31, 34, 40, 47, 50, at . . . . . **8s. 6d.**
 Nos. 21, 24, 28, 30, 35, 46, 48, 51, 53, 55, 56, 58, 60 to 81, at . . **10s.**
 Nos. 20, 27, 33, 38, 41 to 45, 49, 52, 57, at . . . . **15s.**
 Nos. 54 and 59, at . . . . **20s.**
 *** Subject in case of Members to a discount of 15%.
 The volumes of the SECOND SERIES *can only be obtained by paying the arrears of subscription.*

A list of works in preparation is given at page 11. The Secretary will be happy to furnish any further information that may be desired.

Gentlemen desiring to be enrolled as members should send their names to the Secretary. Applications for back volumes should be addressed to MR. QUARITCH.

WORKS ALREADY ISSUED.

FIRST SERIES.

1 The Observations of Sir Richard Hawkins, Knt.,
In his Voyage into the South Sea in 1593. Reprinted from the edition of 1622, and edited by Capt. C. R. D. BETHUNE, R.N., C.B.
(*First Edition out of print. See No.* 57.) *Issued for* 1848.

2—Select Letters of Columbus,
With Original Documents relating to the Discovery of the New World. Translated and Edited by R. H. MAJOR.
(*First Edition out of print. See No.* 43.) *Issued for* 1849.

3—The Discoverie of the Empire of Guiana.
By Sir Walter Raleigh, Knt. Edited by SIR ROBERT H. SCHOMBURGK, Ph.D.
(*First Edition out of print. Second Edition in preparation.*) *Issued for* 1850.

4—Sir Francis Drake his Voyage, 1595,
By Thomas Maynarde, together with the Spanish Account of Drake's attack on Puerto Rico. Edited by W. D. COOLEY.
(*Out of print.*) *Issued for* 1850.

5—Narratives of Early Voyages to the North-West.
Edited by THOMAS RUNDALL.
(Out of print.) *Issued for* 1851.

6—The Historie of Travaile into Virginia Britannia,
Expressing the Cosmographie and Commodities of the Country, together with the manners and customs of the people, collected by William Strachey, Gent., the first Secretary of the Colony. Edited by R. H. MAJOR.
(Out of print.) *Issued for* 1851.

7 Divers Voyages touching the Discovery of America
And the Islands adjacent, collected and published by Richard Hakluyt, Prebendary of Bristol, in the year 1582. Edited by JOHN WINTER JONES.
(Out of print.) *Issued for* 1852.

8—A Collection of Documents on Japan.
With a Commentary by THOMAS RUNDALL.
(Out of print.) *Issued for* 1852.

9—The Discovery and Conquest of Florida,
By Don Ferdinando de Soto. Translated out of Portuguese by Richard Hakluyt; and Edited by W. B. RYE.
(Out of print.) *Issued for* 1853.

10—Notes upon Russia,
Being a Translation from the Earliest Account of that Country, entitled Rerum Muscoviticarum Commentarii, by the Baron Sigismund von Herberstein, Ambassador from the Court of Germany to the Grand Prince Vasiley Ivanovich, in the years 1517 and 1526. Two Volumes. Translated and Edited by R. H. MAJOR. Vol. 1.
(Out of print.) *Issued for* 1853.

11—The Geography of Hudson's Bay,
Being the Remarks of Captain W. Coats, in many Voyages to that locality, between the years 1727 and 1751. With Extracts from the Log of Captain Middleton on his Voyage for the Discovery of the North-west Passage, in H.M.S. "Furnace," in 1741-2. Edited by JOHN BARROW, F.R.S., F.S.A.
Issued for 1854.

12—Notes upon Russia.
Vol. 2. *(Out of print.)* *Issued for* 1854.

13—Three Voyages by the North-East,
Towards Cathay and China, undertaken by the Dutch in the years 1594, 1595 and 1596, with their Discovery of Spitzbergen, their residence of ten months in Novaya Zemlya, and their safe return in two open boats. By Gerrit de Veer. Edited by C. T. BEKE, Ph.D., F.S.A.
(See also No. 54.) *Issued for* 1855.

14-15—The History of the Great and Mighty Kingdom of China and the Situation Thereof.
Compiled by the Padre Juan Gonzalez de Mendoza. Reprinted from the Early Translation of R. Parke, and Edited by SIR GEORGE T. STAUNTON, Bart. With an Introduction by R. H. MAJOR. 2 vols.
Issued for 1855.

16—The World Encompassed by Sir Francis Drake.
Being his next Voyage to that to Nombre de Dios. Collated with an unpublished Manuscript of Francis Fletcher, Chaplain to the Expedition. Edited by W. S. W. VAUX, M.A. *Issued for* 1856.

17—The History of the Tartar Conquerors who subdued China.
From the French of the Père D'Orleans, 1688. Translated and Edited by the EARL OF ELLESMERE. With an Introduction by R. H. MAJOR.
Issued for 1856.

18—A Collection of Early Documents on Spitzbergen and Greenland.
Edited by ADAM WHITE. *Issued for* 1857.

19—The Voyage of Sir Henry Middleton to Bantam and the Maluco Islands.
From the rare Edition of 1606. Edited by BOLTON CORNEY.
(*Out of print*). *Issued for* 1857.

20—Russia at the Close of the Sixteenth Century.
Comprising "The Russe Commonwealth" by Dr. Giles Fletcher, and Sir Jerome Horsey's Travels. Edited by E. A. BOND.
Issued for 1858.

21—The Travels of Girolamo Benzoni in America, in 1542-56.
Translated and Edited by ADMIRAL W. H. SMYTH, F.R.S., F.S.A.
Issued for 1858.

22—India in the Fifteenth Century.
Being a Collection of Narratives of Voyages to India in the century preceding the Portuguese discovery of the Cape of Good Hope; from Latin, Persian, Russian, and Italian Sources. Edited by R. H. MAJOR.
Issued for 1859.

23—Narrative of a Voyage to the West Indies and Mexico,
In the years 1599-1602, with Maps and Illustrations. By Samuel Champlain. Translated from the original and unpublished Manuscript, with a Biographical Notice and Notes by ALICE WILMERE. *Issued for* 1859.

24—Expeditions into the Valley of the Amazons
During the Sixteenth and Seventeenth Centuries: containing the Journey of Gonzalo Pizarro, from the Royal Commentaries of Garcilasso Inca de la Vega; the Voyage of Francisco de Orellana, from the General History of Herrera; and the Voyage of Cristoval de Acuna. Translated and Edited by CLEMENTS R. MARKHAM. *Issued for* 1860.

25—Early Indications of Australia.
A Collection of Documents shewing the Early Discoveries of Australia to the time of Captain Cook. Edited by R. H. MAJOR.
(*Out of print.*) *Issued for* 1860.

26—The Embassy of Ruy Gonzalez de Clavijo to the Court of Timour, 1403-6.
Translated and Edited by CLEMENTS R. MARKHAM.
Issued for 1861.

27—Henry Hudson the Navigator.
The Original Documents in which his career is recorded. Edited by GEORGE ASHER, LL.D. *Issued for* 1861.

28—The Expedition of Ursua and Aguirre,
In search of El Dorado and Omagua, A.D. 1560-61. Translated from the "Sexta Noticia Historiale" of Fray Pedro Simon, by W. BOLLAERT, with an Introduction by CLEMENTS R. MARKHAM.
Issued for 1862.

29—The Life and Acts of Don Alonzo Enriquez de Guzman.
Translated and Edited by CLEMENTS R. MARKHAM.
Issued for 1862.

30—Discoveries of the World

From their first original unto the year of our Lord 1555. By Antonio Galvano. Reprinted, with the original Portuguese text, and edited by VICE-ADMIRAL BETHUNE, C.B. *Issued for* 1863.

31—Marvels described by Friar Jordanus,

From a parchment manuscript of the Fourteenth Century, in Latin. Edited by COLONEL H. YULE, C.B. *Issued for* 1863.

32—The Travels of Ludovico di Varthema

In Syria, Arabia, Persia, India, etc., during the Sixteenth Century. Translated by J. WINTER JONES, F.S.A., and Edited by the REV. GEORGE PERCY BADGER. *Issued for* 1864.

33—The Travels of Cieza de Leon in 1532-50

From the Gulf of Darien to the City of La Plata, contained in the first part of his Chronicle of Peru (Antwerp, 1554). Translated and Edited by CLEMENTS R. MARKHAM. *Issued for* 1864.

34—The Narrative of Pascual de Andagoya.

Containing the earliest notice of Peru. Translated and Edited by CLEMENTS R. MARKHAM. *Issued for* 1865.

35—The Coasts of East Africa and Malabar

In the beginning of the Sixteenth Century, by Duarte Barbosa. Translated from an early Spanish manuscript by the HON. HENRY STANLEY. *Issued for* 1865.

36-37—Cathay and the Way Thither.

A Collection of all minor notices of China, previous to the Sixteenth Century. Translated and Edited by COLONEL H. YULE, C.B. Two Vols. (*Out of print.*) *Issued for* 1866.

38—The Three Voyages of Sir Martin Frobisher.

With a Selection from Letters now in the State Paper Office. Edited by REAR-ADMIRAL COLLINSON, C.B. *Issued for* 1867.

39—The Philippine Islands,

Moluccas, Siam, Cambodia, Japan, and China, at the close of the 16th Century. By Antonia de Morga. Translated from the Spanish, with Notes, by the LORD STANLEY of Alderley. *Issued for* 1868.

40—The Fifth Letter of Hernan Cortes

To the Emperor Charles V., containing an Account of his Expedition to Honduras in 1525-26. Translated from the Spanish by DON PASCUAL DE GAYANGOS. *Issued for* 1868.

41—The Royal Commentaries of the Yncas.

By the Ynca Garcilasso de la Vega. Translated and Edited by CLEMENTS R. MARKHAM. Vol. I. *Issued for* 1869.

42—The Three Voyages of Vasco da Gama,

And his Viceroyalty, from the Lendas da India of Gaspar Correa; accompanied by original documents. Translated and Edited by the LORD STANLEY of Alderley. *Issued for* 1869.

43—Select Letters of Christopher Columbus,

With other Original Documents relating to his Four Voyages to the New World. Translated and Edited by R. H. MAJOR. 2nd Edition (see No. 2). *Issued for* 1870.

44 History of the Imâms and Seyyids of 'Omân,
By Salil-Ibn-Razîk, from A.D. 661-1856. Translated from the original Arabic, and Edited, with a continuation of the History down to 1870, by the REV. GEORGE PERCY BADGER. *Issued for* 1870.

45—The Royal Commentaries of the Yncas.
Vol. 2. *Issued for* 1871.

46—The Canarian,
Or Book of the Conquest and Conversion of the Canarians in the year 1402, by Messire Jean de Bethencourt, Kt. Composed by Pierre Bontier and Jean le Verrier. Translated and Edited by R. H. MAJOR.
Issued for 1871.

47—Reports on the Discovery of Peru.
Translated and Edited by CLEMENTS R. MARKHAM, C.B.
Issued for 1872.

48—Narratives of the Rites and Laws of the Yncas.
Translated and Edited by CLEMENTS R. MARKHAM, C.B., F.R.S.
Issued for 1872.

49—Travels to Tana and Persia,
By Josafa Barbaro and Ambrogio Contarini ; Edited by LORD STANLEY of Alderley. With Narratives of other Italian Travels in Persia. Translated and Edited by CHARLES GREY. *Issued for* 1873.

50 Voyages of the Zeni
To the Northern Seas in the Fourteenth Century. Translated and Edited by R. H. MAJOR. *Issued for* 1873.

51—The Captivity of Hans Stade of Hesse in 1547-55,
Among the Wild Tribes of Eastern Brazil. Translated by ALBERT TOOTAL, Esq., and annotated by SIR RICHARD F. BURTON.
Issued for 1874.

52—The First Voyage Round the World by Magellan.
Translated from the Accounts of Pigafetta and other contemporary writers. Edited by LORD STANLEY of Alderley.
Issued for 1874.

53—The Commentaries of the Great Afonso Dalboquerque,
Second Viceroy of India. Translated from the Portuguese Edition of 1774, and Edited by WALTER DE GRAY BIRCH, F.R.S.L. Vol. 1.
Issued for 1875.

54—Three Voyages to the North-East.
Second Edition of Gerrit de Veer's Three Voyages to the North-East by Barents. Edited by Lieut. KOOLEMANS BEYNEN, of the Royal Dutch Navy.
Issued for 1876.

55—The Commentaries of the Great Afonso Dalboquerque.
Vol. 2. *Issued for* 1875.

56—The Voyages of Sir James Lancaster.
With Abstracts of Journals of Voyages preserved in the India Office, and the Voyage of Captain John Knight to seek the N.W. Passage. Edited by CLEMENTS R. MARKHAM, C.B., F.R.S.
Issued for 1877.

57—The Observations of Sir Richard Hawkins, Knt.,
In his Voyage into the South Sea in 1593, with the Voyages of his grandfather William, his father Sir John, and his cousin William Hawkins. Second Edition (see No. 1). Edited by CLEMENTS R. MARKHAM, C.B., F.R.S. *Issued for* 1877.

58—The Bondage and Travels of Johann Schiltberger,
From his capture at the battle of Nicopolis in 1396 to his escape and return to Europe in 1427. Translated by Commander J. BUCHAN TELFER, R.N.; with Notes by Professor B. BRUUN. *Issued for* 1878.

59—The Voyages and Works of John Davis the Navigator.
Edited by Captain ALBERT H. MARKHAM, R.N. *Issued for* 1878.

The Map of the World, A.D. 1600.
Called by Shakspere "The New Map, with the Augmentation of the Indies." To illustrate the Voyages of John Davis. *Issued for* 1878.

60-61—The Natural and Moral History of the Indies.
By Father Joseph de Acosta. Reprinted from the English Translated Edition of Edward Grimston, 1604; and Edited by CLEMENTS R. MARKHAM, C.B., F.R.S. Two Vols. *Issued for* 1879.

Map of Peru.
To Illustrate Nos. 33, 41, 45, 60, and 61. *Issued for* 1879.

62—The Commentaries of the Great Afonso Dalboquerque.
Vol. 3. *Issued for* 1880.

63 The Voyages of William Baffin, 1612-1622.
Edited by CLEMENTS R. MARKHAM, C.B., F.R.S. *Issued for* 1880.

64—Narrative of the Portuguese Embassy to Abyssinia
During the years 1520-1527. By Father Francisco Alvarez. Translated and Edited by LORD STANLEY of Alderley. *Issued for* 1881.

65—The History of the Bermudas or Somer Islands.
Attributed to Captain Nathaniel Butler. Edited by General Sir J. HENRY LEFROY, R.A., K.C.M.G. *Issued for* 1881.

66-67—The Diary of Richard Cocks,
Cape-Merchant in the English Factory in Japan, 1615-1622. Edited by EDWARD MAUNDE THOMPSON. Two Vols. *Issued for* 1882.

68—The Second Part of the Chronicle of Peru.
By Pedro de Cieza de Leon. Translated and Edited by CLEMENTS R. MARKHAM, C.B., F.R.S. *Issued for* 1883.

69—The Commentaries of the Great Afonso Dalboquerque.
Vol. 4. *Issued for* 1883.

70-71—The Voyage of John Huyghen van Linschoten to the East Indies.
From the Old English Translation of 1598. The First Book, containing his Description of the East. Edited by A. C. BURNELL, Ph.D., C.I.E., and P. A. TIELE, of Utrecht. *Issued for* 1884.

72-73—Early Voyages and Travels to Russia and Persia,
By Anthony Jenkinson and other Englishmen, with some account of the first Intercourse of the English with Russia and Central Asia by way of the Caspian Sea. Edited by E. DELMAR MORGAN, and C. H. COOTE. *Issued for* 1885.

74—The Diary of William Hedges, Esq.,
Afterwards Sir William Hedges, during his Agency in Bengal; as well as on his Voyage out and Return Overland (1681-1687). Transcribed for the Press, with Introductory Notes, etc., by R. BARLOW, and Illustrated by copious Extracts from Unpublished Records, etc., by Col. Sir H. YULE, K.C.S.I., R.E., C.B., LL.D. Vol. 1, The Diary. *Issued for* 1886.

75—The Diary of William Hedges, Esq.
Vol. 2. Sir H. Yule's Extracts from Unpublished Records, etc.
Issued for 1886.

76-77—The Voyage of François Pyrard to the East Indies,
The Maldives, the Moluccas and Brazil. Translated into English from the Third French Edition of 1619, and Edited by ALBERT GRAY, assisted by H. C. P. BELL. Vol. 1. Vol. 2, Part I.
Issued for 1887.

78 The Diary of William Hedges, Esq.
Vol. 3. Sir H. Yule's Extracts from Unpublished Records, etc.
Issued for 1888.

79—Tractatus de Globis, et eorum usu.
A Treatise descriptive of the Globes constructed by Emery Molyneux, and Published in 1592. By Robert Hues. Edited by CLEMENTS R. MARKHAM, C.B., F.R.S. To which is appended,

Sailing Directions for the Circumnavigation of England,
And for a Voyage to the Straits of Gibraltar. From a Fifteenth Century MS. Edited by JAMES GAIRDNER; with a Glossary by E. DELMAR MORGAN.
Issued for 1888.

80—The Voyage of François Pyrard to the East Indies, etc.
Vol. 2, Part II. *Issued for* 1889.

81—The Conquest of La Plata, 1535-1555.
I.—Voyage of Ulrich Schmidt to the Rivers La Plata and Paraguai. II.—The Commentaries of Alvar Nunez Cabeza de Vaca. Edited by DON LUIS L. DOMINGUEZ.
Issued for 1889.

82-83—The Voyage of François Leguat
To Rodriguez, Mauritius, Java, and the Cape of Good Hope. Edited by Captain PASFIELD OLIVER. Two Vols.
Issued for 1890.

84-85—The Travels of Pietro della Valle to India.
From the Old English Translation of 1664, by G. Havers. Edited by EDWARD GREY. Two Vols.
Issued for 1891.

86—The Journal of Christopher Columbus
During his First Voyage (1492-93), and Documents relating to the Voyages of John Cabot and Gaspar Corte Real. Translated and Edited by CLEMENTS R. MARKHAM, C.B., F.R.S.
Issued for 1892.

87—Early Voyages and Travels in the Levant.
I.—The Diary of Master Thomas Dallam, 1599-1600. II.—Extracts from the Diaries of Dr. John Covel, 1670-1679. With some Account of the Levant Company of Turkey Merchants. Edited by J. THEODORE BENT, F.S.A., F.R.G.S.
Issued for 1892.

88-89—The Voyages of Captain Luke Foxe and Captain Thomas James
In Search of a N.-W. Passage, 1631-32; with Narratives of Earlier N.-W. Voyages. Edited by MILLER CHRISTY, F.L.S. Two Vols.
Issued for 1893.

90—The Letters of Amerigo Vespucci
And other Documents relating to his Career. Translated and Edited by CLEMENTS R. MARKHAM, C.B., F.R.S.
Issued for 1894.

91—The Voyage of Pedro Sarmiento to the Strait of Magellan, 1579-80.
Translated and Edited, with Illustrative Documents and Introduction, by CLEMENTS R. MARKHAM, C.B., F.R.S.
Issued for 1894.

92-93-94—The History and Description of Africa,
And of the Notable Things Therein Contained. The Travels of Leo Africanus the Moor, from the English translation of John Pory (1600). Edited by ROBERT BROWN, M.A., Ph.D. Three Vols.
Issued for 1895.

95—The Discovery and Conquest of Guinea.
Written by Gomes Eannes de Azurara. Translated and Edited by C. RAYMOND BEAZLEY, M.A., and EDGAR PRESTAGE, B.A. Vol. 1.
Issued for 1896.

96-97—Danish Arctic Expeditions.
Book 1. The Danish Expeditions to Greenland, 1605-07; with James Hall's Voyage in 1612. Edited by C. C. A. GOSCH. *Issued for* 1896.
Book 2. Jens Munk's Voyage to Hudson's Bay in 1619-20. Edited by C. C. A. GOSCH. *Issued for* 1897.

98—The Topographia Christiana of Cosmas Indicopleustes.
Translated and Edited by J. W. MCCRINDLE, M.A., M.R.A.S.
Issued for 1897.

99—The First Voyage of Vasco da Gama.
Translated from the Portuguese, with an Introduction and Notes, by E. G. RAVENSTEIN. *Issued for* 1898.

100—The Discovery and Conquest of Guinea.
Written by Gomes Eannes de Azurara. Translated and Edited by C. RAYMOND BEAZLEY, M.A., and EDGAR PRESTAGE, B.A. Vol. 2.
Issued for 1898.

SECOND SERIES.

1-2—The Embassy of Sir Thomas Roe to the Court of the Great Mogul, 1615-19.
Edited from Contemporary Records by WILLIAM FOSTER, B.A.
Issued for 1899.

3—The Voyage of Sir Robert Dudley to the West Indies and Guiana in 1594.
Edited by GEO. F. WARNER, M.A., F.S.A., Assistant Keeper of Manuscripts, British Museum. *Issued for* 1899.

OTHER WORKS UNDERTAKEN BY EDITORS.

The Journeys of William of Rubruck and John of Pian de Carpine to Tartary in the 13th century. Translated and Edited by the Hon. W. W. ROCKHILL.

Raleigh's Empire of Guiana. Second Edition (see No. 3). Edited, with Notes, etc., by EVERARD F. IM THURN, C.B., C.M.G.

The Strange Adventures of Andrew Battell of Leigh in Essex. Edited by E. G. RAVENSTEIN.

Histoire de la Grande Isle Madagascar, par le Sieur De Flacourt, 1661. Translated and Edited by Captain S. PASFIELD OLIVER.

The Voyages of Cadamosto, the Venetian, along the West Coast of Africa, in the years 1455 and 1456. Translated from the earliest Italian text of 1507, and Edited by H. YULE OLDHAM, M.A., F.R.G.S.

The Voyages of the Earl of Cumberland, from the Records prepared by order of the Countess of Pembroke. Edited by W. DE GRAY BIRCH, LL.D., F.S.A.

The Voyage of Alvaro de Mendaña to the Solomon Islands in 1568. Edited by the LORD AMHERST OF HACKNEY and BASIL H. THOMSON.

De Laët's Commentarius de Imperio Magni Mogolis (1631). Translated and Edited by Sir ROPER LETHBRIDGE, K.C.I.E., M.A.

The Voyages of Willoughby and Chancellor to the White Sea, with some account of the earliest intercourse between England and Russia. Reprinted from Hakluyt's Voyages, with Notes and Introduction by E. DELMAR MORGAN.

Dr. John Fryer's New Account of East India and Persia (1698). Edited by ARTHUR T. PRINGLE.

The Expedition of Hernan Cortes to Honduras in 1525-26. Second Edition (see No. 40), with added matter. Translated and Edited by A. P. MAUDSLAY.

The Letters of Pietro Della Valle from Persia, &c. Translated and Edited by MAJOR M. NATHAN, C.M.G., R.E.

The Journey of Pedro Teixeira from India to Italy by land, 1604-05; with his Chronicle of the Kings of Ormus. Translated and Edited by W. F. SINCLAIR, late I.C.S.

The First English Voyage to Japan, 1611-14. Edited by H. E. SIR ERNEST M. SATOW, K.C.M.G.

LAWS OF THE HAKLUYT SOCIETY.

I. The object of this Society shall be to print, for distribution among its members, rare and valuable Voyages, Travels, Naval Expeditions, and other geographical records, from an early period to the beginning of the eighteenth century.

II. The Annual Subscription shall be One Guinea (for America, five dollars, U.S. currency), payable in advance on the 1st January.

III. Each member of the Society, having paid his Subscription, shall be entitled to a copy of every work produced by the Society, and to vote at the general meetings within the period subscribed for; and if he do not signify, before the close of the year, his wish to resign, he shall be considered as a member for the succeeding year.

IV. The management of the Society's affairs shall be vested in a Council consisting of twenty-two members, viz., a President, two Vice-Presidents, a Treasurer, a Secretary, and seventeen ordinary members, to be elected annually; but vacancies occurring between the general meetings shall be filled up by the Council.

V. A General Meeting of the Subscribers shall be held annually. The Secretary's Report on the condition and proceedings of the Society shall be then read, and the meeting shall proceed to elect the Council for the ensuing year.

VI. At each Annual Election, three of the old Council shall retire.

VII. The Council shall meet when necessary for the dispatch of business, three forming a quorum, including the Secretary; the Chairman having a casting vote.

VIII. Gentlemen preparing and editing works for the Society, shall receive twenty-five copies of such works respectively.

LIST OF MEMBERS.

1900.

Aberdare, The Right Hon. Lord, Longwood, Winchester.
Adelaide Public Library, per Messrs. Kegan Paul, Trench, Trübner & Co.
Admiralty, The (2 copies), per Messrs. Eyre and Spottiswoode.
Advocates' Library, Edinburgh, per Mr. Eccles, 96, Great Russell-street.
Alexander, W. L., Esq., Pinkieburn, Musselburgh, N.B.
All Souls College, Oxford.
American Geographical Society, 11, West 29th-street, New York City, U.S.A.
Amherst, of Hackney, The Right Hon. Lord, Didlington Hall, Brandon, Norfolk.
Antiga Casa Bertrand, José Bastos, 73, Rua Garrett, Lisbon.
Antiquaries, the Society of, Burlington House, Piccadilly, W.
Army and Navy Club, 36, Pall-mall.
Athenæum Club, Pall Mall.

Baer. Joseph & Co., Messrs., per Messrs. Epstein, 47, Holborn Viaduct, E.C.
Bain, Mr., 1, Haymarket, S.W.
Ball, John B., Esq., Ashburton Cottage, Putney Heath, S.W.
Barclay, Hugh G., Esq., Colney Hall, Norwich.
Barlow. R. Fred., Esq., 71, Marine Parade, Worthing, Sussex.
Basano, Marquis de, per Messrs. Hatchard, Piccadilly W.
Basset, M. René, Correspondant de l'Institut de France, Directeur de l'Ecole supérieure des lettres d'Alger, L'Agha 77, rue Michelet, Alger-Mustapha.
Baxter, James Phinney, Esq., 61, Deering-street, Portland, Maine, U.S.A.
Beaumont, Rear-Admiral L. A., 3, Sloane-gardens, S.W.
Beazley, C. Raymond, Esq., 13, The Paragon, Blackheath, S.E.
Belhaven and Stenton, Col. the Lord, R.E., 41, Lennox-gardens, S.W.
Berlin Geographical Society, per Messrs. Sampson Low.
Berlin, the Royal Library of, per Messrs. Asher and Co.
Berlin University, Geographical Institute of (Baron von Richthofen), 6, Schinkelplatz, Berlin, W., per Messrs. Sampson Low.
Birch, Dr. W. de G., British Museum.
Birmingham Central Free Library, Ratcliff-place, Birmingham.
Birmingham Old Library (The), Birmingham.
Bodleian Library, Oxford *(copies presented)*.
Bonaparte, H. H. Prince Roland, 10, Avenue d'Jéna, Paris.
Boston Athenæum Library, U.S.A., per Messrs. Kegan Paul.
Boston Public Library, per Messrs. Kegan Paul.
Bowdoin College, Brunswick, Maine, U.S.A., per Messrs. Kegan Paul.
Bower, Major Hamilton, per Messrs. Grindlay & Co., 54, Parliament Street.
Bowring, Thos. B., Esq., 7, Palace Gate, Kensington, W.
Brewster, Charles O., Esq., University Club, New York City, U.S.A.
Brighton Public Library.
Brine, Vice-Admiral Lindesay.
British Guiana Royal Agricultural and Commercial Society, Georgetown, [Demerara.
British Museum *(copies presented)*.
Brock, Robert C. H., Esq., 1612, Walnut-street, Philadelphia.
Brodrick, Hon. G., Merton College, Oxford.
Brooke, Thos., Esq., Armitage Bridge, Huddersfield.
Brookline Public Library, Mass., U.S.A.
Brooklyn Mercantile Library, per Mr. E. G. Allen.
Brown, Arthur W. W., Esq., 37, Evelyn Mansions, Carlisle-place, Victoria-street, S.W.
Brown, General J. Marshall, 218, Middle-street, Portland, Maine, U.S.A.

Brown, H. T., Esq., Roodeye House, Chester.
Brown, J. Allen, Esq., J.P., 7, Kent-gardens, Ealing.
Brown, J. Nicholas, Esq., per Messrs. Ellis & Elvey, 29, New Bond-st., W.
Brown University, Providence, Rhode Island (H. L. Koopman, Librarian).
Buda-Pesth, the Geographical Institute of the University of.
Bunting, W. L. Esq., The Steps, Bromsgrove.
Burgess, Jas., Esq., C.I.E., LL.D., 22, Seton-place, Edinburgh.
Burns, J. W., Esq., Kilmahew, Dumbartonshire.
Buxton, F. North, Esq., Knighton, Buckhurst-hill.

Cambridge University Library, per Mr. Eccles.
Canada, The Parliament Library, per Mr. E. G. Allen.
Cardiff Public Library, Cardiff (J. Ballinger, Esq., Librarian).
Carles, W. R., Esq., British Consulate, Tientsin, China.
Carlton Club, Pall-mall.
Carlisle, The Rt. Hon. the Earl of, Naworth Castle, Bampton, Cumberland.
Carnegie Library, Pittsburgh, U.S.A., per Mr. Stechert.
Cawston, Geo., Esq., Warnford Court, Throgmorton-street, E.C.
Chamberlain, Right Hon. Joseph, M.P., 40, Princes-gardens, S.W.
Chetham's Library, Hunt's Bank, Manchester.
Chicago Public Library, per Mr. B. F. Stevens.
Christ Church, Oxford.
Christiania University Library, c/o Messrs. T. Bennett and Sons, Christiania, per Messrs. Cassell and Co., Ludgate Hill.
Church, Col. G. Earl, 216, Cromwell-road, S.W.
Cincinnati Public Library, Ohio, U.S.A.
Clark, J. W., Esq., Scroope House, Trumpington-street, Cambridge.
Colgan, Nathaniel, Esq., 1, Belgrave-road, Rathmines, Dublin.
Colonial Office (The), Downing-street, S.W.
Constable, Archibald, Esq., India.
Conway, Sir W. Martin, The Red House, Hornton-street, W.
Cooper, Lieut.-Col. E. H., 42, Portman-square, W.
Copenhagen Royal Library, c/o Messrs. Lehman and Stage, Copenhagen, per Messrs. Sampson Low.
Cora, Professor Guido, M.A., Via Goito, 2, Rome.
Cornell University, per Mr. E. G. Allen.
Corning, C. R., Esq. } Vesaleanum, Bâle, Switzerland.
Corning, H. K., Esq.
Cortissoz, Royal, Esq., Editorial Room, *New York Tribune*, New York, U.S.A.
Cow, J., Esq., Elfinsward, Hayward's Heath.
Cruising Club, The, 40, Chancery Lane, W.C.
Cunningham, Lieut.-Col. G., Junior U.S. Club, Charles-street, S.W.
Curzon of Kedleston, Right Hon. Lord, Carlton-gardens, S.W.

Dalton, Rev. Canon J. N., M.A., C.M.G., The Cloisters, Windsor.
Danish Royal Naval Library, per Messrs. Sampson Low (Foreign Dept.).
Davis, Hon. N. Darnell, C.M.G., Georgetown, Demerara, British Guiana.
De Bertodano, B., Esq., 22, Chester-terrace, Regent's-park, N.W.
Derby, The Earl of, c/o the Rev. J. Richardson, Knowsley, Prescot.
Detroit Public Library, Michigan, U.S.A.
Dijon University Library, Rue Monge, Dijon.
Dorpat University, per Herr Koehler, 21, Täubchenweg, Leipzig.
Doubleday, H. Arthur, Esq., 2, Whitehall-gardens, S.W.
Dresden Geographical Society, per Herr P. E. Richter, Kleine Brüdergasse, 11, Dresden.
Droutskoy Lubetsky, S.A.S. le Prince, Kovensky per, 2, St. Petersburg.
Ducie, The Right Hon. Earl, F.R.S., Tortworth Court, Falfield.

Eames, Wilberforce, Esq., Lenox Library, 890, Fifth-avenue, New York, U.S.A., per Mr. B. F. Stevens.
Edinburgh Public Library.
Edwards, Francis, Esq., 83, High-street, Marylebone, W.
Ellsworth, James W., Esq., 2, West 16th Street, New York, U.S.A.
Elton, Charles I., Esq., Q.C., F.S.A., 10, Cranley-place, Onslow-square, S.W.

Faber, Reginald S., Esq., 90, Regent's Park-road, N.W.
Fanshawe, Admiral Sir Edw., G.C.B., 74, Cromwell-road, S.W.
Fellows Athenæum, per Messrs. Kegan Paul, Trench, Trübner, & Co.
Ferguson, D. W., Esq., 5, Bedford-place, Croydon.
Field, W. Hildreth, Esq., 923, Madison-avenue, New York City, U.S.A.
Fisher, Arthur, Esq., St. Aubyn's, Tiverton, Devon.
Fitzgerald, Edward A., Esq., per Mr. Jas. Bain, 1, Haymarket, S.W.
Foreign Office (The), per Messrs. Eyre and Spottiswoode.
Foreign Office of Germany, Berlin, per Messrs. Asher and Co.
Forrest, G. W., Esq., C.I.E., Savile Club, 107, Piccadilly, W.
Foster, William, Esq., India Office, S.W.
French, H. B., Esq., 429, Arch Street, Philadelphia, U.S.A.

Georg, Mons. H., Lyons, per Messrs. Sampson Low.
George, C. W., Esq., 51, Hampton-road, Bristol.
Gladstone Library, National Liberal Club, Whitehall-place, S.W.
Glasgow University Library, per Mr. Billings, 59, Old Bailey, E.C.
Godman, F. Ducane, Esq., D.C.L., F.R.S., 10, Chandos-street, Cavendish-square, W.
Gosch, C. A., Esq., 21, Stanhope-gardens, S.W.
Gosset, General M. W. E., C.B., Island Bridge House, Dublin.
Göttingen University Library, per Messrs. Asher and Co.
Grant-Duff, Rt. Hon. Sir M. E., G.C.S.I., 11, Chelsea Embankment, S.W.
Gray, Albert, Esq., Catherine Lodge, Trafalgar Square, Chelsea, S.W.
Gray, M. H., Esq., India-rubber Company, Silvertown, Essex.
Greever, C. O., Esq., 1345, East Ninth-street, Des Moines, Iowa.
Grosvenor Library, Buffalo, U.S.A.
Guildhall Library, E.C.
Guillemard, Arthur G., Esq., Eltham, Kent.
Guillemard, F. Henry H., Esq., M.A., M.D., The Old Mill House, Trumpington, Cambridge.

Haig, Maj.-General Malcolm R., Rossweide, Davos Platz, Switzerland.
Hamburg Commerz-Bibliothek, c/o Herrn Friederichsen and Co., Hamburg, per Messrs. Drolenvaux and Bremner, 36, Gt. Tower-street, E.C.
Hannen, The Hon. H., Holne Cott, Ashburton, South Devon.
Harmsworth, A. C., Esq., Elmwood, St. Peter's, Kent.
Harrison, Edwin, Esq., Church Gates, Cheshunt.
Harvard College, Cambridge, Massachusetts, per Messrs. Kegan Paul.
Harvie-Brown, J. A., Esq., Dunipace, Larbert, Stirlingshire, N.B.
Haswell, Geo. H., Esq., Ashleigh, Hamstead Road, Handsworth, Birmingham.
Hawkesbury, The Rt. Hon. Lord, 2, Carlton House-terrace, S.W.
Heap, Ralph, Esq., 1, Brick-court, Temple, E.C.
Heawood, Edward, Esq., M.A., F.R.G.S., 3, Underhill-road, Lordship-lane, S.E.
Hervey, Dudley F. A., Esq., C.M.G., 24, Pembroke-gardens, Kensington.
Hiersemann, Herr Karl W., 3, Königsstrasse, Leipzig, per Mr. Young T. Pentland, 38, West Smithfield, E.C.
Hill, Professor G. W., West Nyack, New York.
Hippisley, A. E., Esq., c/o J. D. Campbell, Esq., C.M.G., 26, Old Queen-st., S.W.
Hobhouse, C. E. H., Esq., The Ridge, Corsham, Wilts.
Horner, J. F. Fortescue, Esq., Mells Park, Frome, Somersetshire, per Mr. J. Bain.

Hoskins, Admiral Sir Anthony H., G.C.B., 17, Montagu-square, W.
Hoyt Public Library, per Messrs. Sotheran and Co., 140, Strand.
Hubbard, Hon. Gardiner G., 1328, Connecticut-avenue, Washington, D.C.
Hudson, John E., Esq., 125, Milk-street, Boston, Mass., U.S.A.
Hull Public Library (W. F. Lawton, Esq., Librarian).
Hull Subscription Library, per Messrs. Foster, Fore-street.

Im Thurn, E. F., Esq., C.B., C.M.G., 23, Edwardes-square, Kensington, W.
India Office (21 *copies*).
Inner Temple, Hon. Society of the (J. E. L. Pickering, Esq., Librarian).

Jackson, Major H.M., R.E., 3, Ravelston Place, Edinburgh.
James, Arthur C., Esq., 92, Park-avenue, New York, U.S.A.
James, Walter B., Esq., M.D., 268, Madison-avenue, New York.
Johns Hopkins University, Baltimore, U.S.A., per Mr. E. G. Allen.
Johnson, General Sir Allen B., 60, Lexham-gardens, Cromwell-road, S.W.
Johnson, Rev. S. J., F.R.A.S., Melplash Vicarage, Bridport.
Jones and Evans, Messrs., 77, Queen-street, Cheapside, E.C.

Kearton, G. J. Malcolm, Esq., F.R.G.S., 28, Fenchurch Street, E.C.
Keltie, J. Scott, Esq., LL.D., 1, Savile-row, W.
Kelvin, The Rt. Hon. Lord, F.R.S., LL.D., Netherhall, Largs, Ayrshire.
Kinder, C. W., Esq., M.I.C.E., Tongshan, North China.
King's Inns Library, Henrietta-street, Dublin.
Kimberley Public Library, per Messrs. Sotheran and Co., Strand.
Kitching, J., Esq., Oaklands, Kingston Hill, S.W.
Kleinseich, M., per Mr. Wohlleben, 45, Gt. Russell-street, W.C. (3 *copies*).

Larchmont Yacht Club, Larchmont, N.Y., U.S.A. (F. D. Shaw, Esq., Chairman of Library Committee).
Leechman, C. B., Esq., 10, Earl's-court-gardens, S.W.
Leeds Library, Commercial-street, Leeds.
Lehigh University, U.S.A.
Leipzig, Library of the University of, per Herr O. Harrassowitz, Leipzig.
Lewis, Walter H., Esq., 11, East 35th-street, New York City, U.S.A.
Levy, Judah, Esq., 17, Greville-place, N.W.
Liverpool Free Public Library.
Liverpool Geographical Society (Capt. D. Phillips, R.N., Secretary), 14, Hargreaves-buildings, Chapel-street, Liverpool.
Loch, Right Hon. Lord, G.C.B., G.C.M.G., 23, Lowndes-square, S.W.
Loescher, Messrs. J., & Co., Via del Corso, 307, Rome, per Messrs. Sampson Low.
Logan, Daniel, Esq., Solicitor-General, Penang, Straits Settlements.
Logan, William, Esq., per Messrs. Grindlay & Co., 54, Parliament-street.
London Institution, Finsbury-circus.
London Library, 12, St. James's-square.
Long Island Historical Society, Brooklyn, U.S.A.
Lowrey, Joseph, Esq., The Hermitage, Loughton.
Lucas, C. P., Esq., Colonial Office, S.W.
Lucas, F. W., Esq., 21, Surrey-street, Victoria Embankment, W.C.
Luyster, S. B., Esq., c/o Messrs. Denham & Co., 27, Bloomsbury-square, W.C.
Lydenberg, H. M., Esq., Lenox Library, Fifth Avenue, New York.
Lyttelton-Annesley, Lieut.-Gen. A., Templemere, Weybridge.

Macmillan & Bowes, Messrs., Cambridge, per Messrs. Foster, Fore-street.
Macrae, C. C., Esq., 93, Onslow-gardens, S.W.
Manchester Public Free Libraries.
Manierre, George, Esq., 184, La Salle-street, Chicago, Ill., U.S.A.

Margesson, Lieut. W. H. D., R.N., Findon Place, Worthing.
Markham, Vice-Admiral Albert H., F.R.G.S., 65, Linden-gardens, W.
Markham, Sir Clements, K.C.B., F.R.S., 21, Eccleston-square, S.W.
Marquand, Henry, Esq., 160, Broadway, New York, U.S.A.
Martelli, E. W., Esq., 4, New Square, Lincoln's Inn, W.C.
Massachusetts Historical Society, 30, Tremont-street, Boston, Mass., U.S.A., per Messrs. Kegan Paul.
Massie, Capt. R. H., R.A.
Mathers, E. P., Esq., Glenalmond, Foxgrove-road, Beckenham.
Maudslay, A. P., Esq., 32, Montpelier-square, Knightsbridge, S.W.
McClymont, Jas. R., Esq., 201, Macquarie-street, Hobart Town, Tasmania.
Mecredy, Jas., Esq., M.A., B.L., F.R.G.S., Wynberg, Stradbrook, Blackrock, Dublin Co.
Melbourne, Public Library of, per Messrs. Melville, Mullen & Slade, 12, Ludgate-square, E.C.
Meyjes, A. C., Esq., 42, Cannon-street, E.C.
Michigan, University of, per Messrs. H. Sotheran & Co., 140, Strand, W.C.
Milwaukee Public Library, Wisconsin, per Mr. G. E. Stechert.
Minneapolis Athenæum, U.S.A., per Mr. G. E. Stechert, 2, Star-yard, W.C.
Mitchell Library, 21, Miller-street, Glasgow.
Mitchell, Alfred, Esq., per Messrs. Tiffany, 221, Regent-street, W.
Mitchell, Wm., Esq., 14, Forbesfield-road, Aberdeen.
Monson, The Rt. Hon. Lord, C.V.O., Clarence House, St. James's, S.W.
Morgan, E. Delmar, Esq., 15, Roland-gardens, South Kensington, S.W.
Morris, H. C. L., Esq., M.D., Gothic Cottage, Bognor, Sussex.
Morris, Mowbray, Esq., 59A, Brook-street, Grosvenor square, W.
Moxon, A. E., Esq., c/o Mrs. Gough, The Lodge, Sculdern, near Banbury.
Munich Royal Library, per Messrs. Asher & Co.

Nathan, Major, C.M.G., R.E., 11, Pembridge-square, W.
Natural History Museum, Cromwell-road, per Messrs. Dulau & Co., Soho-sq.
Naval and Military Club, 94, Piccadilly, W.
Netherlands, Geographical Society of the, per Mr. Nutt, 57, Long Acre.
Nettleship, E., Esq., c/o R. S. Whiteway, Esq., Brownscombe, Shottermill, Surrey.
Newberry Library, The, Chicago, U.S.A., per Mr. B. F. Stevens.
Newcastle-upon-Tyne Literary and Scientific Institute.
Newcastle-upon-Tyne Public Library.
New London Public Library, Conn., U.S.A.
New York Athletic Club, Central Park, South, New York (John C. Gulick, Esq., chairman of Library Committee).
New York Public Library, per Mr. B. F. Stevens.
New York State Library, per Mr. G. E. Stechert, 2, Star-yard, Carey-st., W.C.
New York Yacht Club (Library Committee), 67, Madison-avenue, New York City, U.S.A.
New Zealand, Agent-General for, per Messrs. Sotheran & Co.
Nicholson, Sir Charles, Bart., D.C.L., The Grange, Totteridge, Herts.
Nijhoff, M., per Mr. D. Nutt, 57, Long Acre, W.C.
Nordenskiold, Baron, 11, Tradgardsgatan, Stockholm.
North Adams Public Library, Massachusetts, U.S.A. [Station.
Northbrook, The Right Hon. the Earl of, G.C.S.I., Stratton, Micheldever
North, Hon. F. H., C 3, The Albany, W.
Northumberland, His Grace the Duke of, per Mr. Cross, 230, Caledonian-road, N.

O'Byrne, P. Justin, Esq., " British-Indian Commerce," 21, St. Helen's-place, E.C.
Oliver, Captain S. P., Findon, near Worthing.
Oliver, Commander T. W., R.N., 16, De Parys-avenue, Bedford.

Omaha Public Library, Nebraska, U.S.A.
Ommanney, Admiral Sir Erasmus, C.B., F.R.S., 29, Connaught-sq., Hyde Park.
Oriental Club, Hanover-square, W.

Parmly, Duncan D., Esq., 160, Broadway, New York.
Payne, E. J., Esq., 2, Stone Buildings, Lincoln's Inn, W.C.
Peabody Institute, Baltimore, U.S., per Mr. E. G. Allen.
Peckover, Alexander, Esq., Bank House, Wisbech.
Peech, W. H., Esq., St. Stephen's Club, Westminster.
Peek, Sir Cuthbert E., Bart., 22, Belgrave-square, S.W.
Peixoto, Dr. J. Rodrigues, 8, Rue Almte. Comandaré, Rio de Janeiro.
Pequot Library, Southport, Conn., U.S.A.
Petherick, E. A., Esq., 85, Hopton-road, Streatham, S.W.
Philadelphia Free Library, U.S.A., per Mr. G. E. Stechert, 2, Star-yard, W.C.
Philadelphia, Library Company of, U.S.A., per Mr. E. G. Allen.
Poor, F. B., Esq., 160, Broadway, New York, U.S.A.
Poor, Henry W., Esq., per Messrs. Denham & Co., 27, Bloomsbury-square.
Pope, Alexander, Esq., Methven House, King's-road, Kingston-on-Thames.
Portico Library, Manchester.
Pringle, Arthur T., Esq., c/o Messrs. G. W. Wheatley & Co., 10, Queen-st., E.C.

Quaritch, Mr. B., 15, Piccadilly, W. (12 *copies*).

Rabbits, W. Thos., Esq., 6, Cadogan Gardens, S.W.
Raffles Library, Singapore, per Messrs. Jones & Evans, Queen-street, E.C.
Ravenstein, E. G., Esq., 2, York Mansions, Battersea Park, S.W.
Reform Club, Pall-mall.
Reggio, André C., Esq., c/o Messrs. Baring Bros. & Co., 8, Bishopsgate-street Within, E.C.
Rhodes, Josiah, Esq., The Elms, Lytham, Lancashire.
Richards, Admiral Sir F. W., G.C.B., 34, Queen Anne's Gate, S.W.
Riggs, E. F., Esq., 1311, Mass. Avenue, Washington, U.S.
Ringwalt, John S., Jun., Esq., Mt. Vernon, Knox County, Ohio, U.S.A.
Rittenhouse Club, 1811, Walnut-street, Philadelphia, U.S.A.
Rockhill, The Hon. W. W., Department of State, Washington.
Rodd, Sir Rennell, C.B., K.C.M.G., c/o Foreign Office, Downing-street, S.W.
Röhrscheid and Ebbecke, Herrn, Strauss'sche Buchhandlung, Bonn.
Rose, C. D., Esq., 10, Austin Friars, E.C.
Royal Artillery Institute, Woolwich.
Royal Colonial Institute, Northumberland Avenue, W.C.
Royal Engineers' Institute, Chatham.
Royal Geographical Society, 1, Savile-row, W. (*copies presented*).
Royal Scottish Geographical Society, Edinburgh (Jas. Burgess, Esq., LL.D. C.I.E., Librarian).
Royal Societies Club, St. James's-street, S.W.
Royal United Service Institution, Whitehall, S.W.
Russell, Lady A., 2, Audley-square, W.
Rutherford, Rev. W. Gunion, D.D., Westminster School, S.W.
Ryley, J. Horton, Esq..
Ryley, Mrs. Florence, LL.A., } Melrose, Woodwarde-road, Dulwich, S.E.

San Francisco Public Library, per Mr. G. E. Stechert.
Satow, H. E. Sir E., K.C.M.G., 104, The Common, Upper Clapton, E.
Saunders, Howard, Esq., 7, Radnor-place, Gloucester-square, W.
SAXE-COBURG AND GOTHA, H.R.H. the Reigning Duke of (Duke of Edinburgh), K.G., K.T., etc., c/o Col. the Hon. Sir W. J. Colville, K.C.V.O., Clarence House, St. James's.
Schwartz, J. L., Esq., P.O. Box 594, Pittsburg, Pa.

Science and Art Department, South Kensington.
Seawanhaka Corinthian Yacht Club, 7, East 32nd-street, New York, U.S.A.
Seymour, Vice-Admiral Sir E. H., K.C.B., 9, Ovington-square, S.W.
Sheffield Free Public Libraries (Samuel Smith, Esq., Librarian).
Shields, Cuthbert, Esq., Corpus Christi College, Oxford.
Signet Library, Edinburgh (Thos. G. Law, Esq., Librarian), per Mr. D. Nutt.
Silver, S. W., Esq., 3, York-gate, Regent's Park, N.W.
Sinclair, W. F., Esq., c/o Messrs. H. S. King & Co., Pall Mall, S.W.
Smith, F. A., Esq., Thorncliff, Shoot-up-Hill, N.
Smithers, F.O., Esq., F.R.G.S., Dashwood House, 9, New Broad-street, E.C.
Sneddon, Geo. T., Esq., 8, Merry-street, Motherwell.
Società Geografica Italiana, Rome.
Société de Géographie, Paris, per Mr. J. Arnould, Royal Mint Refinery, Royal Mint-street, E.C.
South African Public Library, per Messrs. H. S. King & Co., 65, Cornhill, E.C.
Southam, S. Clement, Esq., F.S.A., F.R.G.S., F.R.Hist.S., F.R.S.L., Elmhurst, Shrewsbury.
Springfield City Library Association, Mass., U.S.A.
Stairs, James W., Esq., c/o Messrs. Stairs, Son and Morrow, Halifax, Nova Scotia.
Stanley, Right Hon. Lord, of Alderley, 15, Grosvenor-gardens, S.W.
St. Andrew's University.
St. John's, N. B., Canada, Free Public Library (J. R. Ruel, Esq., Chairman).
St. Louis Mercantile Library, per Mr. G. E. Stechert, 2, Star-yard, W.C.
St. Martin's-in-the-Fields Free Public Library, 115, St. Martin's-lane, W.C.
St. Petersburg University Library, per Messrs. Kegan Paul.
St. Wladimir University, Kief, per Messrs. Sotheran & Co., 140, Strand.
Stephens, Henry C., Esq., M.P., Avenue House, Finchley, N.
Stevens, J. Tyler, Esq., Park-street, Lowell, Mass., U.S.A.
Stevens, Son, & Stiles, Messrs., 39, Great Russell-street, W.C.
Stockholm, Royal Library of, per Messrs. Sampson Low.
Stockton Public Library, per Messrs. Sotheran & Co., 140, Strand.
Strachey, Lady, 69, Lancaster-gate, Hyde-park, W.
Stride, Mrs. Arthur L., Bush Hall, Hatfield, Herts.
Stringer, G. A., Esq., 248, Georgia-street, Buffalo, N.Y., U.S.A.
Stubbs, Captain Edward, R.N., 13, Greenfield-road, Stoneycroft, Liverpool.
Sydney Free Library, per Mr. Young J. Pentland, 38, West Smithfield, E.C.
Sykes, Major P. Molesworth, H.M.'s Consul at Kerman, Persia, via Tehran.

Tate, G. P., Esq., c/o Messrs. W. Watson & Co., Karachi, India.
Taylor, Captain William R., 1, Daysbrook-road, Streatham Hill, S.W.
Temple, Lieut.-Col. R. C., C.I.E., per Messrs. Kegan Paul.
Thin, Mr. Jas., 54, 55, South Bridge, Edinburgh, per Mr. Billings, 59, Old Bailey, E.C.
Thomson, B. H., Esq., Governor's House, H.M.'s Prison, Northampton.
Tighe, W. S., Coalmoney, Stratford-on-Slaney, Co. Wicklow.
Toronto Public Library. } per Messrs. Cazenove & Son.
Toronto University.
Transvaal State Library, Pretoria, Transvaal, South Africa, per Messrs. Mudie.
Travellers' Club, 106, Pall-mall, S.W.
Trinder, H. W., Esq., Northbrook House, Bishops Waltham, Hants.
Trinder, Oliver Jones, Esq., Mount Vernon, Caterham, Surrey.
Trinity College, Cambridge, care of Messrs. Deighton, Bell & Co., per Messrs. Simpkin, Marshall & Co. (Enclo. Dept.).
Trinity House, The Hon. Corporation of, Tower-hill, E.C.
Troop, W. H., Esq., c/o Messrs. Black Bros. & Co., Halifax, Nova Scotia.
Trotter, Coutts, Esq., Athenaeum Club, S.W.
Trübner, Herr Karl, Strasburg, per Messrs. Kegan Paul.
Turnbull, Alex. H., Esq., 7, St. Helen's-place, Bishopsgate-street, E.C.

Union League Club, Broad-street, Philadelphia, U.S.A.
Union Society, Oxford, per Messrs. Cawthorn & Hutt, 24, Cockspur-street.
United States Congress, Library of, per Mr. E. G. Allen.
United States National Museum (Library of), per Messrs. W. Wesley & Son, 28, Essex-street, W.C.
United States Naval Academy, per Mr. B. F. Stevens.
University of London, per Messrs. Sotheran & Co., 37, Piccadilly, W.
Upsala University Library, per C. J. Lundstrom, Upsala.

Van Raalte, Charles, Esq., Aldenham Abbey, Watford, Herts.
Vienna Imperial Library, per Messrs. Asher & Co.
Vignaud, Henry, Esq., Ambassade des Etats Unis, 18, Avenue Kleber, Paris.

Wahab, Mrs., Knowle, Godalming.
Ward, Admiral Hon. W. J., 79, Davies-street, Berkeley-square, W.
Warren, W. R., Esq., 81, Fulton-street, New York City, U.S.A.
Washington, Department of State, per Mr. B. F. Stevens.
Washington, Library of Navy Department, per Mr. B. F. Stevens.
Watkinson Library, Hartford, Connecticut, U.S.A.
Watson, Commander, R.N.R., Ravella, Crosby, near Liverpool.
Webster, Sir Augustus, Bart., Guards' Club, 70, Pall-mall.
Weld, Geo. F., Esq., Quincy-street, Cambridge, Mass., U.S.A.
Westminster School (Rev. G. H. Nall, M.A., Librarian).
Wharton, Rear-Admiral Sir W. J. L., K.C.B., Florys, Princes-road, Wimbledon Park, S.W.
Wildy, A.G., Esq., 14, Buckingham-street, W.C.
Williams, O. W., Esq., Fort Stockton, Texas, U.S.A.
Wilson, Edward S., Esq., Melton Grange, Brough, East Yorkshire.
Wisconsin State Historical Society, per Messrs. Sotheran & Co., 140, Strand.
Worcester, Massachusetts, Free Library, per Messrs. Kegan Paul.
Wright, John, Esq., 2, Challoner Terrace West, South Shields.
Wyndham, Geo., Esq., M.P., 35, Park Lane, W.

Yale College, U.S.A., per Mr. E. G. Allen.
Young, Alfales, Esq., Salt Lake City, Utah, U.S.A.
Young, Sir Allen, C.B., 18, Grafton-street, W.
Young & Sons, Messrs. H., 12, South Castle Street, Liverpool.

Zürich, Bibliothèque de la Ville, care of Messrs. Orell, Turli & Co., Zürich, per Mr. D. Nutt.

www.ingramcontent.com/pod-product-compliance
Lightning Source LLC
Chambersburg PA
CBHW032230230426
43666CB00033B/1656